CONTEMPORARY

JAN 31 1974

PSYCHOLOGY

L

SUFI STUDIES:
EAST
AND WEST

E. P. Dutton & Co., Inc.

New York

SUFI STUDIES: EAST AND WEST

*A Symposium
in honor
of Idries Shah's services
to Sufi studies
by twenty-four contributors
marking
the 700th anniversary
of the death
of Jalaluddin Rumi
(A.D. 1207–1273)*

Edited by
Professor L. F. Rushbrook Williams

ACKNOWLEDGMENTS

The publishers gratefully acknowledge the help, encouragement, and interest of many scholars and men of letters who have contributed to the preparation of this volume. The following are among those to whom particular thanks are due:

Dr. Abdel-Aziz el-Sayed (Director-General, The Arab Scientific, Cultural, and Educational Organisation); Professor Dr. Abdel-Rahman el-Sadr (Vice-Rector for Graduate Studies and Research, University of Alexandria); Hazrat Sahib-al-Siyada Abul-Hadi Shah, Janfishani; Hazrat Sahib-al-Siyada Ally Mohamed Shah (quondam Nazim of the Ajmer Dargah; Mussoorie); Dr. Mulk Raj Anand (Bombay); The Sardar Aqil Hussain Khan, Barlas (Trustee of the Waqf of the Nawab Saiyid Amjad Ali Shah);

Professor John Bowman (Head of the Department of Middle East Studies, University of Melbourne); Dr. Tara Chand (Emeritus Professor, Allahabad University); Professor Saros Cowasjee (University of Saskatchewan); His Excellency Dr. Kazem Naguib El-Daghestani (The Presidency Council, Damascus); Hadrat Ali Dajani (Amman); Lt. Col. M. K. Durrani, G.C. (Multan); Sir Colin Garbett, K.C.I.E., C.S.I., C.M.G., F.R.S.A., M.A., LL.B., (South Africa); Professor A. W. Halipota (Head of the Department of Comparative Religion, University of Sind); Dr. Sami Hamarneh (Smithsonian Institution, Washington); Hazrat Sahib-al-Siyada Major Ibn-e-Hasan Shah (Peshawar); Professor Chafic Jabri (Damascus); Professor Majid Khadduri (Director, Research and Education, Middle East Institute, The Johns Hopkins University); Professor Aqila Khanum Kiani (University of Karachi); Riyadh Kokache Effendi (Beirut); Professor G. M. Meredith-Owens (Department of Islamic Studies, University of Toronto); Professor Khosrow Mostofi (Director, Middle East Center, University of Utah); Shaghali Haidar Nayssan (Kabul); Dr. Sayed Nofal (Assistant Secretary-General, League of Arab States); Sayed Khalifa Abbas El Obeid (former Undersecretary of State for Foreign Affairs, Khartoum); Professor Heikki Palva (Gothenburg); Aghai Ardalan Panahi-Azar (Tehran); Qadi Zain-alabidin Sajjad (The Qadi of Meerut) Jamia Millia, Delhi; Professor M. Shafi'i (Professor of Persian Literature, Pehlavi University, Shiraz); Dr. Ahmed Soussa (Baghdad); The Nawab Sultan Yar Khan; Sheikh Mahmud Zayid (Department of Islamic History, American University of Beirut); His Excellency Dr. Hassan Abbas Zaki (Adviser to His Highness, Abu Dhabi); The Mufti Ziaul Haq of Delhi (Jamiyyat al-Ulema); The Sardar Faiz M. Khan, Zikria (former Minister of Education, Afghanistan).

EDITOR'S NOTE: *The transliteration into the Roman alphabet from the Perso-Arabic script adopted by each contributor to this book has been retained in each paper. Some scholarly opinions on this point may be found in Appendix I.*

LIST OF CONTRIBUTORS

Professor A. Reza Arasteh
Mir S. Basri
Dr. Bankey Behari
Sir Edwin Chapman-Andrews
Professor John H. M. Chen
Judge Hilmi Makram Ebeid
Sir Razik Fareed
Professor Nasrollah S. Fatemi
Professor A. K. Julius Germanus

Sir John Glubb
Dr. Saleh Hamarneh
Professor M. Y. Haschmi
Mr. Justice M. Hidayatullah
Professor James Kritzeck
Professor Rom Landau
Dr. Zeki el-Mahassini
Adnan Mardam Bey
Professor I. H. Qureshi
Aga Ahmad Saidi
Professor M. Y. Shawarbi
The Reverend Sidney Spencer
Emir Aref Tamer
Professor L. F. Rushbrook Williams
Dr. Ahmed Emin Yalman

CONTENTS

The breaking down of some contemporary assumptions in the first fourteen books by Idries Shah: "Something so new that the modern reader is at once struck by it." The meeting of East and West in the spiritual life of man. Understanding and speech as "extra senses." The development of man as outlined by Jalaluddin Rumi in his *Couplets of Inner Meaning*. The function of austerity and simplicity; raising man to

the state of Union with the Eternal. Meaning of the death of
the (conditioned) Self through Sufi exercises: remembering
and meditation. The great thinker al-Ghazzali's work in relating Sufism to attainment of the highest kind of life and the
present activity of Shah's work as similarly oriented. Background and presentation of Idries Shah as a fulfillment of
action-philosophy. Mistakes in regarding Sufism as only a
cult belonging to "pantheistic mystics." The use of the
parables and other material. The Sufi orders and the employment of literary materials in human development. Opposition
to the narrowness of guru-ism.

in the West as a man of letters; my first contact with him; ideas of Sufism current in India; experimentation with varieties of religious experience; conversion through love, and acceptance by the Hindus as saints. The four orders that operated in India: specific Sufi teachers of the past. The influence of the Sufis in the Middle East and Central Asia. The activities of Sirdar Ikbal and his son in making known this tradition and its adaptation to contemporary thought. Interest to a historian as to how this was done. Activities in the Middle East, friendships with the most diverse people— the orthodox and the revolutionaries. Books on the Middle East. Idries Shah's choice of vocation, my meeting with him as a youth. Summary: "The truth seems to be that Sufi doctrine and practice hold something for everyone who has the wit to find it."

by Professor Ishtiaq Husain Qureshi M.A., Ph.D. (Cantab.)

The great diversity of Sufi thought; being grounded on experience, some of its manifestations are unrecognizable to literal thinkers: examples of Ibn al-Arabi's work. The use of tales and illustrative encounters; the literary artifact not employed for historical accuracy and not susceptible to such treatment. Limitations of trying to study Sufism by tracing it to supposed origins. Shah's contributions in collecting Sufi materials. Interpretations of Sufi classics reconcile what have been erroneously regarded as "different traditions" within Sufism. Shah's employment of teaching-stories from *Tariqas* ("orders"). The increasing tendency in the West to adopt extravagant religious beliefs from Oriental sources; reconciliation of authentic materials with Western thought patterns.

by Mir S. Basri

The relationship between the ancient Imams and the spread of knowledge of Eastern thought in the West. The develop-

ment of culture in the medieval civilization in the area between China and Central Africa: its synthesis and catalysis
of ideas. The travelers and polymaths; the translation of
Greek literature, recycled into the new civilization after its
derivation from Babylonian, Egyptian, and other cultures of
earlier times. The peoples who joined in this effort. The use
of Sufism as a modern instrument in human development, in
science, and in thought. The centers of study (*Takias*), the
"orders" (*Tariqas*), the teachers (*Murshids*), and the disciples (*Murids*). Modern investigations of Sufism in the West
—my experience with learned men and the prevailing attitude
toward Hallaj. The influence of Sufi poetry, such as
Sheikh ibn al-Farid's, and Idries Shah as a connecting link.
Shah and his presentation of Mulla Nasreddin, and my own
poem on him, in his personalization of Joha. The function of
wit to enshrine and ensure the preservation of essential material. Jamal al-Din Afghani awakened the people of the
East a century ago to modern ideas: an analogous function
seen in Sufi teaching. There is no hostility between the East
and West on fundamental levels, as the Sheikh of al-Azhar
has affirmed. Durability of current work.

V LITERARY COMPARISONS AND EFFECTS 33

by Professor John H. M. Chen, M.A., M.S., Ph.D., Ed.D.
Sufism and Sufi literature; the use of Shah's work in enabling
Westerners to enjoy the tradition and literature. Familiar and
other instruction in the teaching-stories; considerations of
certain narratives and their overt meaning. Use of the stories
in situational advice; Sufi recommendations through the
stories. Similarity of recitals and stories in *Tales of the Dervishes* and *Reflections* to New Testament parables; affinities
with Shakespearean and other literature. The use of humor
and illustration of deceitfulness; the psychological situation
of man, in isolation and in company. The question of individuality and conformity. The limitations of intellectuality.
Affinity with Taoist and other Chinese thinking. The common thread in different traditions using the story format.

the Dervishes as an authoritative series: overt and symbolic —and deeper—meanings. The value of *The Sufis:* the representation of Nasreddin as a Sufi figure, and the esoteric meaning of the tales. Memories of the dervish Dede Hajji Khan in 1903. My preparation of the centenary edition of Omar Khayyam published in London, and the possibility of Khayyam's being a Sufi exponent. Association with the Mevlevi and Bektashi dervishes.

The historical developments leading to a better knowledge of Eastern thought and traditions. An analysis of the obstacles to free communication of the Eastern heritage to the West that still remain. The activity of Idries Shah in both cultural spheres; the need to discount inevitable opposition, just as much as overenthusiastic support. Requirements for the Eastern thinker who is to surmount certain barriers: conflicts between Eastern and Western cultures, the possibilities of being considered a national or other propagandist; the difficulties of the linguistically oriented student; the "Arab" and "Ajam" (non-Arab) areas. Problems of marked ideological commitment; credentials of Idries Shah; capacity to transpose "flavor"; ability to blend the nuances of the various forms of Sufi thought: Persian, Turkic, Arabian, and Central Asian. Emphasis upon the discoveries, knowledge, and operation of the Sufi thinkers and sages, as against the oversentimentalization of the studies. Unconscious chauvinism can operate against a correct evaluation of this material; the "rapid learning" technique; the importance of *The Book of the Book;* misunderstanding of trenchant attitudes. The uniqueness of this contemporary approach may presage the opening of a door to interpretation that is unlikely ever to be shut again.

Scholastic monopoly of Sufi studies in the West, followed by reinterpretations that are now beginning to reveal the profound humanism of Islamic culture. The work of Idries Shah in the current reinterpretation needed to impart Sufism to modern man. Sufi literature in its humanizing effect and its misuses; problems of using the traditional Western frame for interpreting Sufism; the work of Freud and others. The path of individuation: Taoism, Sufism, and Christianity. The nature of Sufism, different kinds of Sufis: their varying emphases. The "I-Thou" relationship; resensitization and gaining naturalness. The use of the dance; the various "selves" and their manifestations. The Guide; the Stages and States; the meaning of technical terms. The unfolding of unconsciousness. The difference between the Sufi and the man of obsession. Psychotherapeutic results, processes, and attainment of the goal.

Original scientific work lacking interest in Sufism. Realization, after fourteen years' study, of the harmonization of Sufi thought with a contemporary outlook. Personal trials, lectures on "Islamic Mysticism and a Modern World Outlook" in Germany. Consideration of Idries Shah's work. Errors in some attitudes toward mysticism, leading to its study being treated as are other subjects. Hamidullah's statement on the derivation of Sufism, and the possibility of Sufi thought being perceived analogically by reference to other constructs of thought. Reasons for this. Observations of Sirdar Faiz Mohammed Khan Zikria, grandfather of Idries Shah; the Persian and Arabian connections of this family. The position of the Hashimites; genealogy and the Koran. The widespread existence of Sufism among people of all kinds in the East, often unsuspected even by Easterners themselves. Reasons for this anonymity; the increase in the influence of the Sufis today. The first writer to take a panoramic view of Sufism rather than assuming that it is a sequential development. The vitality, variety, and effectiveness of Sufi thought thus susceptible to display in *The Sufis* and *The Way of the Sufi*. The illustration of the specific roles of Sufis of the past (Ibn-al-Arabi, Bektash, Rumi) as specializations, not manifestations, of human personality. Consideration of *Thinkers of the East*, *Wisdom of the Idiots*, and *The Study of Sufism in the West*, with analyses of the intention, function, and effect of these books. Relationships of ancient Sufis with Eastern and Western formulations, such as Vedanta, alchemy, and Christian mysticism. Conclusion: what Sufism is, and the awakening of the desire to study it further.

impossibility of definition, of a spirit in a community. Experience as valid as academic learning: the theoreticians who are experts in subjects that they have never practiced. Problems of Sufic encoding; Sufic reconciliation of apparent opposites; the meaning of renunciation leading to perception of oneself. Love and its effect. Affinities of Sufism and Christian mysticism. The transmission of Eastern ideas in Europe through Southern Europe: Dante, Thomas Aquinas, Albertus Magnus, Ibn Sina. The need to transcend rigid concepts for mutual understanding.

Studying and writing about contemporary celebrated people of the world of thought and literature my concern for twenty-five years. The influence of Idries Shah compared with that of Jamal'udin al-Afghani, the reformer. The importance of *The Way of the Sufi* residing in arrangement and presentation as much as in content; the scope and range of the book. The unique method employed to display and communicate Sufi knowledge. The use of the Ghazzalian approach; treatment of Ibn al-Arabi, Rumi, and Saadi. The work of the great Bahau'din Naqshband of Bokhara. Examination of the teaching-story of the King and the Wolf. The reconciliation of Sufi ideas on the psychological plane and harmonization with the attitudes of Islam. Breadth and importance of *The Sufis*, its content, and the place of Robert Graves's Introduction. *Thinkers of the East:* the storehouse of Sufi materials, after sixteen books, shows no sign of depletion.

Origins of the Sufis, deterioration marked by formation of orders and lodges, whirling, mediocre students, etc. Teaching in parables. Not necessary to know much about Sufi tales to enjoy them; but greater benefits with knowledge of their origin, structure, and context. Difference from the Zen structures, "full of wonders and strange ideas." Saints did not disdain the wag Nasreddin—why should we? Each story can be used to illustrate points of Sufi doctrine. "The clearest thing that comes through is that by discipline and initiation the many hidden meanings in everything can be discovered and passed along." The order of ingestion of tales. Examination of the tale "The Founding of a Tradition." Ordinary transmission of knowledge subject to distortion; relevance of direct perception of fact. Subjectivity of the human brain.

Background: entry of Central Asia into the Islamic domain, extension of the caliphal hegemony over parts of Europe and Africa; resultant unification of diverse peoples. Emergence of an Eastern wisdom from this setting, in which the Persian, Byzantine, Indian, Greek, and other heritages were represented. The coloring of this wisdom distinguishing it from European thought. The attitude of Eastern man. The evocative power, in the East, of Sufi names such as those of Rabia, Hallaj, Rumi, Saadi, and others. Two examples: the emphases of Rabia and of Saadi. *Thinkers of the East* and *The Dermis Probe* and their citations of these personages. The function of these books in distilling the traditional wisdom and presenting it usably in contemporary terms. The capacity to absorb and transpose basic ideas, giving fresh possibilities to a new age. The presentation of the concept of different levels of understanding, and its success with people all over the world from every religious and ideological background. The communication of meanings not perceptible to all. How Shah has worked in the spirit of the various poets: Saadi and the moral tale; Rumi and the immediate relevance to current situations. The value of being forthright, especially where "humility" means that one allows injustice to be done. Symbolism shared with al-Hallaj, al-Arabi, Attar, and others of equal note. Shah's work as an extension in a new setting of the past thousand years of

Sufi workers: bringing them, by way of Eastern models, into the present day, for all cultures.

Idries Shah adheres to the tradition—and also to the inner freedom of spirit—in a way characteristic of Sufis. *Caravan of Dreams* and the description of the pilgrimage to Mecca. Islamic devotion as a reaffirmation of a religious tradition that Islam itself states originates beyond recorded history. The distinctive use by Shah of narratives from many sources, written and oral. Purpose of the stories to communicate with the inner mind; the greater self, which the Sufis, like all mystics, affirm lies beyond the normal and superficial self. Resemblance to Buddhist koans. The tale of "The "Shrine," interpretation and usage in teaching. Consideration of John of Antioch and quotation of sayings of the Master Ahrar. The tale of Ahangar the Smith and its implications. The snare of apparent godliness as a form of self-esteem. The Sufi opposition to debased intellectual activity of some unworthy scholars.

The tradition that aims at achievement in spiritual and temporal action, represented by the contributions of the "People of the House." My feelings and attitudes as a historian of Islam and my studies in the subject of Sufism throughout my career. Interest in the works of al-Arabi, Suhrawardi, Khayyam, Hafiz, and others. My own research and publications on Rumi and Shams-i-Tabriz. The Sufi schools of Iran, Turkey, and Iraq and their function in focusing attention and producing freedom of thought. The genius of their directors in establishing a "thinking method" that extended its influence over chosen educated men. Spread of the teaching throughout the Saracen world; stressing of the activities of liberating mental processes and contact with right guidance. The capacity to demonstrate the underlying unity in fact, in spite of apparent differences: influence of Shah's work on Christians, a Hindu monk, Persians, Afghans, Africans, and others. Drastic misunderstandings by some Eastern and Western authors as to the quality, nature, and texture of Sufi thought. Western reaction to *The Dermis Probe*. How analogical systems of thought are used. The teacher and his manifestation in Sufism.

ment of the Sufi technique of portraying subjects in a manner suited to the audience. Answer to "What is Sufism?" found in these books; different approaches and definitions; the need for love and the abandonment of greed. The use of parables and stories. Shah's *Reflections* and its pointing out the effect of subjectivity in human thought.

Threat to earthly life due to acts of injustice; need for authoritative and apposite voice. The dynamic of Sufi thought as seen by a Christian Arab. The need for a combination to eradicate malicious rivalry: the Christian disciples of Rumi; the acceptance of the Jew Sarmad as a Sufi; the Hasidic use of Sufic methods; Sufi thought and Bhakti Hinduism. Affinities of Sufic action and Christian monasticism as practiced in the Egyptian deserts. The contacts of Western civilization with the Eastern current in Spain. The anchorites of the desert and the intercultural effect of their lives. Feelings of modern Western thinkers that such traditions should not be allowed to decay. The synthesis achieved by the Arabian writers and researchers of ancient times. The contemporary work of Ahmad Shawqi and Bernard Lewis; the diffusion from Egypt: Pharaonic Egypt, Coptic Egypt, and Arab Egypt. The part played by Central Asian civilizations, and the new availability of the products of Eastern culture. The East must show an attitude of service toward the rest of the world, as a cooperative entity. The nature of modern Egypt as a combination of an Islamic majority and an important Christian minority—mutual amity and tolerance. Sufi thought could play a large, perhaps decisive, part in reform and regeneration in this area. The need for the use of every conceivable method in spreading cooperation and understanding, as is employed in Sufi action—and the likely support of Christians. The convergence of a common front from a mutual heritage toward the goal of sanity.

The Magic Monastery. The role of Sufi exercises, and the importance and scope of the teaching-stories. Paradoxical behavior of the Sufis. The dervish training system and how it works.

"*Traces of Sufi-doctrine exist in every country; in the theories of ancient Greece; in the modern philosophies of Europe; in the dream of the ignorant and of the learned; in the shade of ease and the hardship of the desert.*"
—LT. COL. H. WILBERFORCE CLARKE, *The Awarif-l-Ma'arif*

"*No trifling word is said to a master of awareness, but he will grasp its wisdom.*

"*And if a hundred chapters of wisdom are read to an ignorant one—it will reach his ears as a trifle.*"
—SHEIKH SAADI, *Gulistan*, CHAPTER II

FOREWORD

by

Sir Edwin Chapman-Andrews,

K.C.M.G., O.B.E., K. St. J., K.C.S.G.

From the pulpit one day, Nasreddin asked his congregation: "Do you know what I am going to preach about?"

"No," they replied.

"In that case," he said, "it would take too long to explain." And he went home.

Next day he again ascended the pulpit and asked the same question.

"Yes," the people replied, determined to put him on the spot.

"In that case," said Nasreddin, "there is no need for me to say more." And he went home.

Yet again the following day he put the same question: "Do you know what I am going to preach about?"

But now the congregation were ready to corner him. "Some of us do and some of us don't," they answered.

"In that case," said Nasreddin, "let those who know tell those who don't."

INTRODUCTION:
SCOPE AND EFFECT
OF
SUFI WRITINGS
BY
IDRIES SHAH

by

The Hon. Mr. Justice Hidayatullah

Whoever wishes to experience something of the feelings of Keats when he first came across Chapman's Homer should read any of the fourteen Sufi books written by Idries Shah. They contain a wealth of information about Sufis and their special practices unknown, but of great importance, to our material world. They prove that man's happiness does not truly depend on the outward and visible blessings of fortune, but on the inward and unseen perfections and riches of the mind. The spiritual mind of man in contemporary life has weakened and requires to be toned. These books undermine modern orthodoxies and the cult of luxurious living; they awaken in man a new spiritual force through a synthesis of Sufi learning and experience. This is something so novel that the modern reader is struck by it at once.

The mind has always been the true man and the Inner Knowledge of the mind contributes to the Spiritual Force of man. The Lord gave us not only the five senses but He added a sixth when He imparted understanding and then a seventh, speech to be the interpreter of the cogitations thereof. The thin partitions that divide the sixth and seventh faculties from the other five are pierced by Sufi philosophy and exercises. By turning to it one can obtain a catharsis of vanity and greed, the two most deadly failings of man today. Idries Shah, a living exponent of Sufi thought and exercises, has given us entry into the boundless area of spiritual experience of the Sufi savants. As he explains in *The Way of the Sufi* (1968):

> The Sufis claim that a certain kind of mental and other activity can produce, under special conditions and with particular efforts, what is termed a higher working of the mind, leading to special perceptions whose apparatus is latent in the ordinary man. Sufism is therefore the transcending of ordinary limitations.

These powers are illustrated by Idries Shah in the following verses of Jalaluddin Rumi (d. 1273) in his *Couplets of Inner Meaning:*

> From realm to realm man went, reaching his present reasoning, knowledgeable, robust state—forgetting earlier forms of intelligence. So, too, shall he pass beyond the current forms of perception. . . . There are a thousand other forms of Mind. . . .

> The degree of necessity determines the development of organs in man . . . therefore increase your necessity.

The ancient Sufis lived an austere and simple life, in protest against the luxuries of the world, searching for Truth. They sought to realize God in themselves and the answer to the question: What is God in relation to man and the creation? The Sufis show the Way and impart knowledge of God both pantheistically and monistically. They believe in *Fana* and *Baqa* and try to rise to a state of Union with the Eternal One. God is immanent but can be realized through *Dikhr* and *Muraqabat*. *Fana* is the death of self and merger with the Eternal One. *Baqa* is the continued existence of self in this condition of Union. *Dikhr* is remembering God, and *Muraqabat* is meditation. The Sufi must pass through several stages of spiritual existence and development known as *Maqamat*. Contemplation, renunciation, abstinence, love, poverty, and belief in God are the spiritual exercises. They enable the initiated to pass through contemplation, which is a sensing exercise, to a special knowledge of the Inner Self. Sufis hold that the superior experience and knowledge comes to a man or woman in exact accordance with his worth, capacity, and earning of it. Their objective is to achieve, by the understanding of the Origin, the Knowledge that comes through experience. Guidance by a teacher (*Murshid*) is needed—"*Ba Murshid beshudi Insan/Be Murshid mandi Haiwan*" ("With a guide you may become a real man, without one you will remain an animal").

"Two hundred years earlier in Baghdad," says Aldous Huxley in his *Perennial Philosophy* (1945), "the great Mahomedan theologian, Al-ghazzali, turned from consideration of truths about God to the contemplation and direct apprehension of Truth-the-Fact, from the purely intellectual discipline of the philosophers to the moral and spiritual discipline of the Sufis." Al-ghazzali wrote a treatise on Sufism as the highest kind of life. The present volume is a modern attempt to do the same.

When Idries Shah appeared in the BBC program "One Pair of Eyes," it was a new experience for a Western audience accustomed to Nobel Prizewinners, diplomats, and others. Now a man from an Eastern and Islamic background was addressing them on human behavior and thought. He did this by disclosing the perennial and preexisting truths that are timeless in their reach and universal in their appeal. They were derived from the treasures of Sufi thought and action, not in an esoteric or mystic way but as a part of our lives spiritual and material.

Before other audiences, Idries Shah has pointed out some of the "anomalies" that established Sufism as a determining force in shaping psychology and even science and technology, recalling the Western debt to Sufism as acknowledged by Rom Landau and Asín Palacios. As illustrations he mentioned Jabir and Jafar Sadiq, revered Sufis and the fathers of Western chemistry; Hujviris' theory of identity of time and space; Ibn-al-Arabi's pioneering of theories later called "Freudian"; Rumi's statement of human evolution from earth through mineral, vegetable, and animal, long before Darwin propounded his theory of evolution; Shabistari's revelation of the power of the atom in the thirteenth century; and the Majorcan Lull's position as an inventor of the computer.

Before Idries Shah explained the action philosophy of the Sufis, there was considerable misunderstanding about it. Professor Arberry in his *Oriental Essays* (1960) expressed the hope that Eastern thought would some day get a more effective presentation to the West. Arberry himself through his voluminous writings (over forty books) attempted this breakthrough; but his efforts to popularize Eastern philosophy did not succeed. His academic approach and esoteric Orientalism baffled his readers. Idries Shah writes in the language of the West and through him ordinary people realized for the first time that there is nothing specially Oriental in Sufi philosophy and that Sufi thought is human thought. He thus neutralized the prejudice of the West toward the East of which Arberry himself wrote:

> Before the truth about the East, and its peoples can be established in the common consciousness of the West, a vast accumulation of nonsense and misapprehension and deliberate lies will need to be cleared away—nothing distresses the public, and its faithful servants the popular reviewers, more than the demolition of cherished though fantastic images.

The Professor did not realize that the answer lay in presenting Eastern ideas and materials as applicable in today's life in the West. This task is being performed by Idries Shah.

Before his advent, such works as Saiyid Amir Ali's *A Short History of the Saracens* and *The Spirit of Islam* showed that the West owed a part of its civilization to the East. Idries Shah has now made a fresh breakthrough. Born and bred in the ancient Sufi tradition, Shah's first book on the subject, *The Sufis* (1964), was published when he had already made a name for himself. Three previous books had been well received. The first—a survey of human beliefs in Asia and Africa—was warmly introduced by Professor Louis Marin, Director of the School of Anthropology at the University of Paris, as a real contribution to knowledge. The second—an exhaustive bibliographical study of minority beliefs in Europe—and the third—a journal of travel and residence in the Middle East—had consolidated his position. *The Sufis* made an instant appeal. It has been said that if you want to be read, still more if you want to be read widely, you must be readable. *The New York Times Book Review* described it as "eminently readable." It had an introduction by Robert Graves and he feelingly said there, "yes, this is for me."

The West had till then regarded Sufism as a cult of pantheistic mystics. There is really no "mysticism" in Sufism. It is a misleading word to apply to the practical wisdom that Sufi philosophers have culled from everyday experience. Idries Shah put this wisdom before the West in a way that enabled it to sink deeper and deeper into the Western mind as a heritage of intellectual experience that the Sufi savants had gathered over centuries.

As the books appeared in steady stream (almost a book a year), covering Sufi literature, history, activities, thought, and philosophy, they opened a new world of understanding. In his *Wisdom of the Idiots* (1971), Idries Shah collected parables from great Sufi teachers such as Bahauddin Naqshband, Ibn-al-Arabi, Haider Ali Jan, and others. He told the stories of action philosophy of these thinkers who call themselves "Idiots" in contrast to the self-styled "wise." These stories are deep in moral meaning, which is conveyed to the reader in a practical way. They teach the secret of an eternally durable existence and the Way of the Sufis.

In his *Thinkers of the East* (1971) and *The Way of the Sufi* (1968), we get more action stories, themes for contemplation, group recitals, and exercises. Ritual is public worship. Spiritual exercise is private devotion. The latter gives a highly emotional rapport with the Eternal One. *The Way of the Sufi* provides a documented and authoritative account of the origin and development of Sufism and includes representative pieces from great Sufis including among others already mentioned, Saadi, Jami, and Sanai. There are approximately seventy Sufi orders. Here we get a full account of four main orders—Chishti, Qadiri, Suhrawardi, and Naqshbandi—with parables and anecdotes of the teachers.

In this way, each of his fourteen books is a treasury of intellectual teaching. Although Western in expression, they eschew the materialism that is poisoning the existence of man. Here we have parables that disclose deep philosophy—and philosophy is even better imparted in parable than in verse. Sufism is shown to be a living exercise; as Doris Lessing said: "Sufism is of today or it is nothing." These books cut across the ingrained belief, both in the East and in the West, that Sufi thought was a minority interest, something for a small circle of initiates, belonging to the world of mysticism.

Thus Idries Shah has presented Sufi thought and action as part of the life we live. The secret of his success in the West was correctly explained by *The Guardian* (November 26, 1970) when discussing *The Dermis Probe* (1970) (now the subject of a film), based on the parable of "The Elephant in the Dark" from Rumi's *Mathnavi-i-Maanvi* (Couplets of Inner Meaning):

> One reason why Shah's materials take people by surprise is that we are not prepared for penetrating insights into our supposedly unique society from the dreamy East. Generations of students who have found what they believed was there have conditioned us to ignore the other content—if you like, the practical—in such things as Sufi thought.

Many people in the West have now ceased to think of Sufis as Orientals or religious mystics and they find Idries Shah's books as penetrating as *Spiritual Exercises* by Ignatius Loyola, Pourrat's *Christian Spirituality*, Bede Frost's *The Art of Mental Prayer*, Edward Leen's *Progress through Mental Prayer*, or Aelfrida Till-yard's *Spiritual Exercises*. They have become bedside companions. This is because religion, properly understood, is not the adoption of any particular mode. Sufism, cultivated through exercises of deep contemplation, is only a doorway to Inner Knowledge based on humanity and understanding.

It is not surprising that Shah's materials have been used in a university sociology course at Cairo, in examination papers of an Oxford University honors degree course, and at Stanford University in the psychology department. They have also attracted much favorable attention in the Department of Islamic Studies at Budapest, the Islamic School at Toronto University in Canada, and other centers of philosophical investigation. But Idries Shah has never posed as a guru, although Professor Arberry's hopes have been realized in him.

SUFI STUDIES:
EAST
AND WEST

1

IDRIES SHAH—
BACKGROUND AND WORK
by
Aga Ahmad Saidi

Robert Graves, summoned to receive the Queen's Gold Medal for Poetry in 1969 at Buckingham Palace, availed himself of the opportunity to remind Her Majesty of her Arabian descent and its possible significance in the international field. Among others, the genealogical authority Sir Ian Moncreiffe emphasizes that Queen Elizabeth II could indeed trace her ancestry to Mohammad, King of Seville, in Spain. And, in the same book, Prince Philip's forebears are traced to Mithradates, an ancient Shah of Persia. "The international pool of Blood Royal," says Sir Ian, "has always been so intermingled that ultimately it tends to become one everywhere—however remote its tributaries in space and time. It spans the centuries to link the continents." [1]

[1] Sir Ian Moncreiffe, *Blood Royal* (London: Nelson & Sons, 1956), p. 61.

For the people of the Middle East, the linking of the Persian and Arabian most noble houses, which took place in the seventh century of the Christian era, is of the greatest significance. Hazrat Husayn, grandson of the Prophet Mohammed, married Princess Harar, better known in Iran as Shahribanu, the daughter of the Sasanian Shahinshah Yezdigird III of Persia; [2] and it is from this marriage that the *Saadat*—the *Saiyids*—are descended. Some ruling monarchs of today are products of this line,[3] and the families tracing their ancestry to the Prophet through this line continue to enjoy a special prestige that has no real parallel in the West. True enough, there are indications that the esteem in which such people are held has recently diminished. This is due to the weakening of religious faith among the young and the educated classes, which is a worldwide phenomenon. The weaker the faith the less the reverence in which the Prophet, and consequently his vice-regent and his descendants, are held, but devoted Muslims still constitute the large majority in all Islamic countries, and they still look upon Saiyids as Princes of the Faith.

An important consequence of a pedigree of this type is that its maintenance and conventionalities have ensured, for almost a millennium and a half, the preservation and transmission of traditions, including teachings and codes of behavior, that could hardly have been preserved through the vicissitudes of history in any other manner. At the minimum, the observed effective function of the preservation of the theme of the importance of the Saadat has been to cause them, with perhaps some exceptions, to harbor, from father to son, a tradition of the need to maintain excellence in conduct and performance, and fidelity to certain honored precepts.

This tendency in turn has, not unnaturally, resulted in the continuous production of people from this stock who have made their mark in the world, particularly in matters of spiritual, literary, and scholarly affairs.

Some families from these origins are, again quite naturally, better known for their distinctions in these fields than others. It

[2] See Sir Percy Sykes, *History of Persia*, Vol. I (2d ed., 1930), p. 542, footnote 2.

[3] Including the Sharifian kings of Morocco and the Hashimite kings of Jordan.

is against this background that the achievements and acceptance of the Saiyids must be viewed by those in the West who may not be familiar with the tradition. Idries Shah comes from such a background. Born into the princely family of Sardhana, North India, Idries Shah, the son of the famed Afghan diplomat and scholar, Ikbal Ali Shah, is a direct descendant of the Prophet Mohammed through the Saiyids of Paghman, Afghanistan.[4] His distinguished descent, while requiring, in the East, fulfillment of expectations of attainment, has at the same time helped him to gain the esteem of the populace; in a relatively short time he has certainly established himself in the East, as this book's numerous Eastern authors show, at the forefront of the thinkers of that region.

No such built-in respect or expectation of high achievement exists, of course, for the Saiyids in most Western eyes. For this reason Idries Shah's wide acceptance among thinking people of the West must be ascribed entirely to his own capacities. "Wise men from the East," although they may be passing fads among devotees here and there outside of their own cultural areas, are almost never found to have made their mark quite to this extent in Europe and America. Idries Shah seems to be the singular exception.

One of the striking characteristics of Saiyid Idries Shah's literary work in English is the way in which he has been able to project, almost to reconstitute, the atmosphere of Persian and Arabic literature without in the least giving the sensation of oddity. This feeling is very different from that given by the pseudo-Oriental writings that have been from time to time in vogue in the West and that have, quite rightly, slipped into oblivion.

This transposition of atmosphere, easy to experience but hard to describe, as one Western critic recently put it, must be due to the fact that the author is steeped not only in the classical literatures that contain it, but also in the oral tradition and the social background he can call upon to bring into his work that authenticity that so much Western translation lacks: that extra dimension, which tends to be absent from even the most faithful literal

[4] *Who's Who in the Arab World* (Beirut, 3d ed.), p. 1493.

translations of original works as we find them in various versions.

Another distinctive feature of Shah's literary production lies in the universality of the theme, which, like a cohesive element, combines and interrelates all his writings, producing a correlated, unified piece of work. Each of his books (and he has written many) is a separate, individual fountain that taps the same inexhaustible source. Each book is a distinct, different discourse that expounds the same basic thought—a master instrument playing its part in perfect harmony with others, and the result is a majestic Sufi symphony competently and delightfully presented.

Take, for example, his *Caravan of Dreams*, a treasury of interesting stories, poems, and witty remarks of some famous and some unknown sages of southwestern Asia who were gifted enough to see the world in a different light, and whose standard of valuation rested on spiritual rather than on material considerations. Though containing only a fraction of the rich heritage they left, this book has nevertheless the potential of providing a new perspective, of enabling the reader to realize that there are other, and far better, alternatives to the accustomed way of life with its undue emphasis on materialism. In other words, it has the appeal, the effectiveness, to make him think, and thinking is the prelude to understanding. Pursuing one story after another, he begins to see new vistas, new horizons, gradually appearing before him—a little contemplation, a little reflection, and the process of reorientation is set in motion. "There were once two brothers who jointly farmed a field," so goes one of the stories related by a venerable sage, "and always shared its yield."

> One day one of them woke up in the night and thought: "My brother is married and has children. Because of this he has anxieties and expenses which are not mine. So I will go and move some sacks from my share into his storeroom, which is only fair. I shall do this under cover of night, so that he may not, from his generosity, dispute with me about it."
>
> He moved the sacks, and went back to bed.
>
> Soon afterwards the other brother woke up and thought to himself: "It is not fair that I should have half of all the corn in our field. My brother, who is unmarried, lacks my pleasures in having a family, and I shall therefore try to compensate a little by moving some of my corn into his storeroom."

So saying, he did so.

The next morning, each was amazed that he still had the same number of sacks in his storeroom, and afterwards neither could understand why, year after year, the number of sacks remained the same even when each of them shifted some by stealth.[5]

Simply but most effectively this wonderful narrative portrays brotherhood in its true spirit, teaching us what it involves, what it requires: a sense of equity, charity, generosity, and magnanimity. And by implication it points out what our behavior should, in our daily relations, be toward our fellowmen. Here is the magic formula for peace, if peace is ever to be established on earth: Give more and take less. Surely the idea is not new but the manner in which it is presented is singularly impressive.

Compare his *The Exploits of the Incomparable Mulla Nasrudin*, the translations of the Mulla's remarkable tales, humanizing animals and prompting individuals so interestingly and amusingly as to entertain children, yet illustrating maxims and dicta so effectively and penetratingly as to benefit their elders, and embodying in the meantime "a little extra" as Idries Shah puts it, "which brings the consciousness of the potential mystic a little further on the way to realization." [6]

One day, we are told, "Nasrudin arrived at an all-comers' horse race mounted on the slowest of oxen. Everyone laughed: an ox cannot run.

" 'But I have seen it, when it was only a calf, running faster than a horse,' said Nasrudin, 'so why should it not run faster, now that it is larger?' " [7]

The humor of the story is obvious, and its moral that conclusions based on a logical extension of observed facts may not correspond with reality is not too difficult to grasp. The "little extra," which is enlightening to potential Sufis, is the fallacy of the assumption that "just because a thing—or person—is old, it is necessarily better than something which is young." [8]

[5] Idries Shah, *Caravan of Dreams* (London: Octagon Press, 1968), p. 133.

[6] Idries Shah, *The Sufis* (New York: Doubleday & Co., 1964), p. 56.

[7] Idries Shah, *The Exploits of the Incomparable Mulla Nasrudin* (London: Jonathan Cape, 1966; New York: Dutton Paperbacks, 1972), p. 80.

[8] *The Sufis*, p. 82.

Explore, if you will, his *Wisdom of the Idiots,* a collection of fascinating stories embodying the concepts and ideas, lore and learning of those preeminent Sufi masters who dubbed themselves "idiots" because "narrow-minded thinkers considered to be wisdom what seemed to them to be folly," and left a heritage of sapience, sense, and reason for the reflection of posterity. Let us turn a leaf and reflect, for a moment, about the wandering dervish who "ran to where a Sufi sat deep in contemplation, and said: 'Quick! We must do something. A monkey has just picked up a knife.'

" 'Don't worry,' said the Sufi, 'so long as it was not a *man.*'

"When the dervish saw the monkey again he found, sure enough, that it had thrown the knife away." [9]

Again, there is *Thinkers of the East,* an anthology of proverbs and parables, interviews and interchanges, "selected in accordance with the need of the time." The book is a revelation unfolding before us a world entirely different from contemporary society—a world hard to imagine and harder still to believe once existed in the East. We may have a peep into a remote corner of that world through the story of the rich braggart who took a Sufi on a tour of his house and "showed him room after room filled with valuable works of art, priceless carpets and heirlooms of every kind.

"At the end he asked: 'What impressed you most of all?'

"The Sufi answered: 'The fact that the earth is strong enough to support the weight of such a massive building.' " [10]

Glance over his *Tales of the Dervishes,* an album of eighty-two "teaching stories," as Shah calls them, some Persian, some Turkish, some Arabic, but all of them subtle and witty, wily and spicy, bearing within their folds golden advice and practical wisdom that could be of inestimable value to anyone.

There is, for instance, the story of the idiot who chanced to see a browsing camel and said to it:

"Your appearance is awry. Why is this so?"

The camel replied: "In judging the impression made, you are

[9] Idries Shah, *Wisdom of the Idiots* (2d ed.; London: Octagon Press, 1970; New York: Dutton Paperbacks, 1971), p. 150.

[10] Idries Shah, *Thinkers of the East* (London: Jonathan Cape, 1971), p. 162.

attributing a fault to that which shaped the form. Be aware of this! Do not consider my crooked appearance a fault.

"Get away from me, by the shortest route. My appearance is thus for function, for a reason. The bow needs the bentness as well as the straightness of the bowstring.

"Fool, begone! An ass's perception goes with an ass's nature." [11]

What an effective way to learn that one should not be swayed by subjective impressions and conditioned judgments. "In the distorted mirror of your mind," says Hakim Sanai, "an angel can seem to have a devil's face."

I was fifteen years old when I delved into Omar Khayyam's *Rubaiyat* (Quatrains), Sheikh Saadi's *Kolliyat* (Complete Works), and Jalaluddin Rumi's *Mathnavi* (Multirhymed Couplets), and they have been my constant companions ever since. But I must acknowledge that Shah's *The Sufis* added new dimensions to my understanding of the teachings of these sublime poet-philosophers whose impact on Western civilization may gradually surpass the indelible mark they have left on the culture of the East. In his *The Way of the Sufi*, Shah gives us an idea of the profundity of their teachings, and we may take from each a sample as we pass.

Speaking of the slumber of man, Khayyam writes:

I fell asleep, and Wisdom said to me:
"Sleeping, the rose of happiness never bloomed,
Why do you do a thing which is next to death?
Drink 'wine,' for you will have long to sleep." [12]

Deriding selfishness, aggressiveness, greed, and ambition, Saadi remarks:

Ten dervishes can sleep beneath one blanket; but two kings cannot reign in one land. A devoted man will eat half his bread, and give the other half to dervishes. A ruler may have a realm, but yet plot to overcome the world. [13]

[11] Idries Shah, *Tales of the Dervishes* (London: Jonathan Cape, 1967; New York: Dutton Paperbacks, 1970), p. 152.

[12] Idries Shah, *The Way of the Sufi* (London: Jonathan Cape, 1968; New York: Dutton Paperbacks, 1970), p. 60.

[13] *Ibid.,* p. 91.

Admonishing his fellowmen for their childish infatuation with the material world, the Great Master (Maulana Jalaluddin Rumi) inquires:

How long shall we, in the Earth-world like children
Fill our laps with dust and stones and scraps?
Let us leave earth and fly to the heavens,
Let us leave babyhood and go to the Assembly of Man.[14]

Shah's chief contribution, as may be gathered from this brief notice of some of his books, is the exposition, in easily understandable terms, of an ancient theme challenging the intellectual assumptions and fixed patterns of thought that account, to a large extent, for the disturbed and distressing conditions in contemporary society, thus providing the opportunity of orienting the thinking capacity of Western man in a new direction.

But one may justifiably ask: What is this new direction, the mystic experience called Sufism? Briefly, it is an ascetic, contemplative way of life as a means of attaining the ultimate truth—a moral and spiritual culture that permeates the Sufi's personality, transforms his entire being and elevates him to a point where he becomes cognizant of reality. It is the state of perfection—the state of balance between his physical and spiritual existence, the totality of his rarefied thoughts and spiritual attainment as manifested in his attitude and behavior toward the community. It is what he is, "a king beneath a humble cloak," as Hakim Sanai describes him—the kind of individual fervently sought by the revered Sheikh. The allusion is to the allegorical representation of Maulana Jalaluddin Rumi, who wrote:

With a lantern yesterday
Through the town the Sheikh did go:
"Tired of deuce and devil I
Wish a human being to know."
"None can there be found," they cried,
"Long we searched futilely."
"Him who can't be found," said he,
"I am seeking earnestly." [15]

14 *Ibid.*, p. 109.
15 Author's translation.

Thus in a dramatic way he tells us that "he is hidden—seek him," and the search has steadily continued.

This may sound strange, for individual Sufis are known in their thousands throughout the East. Settlements of Sufis are found in the lands of the Arabs, Turks, Persians, Afghans, Indians, and Malays, and there are even some among the Western nations. But the fact is that the Sufi is "hidden more deeply than the practitioner of any secret school," [16] and cannot be easily found.

No wonder, then, that the more doggedly

> searchers of the Western world have tried to dig out the secrets of the Sufis, the more hopelessly complex the task has seemed to be. Their work thus litters the fields of mysticism, Arabism, Orientalism, history, philosophy and even general literature. "The secret," in the Sufi phrase, "protects itself. It is found only in the spirit and practice of the Work." [17]

To pursue it, however, one need neither give up his religion nor retire to seclusion, for Sufism is a secret teaching within all religions, and does not require its followers to become monks, nuns, or hermits. All that is necessary is to seek assimilation, search for ultimate knowledge, and strive for wisdom.

The role of the classics in Sufism is to act upon the mind and upon the community, so that some sort of real, special understanding develops. A cultivated man, in the Eastern sense, is not a devotee of anything, nor even a man who is word-perfect in the classics, but a man (or woman) who has reached some understanding through the interaction of written materials and social contact and inner cognition. The evident demand for this more rarefied type of consciousness among thinking people in the West may in some measure account for the current interest in this kind of literature.

The ability of Idries Shah to fascinate a Western literary audience is undeniable. The many long discussions of his work are notable both for the eminence of their authors and for the variety of levels of the media in which they appear. This is not

[16] *The Sufis*, p. 16.
[17] *Ibid.*, p. 16.

exceptional in the case of classical writers, but it is exceptional for a contemporary writer to acquire this range of contact with such a varied and immense audience.

Not everyone, of course, can be said to have been fascinated. Some critics, though very few, have said that there is nothing new in his work. Others hold that he is trying to establish a cult. Still others feel affronted by his lack of reverence for the more pedantic type of scholar. So far this kind of reaction has done little more than add "salt to the meal"; and those who read the discussions of Shah's work may acquire certain extra dimensions of experience through studying the critics' reactions. One interesting phenomenon is the way in which Shah can publish a story describing the sensitive subjectivity of critics, and then find reviewers displaying exactly these symptoms—annoyance and so on—when criticizing that very piece. If such critiques are placed side by side they make hilarious reading, for they tend to show the critic behaving just as Shah predicted he would and yet remaining unconscious of it. A man must be very sure of his materials and of his ground before he can do that. A spin-off from this secondary harvest is that some psychologists have been able to use the hostile criticisms to show how standard they are in pattern, thus directly contributing to Shah's work of illustrating the perils of facile assumption and unconscious bias.

Especially interesting, both in its power to ruffle and in its great perceptivity and humor, is Shah's smallest book, *Reflections* (1969). This was chosen on the BBC's "The Critics' Programme" as a Book of the Year. It contains sayings, aphorisms, jokes, fables, and all manner of most entertaining pieces derived from many sources. It is saturated in Sufi lore, and yet it has a fascination that has made it a best seller. Although nobody has called this an "Oriental" book, it is full of names and places connected with the East. Yet, as repeated references to it in all kinds of newspapers show, it is regarded as containing both wise counsel and illustrations of the human condition which are intensely interesting to people in the West.

It is not without significance that although some people instantly attach themselves to its contents, others have observed a secondary effect, which they are hard put to explain: there is a sort of subliminal operation causing passages in the book that do not appear significant at first to gain in interest and increase in meaning, if they are held in the mind. The same sort of effect may also be noted in some of Shah's other books. How this effect is caused must be ascribed, pending any deeper analysis, to a special Sufi power over words.

Another, and for some people no less tantalizing, characteristic of Shah's work is to be found in the sheer variety of what he writes and how it is handled. His *Destination Mecca* (London: Octagon Press, 1957), a travel book with a dash of exploration, his *Oriental Magic* (London: Octagon Press, 1956), a serious study of minority beliefs, and his *The Dermis Probe* (London: Jonathan Cape, 1970; New York: Dutton Paperbacks, 1971), a collection of anecdotes and stories keynoted by a space satire based on an Eastern parable more than seven hundred years old, are all different. But one can find in them, aimed though they may be at different audiences, the same inner coherence of spiritual values that few bodies of writing can display. And, of course, each of these books is a success in its own right, constantly reprinted and widely admired.

I am aware that commentators have remarked how completely master of his subject Shah is, no matter what he seems to be writing about. But it is possible to hold that this very expertise, if one allows oneself to be carried away by it, could tend to mask the operation of the inner content. There are many authors who are masters of their subject but fail to carry an impact so that they take decades to become known.

Shah's own explanation for this capacity of mastery is simple, and seems to be consistent with manifestations of art and effort in many other fields. He says that where there is a real, significant, inner content to anything, it is capable of a powerful, contemporary and effective manifestation. His work is not so much an exposition of Sufism as an extrusion or a manifestation of it. That inner truth must find expression, and that this expression is certain to exercise a definite fascination rooted in its inner reality is something that one cannot ignore. Many of those who ignore the existence of such a phenomenon may be found either denying that Shah's work is of importance (though unable to account for its effects) or else claiming that it is his talent alone that is responsible for his success. Shah himself denies the possession of talent. He reverts to the claim that if something is true or "right," its expression is sure to be superior to that of something that is more shallow. There is no need to embrace a cult, or to resort to occultist thinking to see that there are great possibilities of experiential research here.

II

SHAH
IN HIS EASTERN
CONTEXT

by

Professor L. F. Rushbrook Williams

It is unusual, to say the least of it, for an Oriental exponent of an Eastern philosophy to write books that are best sellers in the Western world; more unusual still that the same author's space-age adaptation of an eight-hundred-year-old Persian parable should have been turned into a prizewinning film, acclaimed at festivals in London and New York. These are considerable achievements, but the fame that they have brought is merely incidental to the contributions to new lines of thinking that have resulted from Saiyid Idries Shah's rescuing of Sufi philosophy and Sufi practice from the accusations of charlatanism and hallucination that have for too long obscured their merits and debarred them from the serious attention of many Western observers. It seems fashionable in these egalitarian days to decry the value to the world of inherited capacity, except perhaps in the case of racehorses; but a study of the background of Saiyid Idries Shah, as disclosed in his birth and upbringing, goes far to explain what he has accomplished.

He belongs to a family of Muswi Saiyids directly descended from Ali Musa Raza, the eighth Imam, and thus from the Prophet Mohammed himself. For centuries, this family has provided scholars, soldiers, and statesmen—including kinsmen of the Sassanid dynasty of Iran—who have played a prominent part in the history of Iran, Iraq, Afghanistan, and India.[1]

The connection of this family with Britain began as recently —considered in the light of their long preceding history—as 1839, at the time of the First Afghan War, when the head of the house was a great landholder and Sufi Murshid in Afghanistan. That intrepid and formidable Englishwoman, Lady Sale, who kept a detailed diary of the tragic events following the British attempt to set Shah Shuja on the Afghan throne, refers to him as "the Laird of Paghman." He was known by his title of Nawab Saiyid Mohammed Jan-Fishan Khan. When the revolt against Shah Shuja began, Jan-Fishan Khan, as Lady Sale says:

> has had his forts and property destroyed; his wives and children, he hopes, may have been saved, but as yet he only knows the fate of one young boy who was burned alive. He had one wife with him in Cabul (*sic*) when the insurrection broke out and urged her to fly to Pughman (*sic*) for safety; the old chief told me, her reply was worth a lakh of rupees, "I will not leave you; if you fall, we die together: and if you are victorious, we will rejoice together." [2]

Paghman and Kohistan remained—and continue to this day —inhabited by local clansmen of the family. The Saiyid established himself on a great estate—some twenty-eight square miles in extent—at Sardhana, near Meerut, in Uttar Pradesh, India.[3]

---

[1] Foster, W., "The Family of Hashim," in *Contemporary Review* (May 1960), deals with the special distinction of this (Paghman-Sardhana) branch of the family.

[2] Lady Sale, *The First Afghan War*, ed. Patrick Macrory (London, 1969), p. 61.

[3] C. E. Buckland, C.I.E., *Dictionary of Indian Biography* (London, 1906), p. 374, cols. 1 and 2.

The Great Nawab's tomb towers over the Sardhana land-scape of Kamra-i-Nawaban ("the Princes' Abode"). It follows the domed pattern of the Sufi masters' mausoleums, which are found everywhere in the Islamic world. His gravestone is made of white marble; on it is inscribed in graceful *nastaliq* script the verses in tribute to him written by the Nawab (Prince) Basharat Ali Khan, a famous poet, whose pen-name was Sidq. The chrono-gram embodied in the poem, to date it, is in the penultimate line:

> *Sidq-i-sukhan-sanj—Sidq, Weigher of Words:*
> *The Stately Prince, exalted and full*
> *of virtue*
> *By the perfume of whose presence Paghman*
> *swelled with pride:*
> *He was of the children of Ali Musa*
> *Raza* [the Eighth Imam].
> *He came to see India from Kabul—*
> *His footsteps turned Sardhana into the*
> *garden of Paradise.*
> *When the desire for a return to Heaven*
> *took him*
> *He left this abode of mortality, throwing*
> *away his outer garment.*
> *For the date: "O Sidq—Weigher of Words!"*
> *Say: Saiyid, Mohammed JAN-FISHAN Khan.*

He was succeeded by his son, Nawab Saiyid Muhammad Ali Shah; he in turn by Nawab Saiyid Amjad Ali Shah, who was the grandfather of Saiyid Idries Shah. These descendants of a great family, although prominent in local affairs, took little part in political life. They maintained great state and at the beginning of the present century, when through their generosity some finan-cial difficulties beset them, the government paid their debts and managed the Sardhana lands for them until a loan was paid off.

Nawab Saiyid Amjad Ali Shah's son, Sirdar Saiyid Ikbal Ali Shah (the father of our Saiyid Idries Shah) at quite an early age initiated what was in fact a new line for the family. For centuries, as we have seen, these descendants of the Prophet had been rulers, statesmen, and soldiers. Saiyid Ikbal Ali Shah was the first of them to become known in the West as a man of letters, as well as the first to travel to Britain to complete an education, which began in the famous Mohammedan Anglo-Oriental College—now the University—at Aligarh. He went to Edinburgh for further studies; and from that time onward, although he never became "Anglicized" and never lost in any way his link with his own great cultural heritage, he formed a deep attachment to the United Kingdom where he made his home, so far as so great a traveler could be said to have a home at all, for many years. This attachment has gone even deeper in the case of his son, Saiyid Idries, who always returns to England, even after traveling, as did his father, in many parts of the world.

Sirdar (as he was generally known) Ikbal Ali Shah was a remarkable man; I delighted in his friendship for more than half a century. I first came to know him at the time of the "Kaiser's War," when I myself had only been in India for a few years. As a student of Muslim history—I held a professorship at Allahabad until I was taken into the Government of India—I appreciated Sirdar Ikbal Ali Shah's long descent; and I expected to find, when I first met him, an aristocrat of conservative, almost reactionary views, wedded to a conviction that the world owed him a living because of his distinguished ancestry. Not a bit of it; I found him a man of most enlightened outlook, of vast reading, and of interests, if anything, wider than my own. Although the family wealth was considerable by any standards, he seemed determined to make his own way in the world, and to take advantage of his privileges of birth only for the purpose of gaining access to persons and places that, because of these privileges, became accessible to him. He had already begun to present a considerable puzzle to the local British officials. That the son of a wealthy United Provinces dignitary of ancient family should choose to go to Europe to undertake higher studies was strange enough; but odder still, in their eyes, was his deep interest in things of the mind and the spirit, which made the comfortable life on the Sardhana estate, of which he was the Nawab's only son and heir, too narrow and limited to satisfy him. Even those British officials who, like myself, were cognizant of his noble ancestry were perplexed by him, if perhaps for a different reason. Why should a Saiyid, of the true Fatimite line, born, as it were, to be a leader of Islam, display this strange interest in the Sufi philosophy? It seemed to us almost as though a cardinal archbishop, in the days of the Holy Roman Empire, were to busy himself with the doctrines and practices of the Albigensian heretics.

As a student of Indian history, I knew something of the Sufis in India. Their name, it was said, derived from their habit of wearing garments of white, undyed wool. Their origin, it was believed, stemmed from Iran, where their zeal for the ties of common humanity and their freedom from doctrinal rigidity made them beloved by the humble folk among whom they worked. They must have been among the earliest students of comparative religion, for they examined Buddhism and Christianity; they studied the philosophies of Greece and India. Against this background, they reexamined the faith of Islam, with the object of extracting, as it were, the timeless and essential elements of the Prophet's message to mankind, as recorded in the Koran and the Traditions. Like the Franciscan and Dominican Friars in thirteenth century Europe, they set great store on poverty and detachment from the shackles of material possessions; but unlike the mendicant orders, they had no uniformity of doctrine. Their purpose was to achieve nearness to God, and to pass on to others the message of the everlasting mercy and compassion that marked His dealings with mankind. Their constant endeavor was to develop the possibilities of "nearness" to Him wherever and whenever they could. They experimented with many varieties of religious experience: among these the ritual repetition of the attributes of God until the worshiper's sense of subjective personality vanished; and the use of calculated music and dancing as aids to the sense of exaltation that facilitated an approach to the threshold of Truth. Inevitably, they came to be regarded as miracle-workers, possessed of magic powers, although many of their practices, in our own times, appear to us to conform with the results of our modern studies in such fields as education and the training of the mind.

As propagandists for Islam as they interpreted it, they were superb; in India they won many more converts by love and understanding than were ever turned to the creed of the Prophet by indoctrination. They destroyed no temples; they slew no infidels. They welcomed converts as friends and equals; they accepted intermarriage with them. As their numbers increased, so did particular leaders—many of them ranked as true saints by both

Muslims and Hindus—emerge. Their followers began to constitute themselves into something like the separate orders of the
Christian Church, some pursuing particular practices that their
leader had found locally effective: but all characterized by the
single basic attitude of seeking God, honoring true learning, and
teaching—by methods that our modern investigations are beginning to rediscover and approve—how knowledge should be applied to the needs of mankind. Among the Sufi orders, those
which have played the greatest part in the history of India were
the Chishtis, the Qadiris, the Suhrawardis, and the Naqshbandis.
All have given to the country saints to whose tombs the multitude
still flocks—men like Moinuddin Chishti of Ajmer, Nizamuddin
Auliya of Delhi, Mian Mir of Lahore, and Shaikh Salim Chisti,
who was the great Mughal Akbar's spiritual counselor. Such saints
exercised great influence during their lives; after their deaths, poor
Muslims who could not perform the hajj to Mecca made pilgrimage to their shrines instead. That distinguished historian of the
Sikhs, Khushwant Singh, who is among the most prominent of
contemporary Indian men of letters, has testified to the formative
influence of the Sufis in the foundation of the Sikh religion. The
two faiths have, indeed, a good deal in common; Mian Mir of the
Qadiri Order, who was a close friend of the fifth of the Sikh
Gurus, Arjun Singh, laid the foundation of the Golden Temple at
Amritsar, greatest and most famous of all the Sikh shrines.

A student of Indian history, like myself, could not avoid
having some knowledge of the Sufis and of their work in India;
but what I had failed to realize, until Sirdar Ikbal Ali Shah explained the point to me, was that their influence was strong in
almost every country in the Middle East, Africa, South and Central Asia. He told me that his ambition was to devote his life to a
study of these widely dispersed communities, and of the message
that they inculcated everywhere they were to be found. He was
convinced, he said, that this message might form a bridge between
the Western and the Eastern ways of thinking; and that the
methods that they were using to convey it—methods well tested
by centuries of successful practice—would certainly be of interest, and might be of value, to the Western world in the quest for
the best ways of promoting independent thought and the reexamination of accepted values to test their suitability to the needs of

modern social organization. These ideas, which Sirdar Ikbal Ali Shah expounded, were quite new to me at the time, but I saw how fruitful they might be, and I did what I could to encourage him in his pursuit of them.

Sirdar Ikbal and his son, both in writing and in other ways, were ultimately to show how Sufi thought and action, educational and adaptive as they are, could be of service to contemporary thinking. As a historian, it was of particular interest to me that they discovered, and utilized in no uncertain manner, a key to those perplexities of Sufi history that have indeed rendered so much previous research on the subject largely unfruitful. This key, chiefly shaped by symbolism, levels of understanding, and adaptation, explains why so many people at different places and times, came to form such varying impressions of the Sufis and their origins and intentions. The Sufis are, in fact, themselves the living parable of "The Elephant in the Dark," [4] half-understood by simple folk, least understood by many eager specialists, even in the East—and that even today. But the very coherence of the doctrine expounded by the Shahs establishes its authenticity. For the first time, it explains Sufism without forcing meanings, without "proof by selected instances."

Sirdar Ikbal Ali Shah was quite the most brilliant of the Asian scholars with whom I worked. He was a master of Urdu, Persian, and Arabic. His reading was wide as well as profound. He had a beautiful English style and enormous facility of expression. He was a remarkably rapid writer, and could turn in his calligraphic "copy" long before the deadline was ever reached.[5] We worked together long enough to lay the foundations of a friendship that endured right up to his death in a motor accident in Tangier in 1969.[6]

By the time that his son Idries Shah was born in 1924, the Sirdar had begun to travel widely. He had reestablished the family links with Afghanistan, where his mastery of Pushtu and Persian, his status as a Saiyid, and his diplomatic gifts made him a most honored visitor. Very sensibly, the Afghan authorities—

[4] Idries Shah, *Tales of the Dervishes* (London: Jonathan Cape, 1967; New York: Dutton Paperbacks, 1970), pp. 25 ff quote this famous story.

[5] See The Sirdar Ikbal Ali Shah, *The Spirit of the East* (London, 1939); *The Oriental Caravan* (London, 1933).

[6] Obituary, *The Times* (London), November 8, 1969.

who were at that time, and indeed up to the recently established reforms in the administration, all members of the royal family— sought his advice and help quite frequently, not only in Kabul itself but also in their embassy in London, to which the Sirdar for long remained attached in various capacities. This did not prevent him from traveling widely through the Middle East, where he became the close and trusted friend of his Hashimite kinsmen, the Sharif of Mecca, King Abdullah of Jordan, the Emir Abdulillah of Iraq, and other prominent statesmen. Purely because of his descent and personality—I can think of no other reasons—he seemed equally trusted by leaders of orthodoxy like the Rector of Azhar University in Cairo and by reformers like Kemal Ataturk.[7]

In addition to his other qualities, Sirdar Ikbal Ali Shah was a born writer with an almost dangerous facility with his pen in English, Arabic, Persian, and Urdu. I say "almost dangerous" be- cause his output was so great, the sphere of his interests was so wide, and his access to persons and places quite inaccessible to other people so remarkable that a certain skepticism grew up, particularly in Britain, about whether he had really been every- where he claimed to have been. This attitude annoyed me very much, for the Sirdar was the soul of honor, and it would have been beneath his dignity, as well as inconsistent with the great traditions of his house, to put forward any statement that was not strictly in accordance with the facts. I did my best to confute his critics, and I think that to some extent at least, I succeeded. Moreover I knew well, even if other people did not, that his ex- cellent travel books,[8] and his biographies of figures like Kemal Ataturk and the late Aga Khan [9] were—in spite of the fact that he wrote about twenty books in English in the course of his lifetime —merely by-products of his determination to study the contem- porary manifestations of Sufism and to seek in the doctrines and practices of the various Sufi communities the link between East- ern and Western thought of which, he was convinced, the world

---

[7] The Sirdar Ikbal Ali Shah, *Kemal—Maker of Modern Turkey* (Lon- don, 1934); and also his *The Controlling Minds of Asia* (London, 1937).

[8] Such as *Eastward to Persia* (London: Wright & Brown, 1930), *West- ward to Mecca* (London: Witherby, 1928), *The Golden East* (London: John Long, 1931), *Arabia* (London: A. & C. Black, 1931).

[9] *The Prince Aga Khan* (London, 1933).

stood in such need. He gradually became recognized as the great living authority on Sufi doctrine and the instructional methods by which this doctrine could be applied to the requirements of modern social organization. Further, he employed his mastery of Arabic and Persian to study and translate the writings of the great' exponents of Sufi philosophy in the past, thus bringing to the notice of the Western world hitherto ignored treasures of thought and practice.[10] He lectured in many of the universities of the Middle East and South Asia as well as of the West, and even in Latin America. For some time he headed a research group in England to which students of Sufism flocked; he held a professorship (covering West Asia) in the Council for Cultural Relations set up by independent India in Delhi, and up to the very day of his death he was active in intercultural work in North Africa.

There can be little doubt that his profound knowledge of the teachings and methods of Sufism, his deep study of the Sufi masters, and his interest in the great mass of proverbial wisdom associated with such figures—real or legendary—as Mulla Nasreddin, Mullah Do-Piyaza, and the anonymous heroes of Dervish tradition opened up to his son, Saiyid Idries Shah, a well-nigh untapped source—so far as the English-speaking world is concerned —of Sufi wit, humor, and acute penetration beneath the surface appearance of conventional human intercourse.

From the time when Saiyid Idries Shah was old enough to travel with his father, he accompanied him on many of his journeys, and at quite an early age was brought into contact with many distinguished personalities to whom the high birth and long lineage of the two Saiyids were the principal—and in some cases the only—passports to real confidence and intimacy. Such an upbringing presented to a young man of marked intelligence, such as Idries Shah soon proved himself to possess, many opportunities to acquire a truly international outlook, a broad vision, and an acquaintance with people and places that any professional diplomat of more advanced age and longer experience might well envy. But a career of diplomacy did not attract Idries Shah; he had witnessed some of the frustrations and disappointments that from time to time beset Sirdar Ikbal Ali Shah in this field of activity,

[10] See The Sirdar Ikbal Ali Shah, *Islamic Sufism* (London, 1933).

and he decided that life in an embassy was not for him. And just as Sirdar Ikbal Ali Shah, as I have already related, had struck out for himself in a career that was something new in the long history of his house, so has his son, Saiyid Idries, continued and enlarged the investigations originally commenced by his father. I first came into contact with the son when Saiyid Idries Shah was quite young, but I remember being impressed by the attention that he paid to the talks between his father and myself, which covered a wide ground in world affairs affecting the Middle East and South and Southeast Asia. Even then, he was plainly a deeply reflective youth; but he had, I thought, a very practical streak that might serve him well in his later career. Time has certainly shown that this impression was justified.

It may well be, I think, that Idries Shah early realized the extent to which his father had suffered from a certain otherworldliness. Sirdar Ikbal Ali Shah was a most lovable man; but he did not understand business affairs very well. He never derived much profit from his excellent books; and he scorned to utilize for personal advantage his innumerable intimate contacts with men in high position. The Sufi philosophy is nothing if not highly practical; yet it is practical in a particular way—spiritually and intellectually rather than economically and financially; and the Sirdar retained in his way of life the ancient Sufi tradition of brushing aside the ties of worldly possessions. From time to time, this trait caused considerable complications: as when he suddenly discovered that because he had not taken the precaution of acquiring British domicile, the tightening-up of residence regulations obliged him to leave the study center for Sufism that he had made significant in England and find a new home in Morocco. This uprooting was quite serious for a man of his age; it could have been avoided if the proper precautions had been taken. Unluckily I heard about it too late to be of any help—which again was characteristic of Sirdar Ikbal Ali Shah, who hated to inflict his personal difficulties upon his friends. Could this episode have inspired Saiyid Idries to include in *The Dermis Probe* [11] the instructive fable of the ichthyologist who, devoting his life to the study of goldfish, discovered too late that he had broken the law

[11] Idries Shah, *The Dermis Probe* (London: Jonathan Cape, 1970; New York: Dutton Paperbacks, 1971), p. 9.

for lack of the necessary certificates under the Cruelty to Animals Regulations?

Idries Shah has never fallen into this kind of trap. He combines shrewdness and business acumen with the inquiring mind and deep philosophical insight that distinguished his father. Moreover, whereas Sirdar Ikbal Ali Shah, who pioneered the effective study of Sufi philosophy in the West, found that the time was not quite ripe for his message to be appreciated at its true value, Idries Shah has discovered that, in this age of spiritual uncertainty and a dawning reaction against the prevalent materialism, the outlook and practices of Sufism are meeting exactly the needs that so many people are now experiencing. I am reminded of the Persian saying, quoted in Saiyid Idries Shah's *The Pleasantries of the Incredible Mulla Nasrudin:* "If the Father cannot, the Son may bring it to its conclusion." [12]

A remarkably large number of people in the Western world seem to find in the Sufi message something that gives a fresh meaning to life. This is partly a consequence, perhaps, of the new and startling way in which the message is conveyed. The outlook of Mulla Nasreddin and the Dervish sages has several facets. One of these stresses the uselessness of knowledge without insight, accumulated merely for its own sake. This reminds one of the saying of Hobbes recorded by Aubrey: "If he had read as much as other men, he would have known no more than they." Another aspect appeals to those now experimenting with extrasensory perception, in which certain Sufi orders were advanced practitioners. Yet a third looks at first sight almost like sheer clowning, as when Mullah Do-Piyaza defeats a learned company of Ulema in an argument by an obscene gesture, which they interpret as a devastating reminder of the unity of the Almighty. And yet the same personage can, on another occasion, with piercing insight, define the cults of orthodoxy as "irrationals united in a belief in the impossible." On occasion the wit is really biting: "The ways of Allah are wonderful—he had Hell and yet he created India." But this last, after all, is only reminiscent of what

---

[12] London: Jonathan Cape, 1968, p. 9. Nasrudin tales are also found in *The Sufis* (1964); *The Exploits of the Incomparable Mulla Nasrudin* (1966), *Caravan of Dreams* (1968), and *The Subtleties of the Inimitable Mulla Nasrudin* (1973).

the Emperor Babur, first of the Mughals, wrote in his powerful invectives against the climate and amenities—or lack of them—in Hindustan.[13] The truth seems to be that Sufi doctrine and practice hold something for everyone who has the wit to find it. No doubt this is why the works of Idries Shah are now attracting a variety of readers in many different professions and ranks of Western society. How many of us wish with all our hearts that we, too, could encounter that famous character in Sufi lore, Mushkil Gusha, the "Remover of Difficulties"! [14]

[13] And the Indians can take a joke. *Caravan of Dreams* was delightedly received in India, with this quotation singled out for special comment.

[14] *Caravan of Dreams*, pp. 115 ff.

III

PROJECTING
SUFI THOUGHT IN AN
APPROPRIATE
CONTEXT

by

Professor Ishtiaq Husain Qureshi

Sufi thought, seen through the great variety of material assembled by Shah, proves to be extremely diverse and manifested in very many forms. The agreement of Sufis themselves upon who constitutes a Sufi is the only test of Sufihood. This is because, as Rumi and others have tirelessly pointed out, Sufism is grounded not on theology but on experience. Manifestations of Sufi teaching may even appear absurd at a given time; for example, local authorities could not comprehend Ibn al-Arabi's *Tarjuman al-Ashwaq*, until he himself wrote a commentary for them.[1] The same is true of such artifacts as *Fusus al-Hikam*.[2]

---

[1] Reynold A. Nicholson, *Tarjuman al-Ashwaq* (by Muhiyuddin Ibn al-Arabi), Vol. XX, New Series (London: Royal Asiatic Society, 1911).

[2] Muhiyuddin Ibn al-Arabi, *Fusus al-Hikam*.

Shah has often illustrated the allegorical use of tales and "illustrative encounters." It is important to realize that one must regard the latter as word-artifacts, constructed for teaching purposes, and not necessarily as historical facts. Many Western students regularly go astray in stating that "such-and-such an event could not have happened at such-and-such a time, because of chronological problems." Yet it is more than seven hundred years since such thinkers as Rumi pointed out that, for example, "Moses and Pharaoh" may not mean the historical Moses and Pharaoh, but can also stand for opposing tendencies between thoughts in an individual's mind.

Today it is fashionable to try to trace Sufism to its roots and to define what influences may have played upon its development and upon the personalities of its outstanding men and women. This approach, admirable though it is likely to be in the tracing of social history or political development, is extremely unlikely to be of value in the study of Sufism itself, and its continued employment may well indicate that "a cobbler is trying to use a watchmaker's tools."

It is most important to note that Shah has taken a good deal of his material from extant traditional oral teaching. Many of the stories and teachings that he has published would be regarded by the folklorist as an outstanding contribution to the preservation of a tradition in the manner of the Brothers Grimm or other important collectors of "people's wisdom." This role of Shah in the literary preservation of important material can hardly be exaggerated. He has traveled in all the Arab countries, in Africa, Turkey, and Central Asia, collecting, tape-recording, and ascertaining the interpretations of these tales. In some cases at least they may well represent true traditions handed down from remote antiquity from some of the great teachers of the past who are named in them.

Shah's originality finds expression in his interpretations of passages from Sufi classics and his reconciling of what many people regard as "different traditions" within Sufism. For instance, he has shown that the "Mulla Nasreddin" corpus of tales is susceptible of inner interpretations, while many people have assumed them to be mere buffoonery. Another original contribution lies in Shah's careful collection of stories from some of the Sufi *Tariqas*, which are less well known for their instructional value.

A point must be made that the subtlety and spiritual merit of the stories used by Shah have been often noted and acclaimed by Western reviewers, who have contrasted them very favorably with the dry and uninteresting didactic and moralistic tales that belong to the lowest level of human instruction. Of the highest form is the tale of Moses and Khidr from the Koran, which inspired Parnell's *The Hermit*. Shah was the first to show that this tale originated in the Koran, and to use it as an illustration of the most advanced and effective type of story, far removed from the stories of folklore.[3]

There is an increasing tendency in the Western world to adopt extravagant religious beliefs from Oriental sources, generally called "guru-ism," because such beliefs are usually ascribed to some "Master." Thousands of people now follow these cults, and their proliferation and absurdities have given rise to real concern among genuinely thinking people. It is thus of the greatest importance to realize that Idries Shah is selecting and publishing materials of real authenticity and high literary merit, and that he has been struggling against the fantasies and absurdities of "guru-ism" for years. It is a good thing to have an active representative of Eastern thought in the West whose mind is free of such absurdities, and who possesses sufficient intellectual caliber to be able to communicate with, and to command the respect of, scholars, literati, and other persons of serious intent. As the false coin can drive out the true, so cheap imitations can debase true spirituality. Shah's obvious task is to make available standard and important materials for those who are willing to take note of them, so that eventually the jewels of Eastern thought in the Sufi tradition come to be recognized and appreciated.

Occult and metaphysical speculation and moralistic training alike are incomplete without a sound basis of genuine material from this tradition. Shah has started by making available, in Western languages, materials that will eventually enable Western students to understand Islamic culture and philosophy. He has done this largely by introducing Western people to the materials in a manner suited to them and to some extent by reconciling these materials with Western thought patterns and traditions.

[3] Idries Shah, *Tales of the Dervishes* (London: Jonathan Cape, 1967; New York: Dutton Paperbacks, 1970), pp. 198 ff, note on p. 200.

IV

IDRIES SHAH:
BRIDGE
BETWEEN EAST AND WEST—
HUMOR, PHILOSOPHY,
AND
ORIENTATION
by
Mir S. Basri

In the year 799, Imam Musa al-Kazim, "The Patient," died in Baghdad. Over eleven centuries later, several books by Idries Shah were published, and they rapidly became known in the West. What is the relationship between these events, widely spaced in time and place? There is indeed more than one connection between them.

Firstly, Saiyid Idries Shah is a direct descendant of the Imam, who is buried at Kadhimain near Baghdad, and who was himself seventh in descent from the Prophet Mohammed through his daughter, the Lady Fatima al-Zahra. And this blood connection is not the only one between Baghdad and the West—the East represented by Idries and the West that reads his books with such interest. Kipling's "Never the twain shall meet" notwithstanding, the two have met, and have continually met many times during their long history.

To help illuminate the continuous meeting and interchange, we may recall the spread of Arabic through the Abbasid Empire, which ruled the Middle East and North Africa for centuries in the Middle Ages. This language formed the *lingua franca* of a territory centered on Basra and Baghdad, and was in use from Spain to India, from Samarkand to the Yemen. Latin was in use as the tongue of culture in Europe, and similarly, Arabic was the language of science and literature, including philosophy and metaphysics, among the multitude of peoples, sects, and nations that lived in peace under the aegis of Islam.

Within this enormous territory, and beyond it to China and inner Africa, there was considerable cultural interchange and a great catalysis of ideas. The amount of travel and study carried out is not even exceeded today. An example is the life of the Moroccan traveler Ibn Batuta. He was born in Tangier and journeyed in Africa, Syria, Arabia, Iraq, Persia, Yemen, the lands of the Tatars, and Transoxania, reaching India, China, and Java.

Such men were polymaths, studying and teaching a vast number of sciences, absorbing and contributing, comparing and excelling in a multitude of fields. Ibn Batuta was appointed a judge in Delhi and was an ambassador to the Emperor of China. During the rule of al-Mamun (in the ninth century) Greek works in the fields of medicine, astronomy, mathematics, and many other sciences and arts were translated extensively into Arabic. In this way the Greek culture, which had itself earlier absorbed from the Babylonian, Egyptian, and other ancient Oriental cultures, returned to the East. The Arabs and people of other nations that joined them advanced literature and science in a way that is a matter of record, and has not yet been outshone. At the time of the European Renaissance the Eastern current returned to Europe, and many of the works and thoughts of the Easterners were translated and communicated to the new society of Europe.

Throughout these processes, Islamic Sufism was an effective instrument of human development, of science, and of thought. It was especially marked in the lives and teachings of ascetics and anchorites, such as Hasan of Basra, Wassel ibn Atta, and the woman Sufi Rabia al-Adawia. Parallels and equivalences in experience in other systems known to the ancient world were discerned; and effective work in this field was associated with Bayazid of Bistam, al-Hallaj, Ibn al-Arabi, Farid al-Din Attar, and Jalaluddin Rumi. Noteworthy organizations and formulations became apparent with the characteristic Sufi organizations known to the public: *takias* and *zawiyas* (centers of study), groups and *tarikas* ("orders"), ceremonies, and litanies. There were Sufi guides, known as *Murshids*, followed by disciples, *Murids; Pirs* (Sages, Elders) and Sheikhs, ancients.

In our century the prominent French professor Louis Massignon has been one of the most indefatigable students of Hallaj in particular. Through his work and interpretations many Western readers have become aware of this area of Sufism. He visited Baghdad several times and met its erudite and learned men. One day I was present in the convent of Father Anastase-Marie the Carmelite when Dr. Massignon was there, continuing, as was his custom, his interaction with the learned, the nobles, and the writers of the capital.

Massignon was praising Hallaj excessively; suddenly our friend the historian and lawyer Professor Abbas al-Azzawi shouted out: "If I were asked, today after a thousand years, to judge the case of Hallaj, I would not hesitate to shed his blood, again!"

There is still a clear division between the literal mind and that of the poetic, the Sufi and the conventional scholar. The best of researchers into the affairs of the Dervishes in our time may well be our friend Ahmad Hamid al-Sarraf. He has translated Omar al-Khayyam, and has written introductory studies about the Dervishes and their states, beliefs, and ceremonies.

Sufi poetry has had a tremendous influence upon Arabian thought and upon Eastern life. Only a few in the Middle East are unaware, for instance, of the Sultan of Lovers, the Knower of God, the Sheikh Ibn al-Faridh, whose poetry is still sung from the Atlantic to the lands of the Persians, inebriating souls with holy wine and making eyes weep with longing and desire.

And all this brings us back to the Saiyid, Idries Shah, worthy scion of the Imam Musa al-Kazim, and a new connecting link between East and West. Idries has studied deeply the knowledge of the East, and he has conveyed it to the West by means of his works, astonishing and delighting Western as well as Eastern literary men and critics. His writings and treatment of Sufism have succeeded in simplifying, through artistry, those principles that Sufi authors have perennially employed to reach and transmit ever-renewing spiritual experience.

Now, Shah has also written about Mulla Nasreddin, a strange Eastern character, who combined wit and simplicity and is known by many different names, including that of Joha al-Rumi. His tales are found all over the world. He usually takes on the habit of fools—but in truth he represents human wisdom. More than thirty years ago I read a book by a Swedish author, called *Philosophy of Mulla Nasrudin*. And, in one of my poems, addressing Joha, or Nasreddin, I said:

> *O Joha al-Rumi, idiocy or wit*
> *Saying this and doing that*
> *Concealing wisdom in the garb of foolishness—*
> *As gaiety so often hides tears.*
> *You have garbed Truth in a comic dress*
> *As if pulling a tail of seashells and trinkets.*
> *Is it really that you feared the Age of Destruction*
> *And so fashioned foolishness to shield you from woe and ill-*
> *will?*

Wit not only penetrates where other things will not go, it ensures the preservation and transmission of the essential material.

Saiyid Idries Shah is well prepared in every sense to deliver his message and to see its effect, in transferring, as it were, the East alive to the West, combining a deep understanding of both worlds. And, as an Afghan of Sharifian blood, he at once calls to mind a kinsman who preceded him and who struggled, too, on the frontiers to awaken the East and to tell the West about our revival.

This man, whose name is constantly mentioned and blessed throughout Islam and beyond, is Saiyid Jamal al-Din al-Afghani (1838–1897) who left his native land and visited India, Turkey, Egypt, and Persia, leaving in every country through which he passed the call for awakening from slumber, and a band of active teaching students. He established an Arabic newspaper (*Al-Urwat al-Wuthqa*, the "Everlasting Bond") in Paris, and lived for some years in St. Petersburg, capital of Tsarist Russia. He fought reactionary thought and imperial domination, and called for freedom and the struggle against tyranny. He returned to Istanbul to die there after his long wanderings, and his remains were taken, not long ago, with the greatest honors, back to his noble land.

The struggles of Jamal al-Din the Afghan had a powerful effect upon the awakening of the East and on its capacity to accept modern ideas. It might be said that there is a great contrast between his method and objectives and those of his contemporary countrymen. But the fact that the resemblance is so often invoked indicates how, in the East at any rate, the theme of awakening and development, of combining separated elements, can readily be seen as integral activities, whatever the plane upon which they are pursued. Saiyid Idries Shah and Saiyid Jamal al-Din are links in the chain between Europe and the East.

The supposed hostility between the East and West does not exist at fundamental levels. A most honored learned man, Mustafa Abdul-Razeq, Sheikh of al-Azhar at Cairo, was among those who believed firmly in this idea. He said, in an introductory article to *Islam and the West* (Paris, 1947):

> I see no real reason for any objection from the Islamic point of view to the West; for Islam in its essence has nothing which contradicts the West in *its* essence. And also, the ideas of the West contain nothing contrary to the ideas of Islam.

In this contemporary world of ours, with its atomic reactors, visits to the Moon, and psychiatric, natural, and philosophical sciences, there is still a place for spiritual Sufism and for Mulla Nasreddin. The works of Saiyid Idries Shah will be important in the fields of human knowledge as long as the human spirit seeks the unknown and yearns for wider horizons and new worlds.

V

LITERARY COMPARISONS
AND
EFFECTS
by
Professor John H. M. Chen

Throughout ancient times, religious beliefs and literature were closely related; teaching stories and proverbs are found in religious masterpieces such as the Bible, the Koran, and the Chinese classics, as well as in various Oriental religious writings by saints, especially in the areas falling within Eastern or Oriental cultures.

The Sufi teaching stories are little known beyond central and southwestern Asia, Asia Minor, and Turkestan, especially Turkey, Iran, and Afghanistan. Idries Shah's efforts to translate such stories from local tongues into English and some European languages have made it possible for many Westerners to enjoy Sufi literature and tradition. His efforts also form a bridge between the Eastern and Western cultures. I was especially interested in reading his two books entitled *Reflections* and the *Tales of the Dervishes*. In order to understand the Sufi teaching stories, a fundamental knowledge of Sufism is necessary.

Both *Reflections* and *Tales of the Dervishes* are collections of fables, legends, sayings, and teaching stories of the Sufis. Idries Shah has succeeded in presenting these in the English language in a manner that still preserves their thought-provoking nature. He has spent much time in tracing these stories and in compiling them into his books. These tales are amusing and entertaining. Yet they challenge the reader, in many cases, to seek a deeper meaning. These fables also present a variety of illustrations on human nature.

A number of these tales deal with how different points of view can lead to different ideas. Perhaps most illustrative of this is "The Blind Ones and the Matter of the Elephant" [1] in which blind men explored different parts of an elephant and came up with a number of descriptions of this strange creature. To the one who touched its tail, it was a rope. It seemed to be a fan to the one who felt its ear. This story quickly showed that looking at parts rather than the whole can lead to different ideas of what the whole must be like. Similarly, in everyday living, it would be advantageous to look first at the whole situation and all its alternatives before making a decision.

Another tale illustrating this idea is "Point of View" in which a man was very surprised to find the Devil handsome and wise rather than ugly and ignorant as he had been told. The Devil quickly clarified this apparent paradox with "My friend, . . . you have been listening to my detractors." [2] Indeed, we have all probably had this experience when meeting someone for the first time after hearing a group discuss that individual.

In "Different Every Time" a Seeker-after-Truth complained to a Sufi master about the problem of getting different answers to the same question. The master easily explained this matter by a short walk during which he asked numerous people the time at various intervals. As he explained to the Seeker, ". . . virtually the same question can elicit almost totally different answers, all

[1] Idries Shah, "The Blind Ones and the Matter of the Elephant," in *Tales of the Dervishes* (London: Jonathan Cape, 1969; New York: Dutton Paperbacks, 1970), pp. 25-26.

[2] "Point of View," in *Reflections* (London: Zenith Books, 1969), p. 7.

of them corresponding to the current truth." [3] This story may be interpreted as saying that a different point of view might be the result of the particular time and situation as well as the individual. It also illustrates that all different points of view may be correct or partially correct. It is not necessarily true that one is correct and all others are false.

Another suggestion set out in many of Shah's stories was not to let opportunity pass you by. In "Gates of Paradise," a man was told to wait alertly for the Gates of Paradise to open, as they did only every hundred years, so that he might enter. He fell asleep only to awaken as the gates snapped shut. Thus, he missed his chance to enter Paradise. [4]

The same idea is briefly expressed in the thought entitled "Hope" which states: "It is not 'Have I got a chance?' It is more often 'Have I seen my chance?' " [5]

Though Shah might lecture the person who let an opportunity slip by, he also has a word of advice for him:

"When a door bangs, people look at it, attracted by the noise.

"How few realize that it is at that time that they might instead be looking at another door opening or preparing to open one." [6] Therefore, if one does forfeit an opportunity in some way, he should not look backward, but, rather, look to the future and the opportunities it holds.

Another piece of advice, offered by the Sufis, is not to get into others' arguments. In one Sufistic tale, a man who understood animal talk attempted to settle an argument between a dog and a donkey. He was knocked out for his efforts. [7] In a similar tale, a man tried to tell a cat and a dog, who were arguing over which was a rat, that neither was a rat. For his helpful intentions, he was chased by both. [8] This admonition is not new to Westerners. Most of us have often been told to stay out of other people's arguments. Those who have failed to heed this advice have generally found the above illustrations borne out.

[3] "Different Every Time," *ibid.*, p. 8.
[4] "Gates of Paradise," in *Tales of the Dervishes*, pp. 75–76.
[5] "Hope," in *Reflections*, p. 123.
[6] "The Door Shuts," *ibid.*, p. 71.
[7] "The Dog and the Donkey," in *Tales of the Dervishes*, p. 81.
[8] "The Cat and the Dog," in *Reflections*, p. 53.

Many of the stories presented in *Reflections* and *Tales of the Dervishes* are very similar to parables and events related in the New Testament. A case in point is "The Rich Man Who Was a Beggar," which concerned a rich man who wished to distribute his wealth to the deserving. He disguised himself as a beggar and kept notes on who was kind to him. These were the ones who received part of his money.[9] This is similar to the parable of Christ, in which he divided the people into those on his right hand, who would go to Heaven because they helped those in need, and those on his left hand, who would go to Hell for refusing to help the needy.[10]

"Why He Was Chosen" compares with a Christian parable advising one not to boast and sit at the head of the table lest he be asked to move to a lower seat. Rather, he should sit at the lower seat and be complimented in front of all if asked to move to a higher seat.[11] In "Why He Was Chosen," a student flattered himself that he was chosen above all others to be a student because of his wisdom. Then he was told that he was chosen because he was the one who most needed to learn.[12] The moral for both was the same: do not boast about your own importance for, perhaps, your bragging will cause you much embarrassment.

"Bayazid and the Selfish Man" tells of a man who complained to Bayazid, a mystic, that he had not found joy though he had carried out the teachings. Bayazid told him he would have to sacrifice his vanity; but the man refused. Thus, he was unable to attain the joy he desired.[13] Similarly, we find the young man who asked Christ how he could find happiness. He was told to give away all his goods and follow Jesus. As he was very rich, he could not bring himself to do this. Like the man in "Bayazid and the Selfish Man," he was not able to find the happiness he sought.[14] Both of these religions teach the idea of self-sacrifice as a stage on the road to true happiness.

There is a parable about two men who went to pray, one

[9] "The Rich Man Who Was a Beggar," *ibid.*, pp. 33–34.
[10] Matthew 25:33–46.
[11] Luke 14:8–11.
[12] "Why He Was Chosen," in *Reflections*, p. 39.
[13] "Bayazid and the Selfish Man," in *Tales of the Dervishes*, p. 180.
[14] Matthew 19:16–24.

loudly praising God for not making him like the lowly tax col-
lector, the other quietly asking God for His forgiveness. Naturally, the latter was the one Jesus commended.[15] The Sufis have
a similar legend in which two men went to pray in the temple.
One removed his shoes and left them on the steps, the other
carried his into the temple. When questioned about his actions,
the former explained that he had left his shoes to provide the
opportunity for a potential sinner to resist the temptation to
steal. The latter said that he had taken his to prevent a potential
sin (theft), which would be his responsibility if it did occur.
However, an objective observer pointed out that while these
two had been boasting about their own goodness, a poor bare-
footed beggar had gone in inconspicuously and prayed. According to this sage, the prayers of this beggar were worth more than
the actions and the prayers of the two "pious" men.[16] Both of
these tales pointed out that it is the true communion between
man and his God that is important. The actions and prayers
whose intent is to show other men how righteous the doer is
are worthless.

Finally, there is a story "The Nature of Discipleship" in
which a young man sought to become the disciple of a certain
sage. The sage took him on a pilgrimage during which he illustrated the idea of discipleship by serving this young man at every
opportunity, despite the protests of the young disciple.[17] This
story is only slightly different from that of Jesus washing the
disciples' feet. When Peter initially refused to be served by his
Master, he was told that he could not be a disciple of Christ's
unless he submitted to being served by Him.[18] According to these
stories, the disciple must first be willing to accept the service of
his leader in order to see what a truly good leader-disciple relationship is to be like. They also show that a good leader is one
willing to show his followers by illustration and common work
rather than by command.

These stories demonstrate only a few instances of where
the ideas of the Christians and those of the Sufis meet. Both pro-

[15] Luke 18:9–14.
[16] "Carrying Shoes," in *Tales of the Dervishes*, pp. 82–83.
[17] "The Nature of Discipleship," *ibid.*, pp. 146–147.
[18] John 13:5–15.

mote the ideas of humility, kindness to all, true devotion to religion rather than a facade of religious show, and emphasize the importance of self-sacrifice for true happiness.

Some of the stories contained in Shah's books also demonstrate the idea that you cannot escape or trick fate. In a story basically like *Oedipus Rex*, a man, hearing that Death was going to "collect" him in Baghdad, left for a distant city to escape. However, Death related to another that he would have to travel to that city to collect that man who was, indeed, on his list.[19] Thus, this story related the Sufi idea of fate being unchangeable. This may be compared with the belief of predestination held by many Westerners.

"Bread and Jewels" is an interesting story with two lessons. It tells of a rich man who, in an effort to give away some jewels to a deserving person, had a baker bake the jewels in a loaf of bread and sell the bread to one of his customers. Two men came in to buy bread. The baker sold the bread with the jewels inside to the man dressed as a religious leader who, in fact, was a fraud, and sold the other man plain bread because he did not like his looks. However, the fraud, feeling the lumps in the bread, swapped with the poor man. So, despite the efforts of the baker, the truly righteous person received the jewels.[20] This, like "When Death Came to Baghdad," illustrates that one cannot trick fate. On the other hand, it also points out that looks can, indeed, be deceiving. It is the man himself that counts, not his looks or his dress. These ideas are certainly not limited to the teachings of the Sufis.

Another topic of the stories of the Sufis was admonishing man not to jump to conclusions. In the tale "The Horseman and the Snake," a horseman who had seen a man unknowingly swallow a snake forced the man to vomit. The man cursed the horseman until he realized the seemingly evil actions of the horseman had been for his own good. Thus, by jumping to conclusions, the man had harshly misjudged the horseman.[21]

---

[19] "When Death Came to Baghdad," in *Tales of the Dervishes*, pp. 191–192.

[20] "Bread and Jewels," *ibid.*, pp. 113–114.

[21] "The Horseman and the Snake," *ibid.*, pp. 140–141.

"The Man Who Looked Only at the Obvious" tells a similar story. In this case, a Seeker-after-Truth had been allowed to follow and observe a Wise One. It seemed to him that when someone did them a favor, the Wise One reacted by doing that person harm. Contrary to this, when someone did them an injustice, the Wise One repaid him with a kindness. The Seeker was very perplexed about this and, to the dismay of the Wise One, continually asked why the Wise One acted in this way. He was finally told that succeeding events would result in the actions that seemed harmful to the well-disposed proving beneficial. On the other hand, the actions that seemed beneficial to the evilly disposed would, in the long run, be beneficial only to the deserving.[22]

Some stories also bring to light a variety of human characteristics in a sometimes humorous, sometimes poignant fashion. Naturally, the greed of humans comes under study. In "The Oath" a man pledged himself to sell his house and give the money to the church if his problems were solved. They were. The man, carrying out his promise sold the house for a small amount which he did, indeed, give to the church. However, the man who bought the house also had to buy a cat that carried a very high price. This money was kept by the man who had made the pledge.[23]

"The Candlestick of Iron" tells of a young man instructed to go into a room of treasures and return with an iron candlestick only. He returned with the candlestick and a pocketful of hidden treasure. His actions were discovered. When given a second chance, greed was again his downfall. In the end he had nothing more than when he started out.[24] The lesson, of course, was that greed, like crime, does not pay.

"The Gnat Namouss and the Elephant" points out that even though a person might feel he is very important, his existence may not even be noticed by others. In this story, a gnat lived much of his life in the ear of an elephant. When he arrived, he made a big production of his arrival. As he left, he announced his departure, feeling very important. In reality, the elephant had not noticed the arrival, residence, or departure of the gnat. It

[22] "The Man Who Looked Only at the Obvious," *ibid.*, pp. 198-200.
[23] "The Oath," *ibid.*, p. 68.
[24] "The Candlestick of Iron," *ibid.*, pp. 51-54.

had made absolutely no difference to him.[25] No one should feel that he is indispensable.

"The Wayward Princess" in some ways compares with *King Lear*. In this story, the daughter who would not acknowledge the absolute supremacy of her father's rule was exiled to a barren land. She learned to exist and eventually married a man who lived there. In the end, their kingdom far overshadowed the kingdom of the princess' father. Thus, the princess was able to overcome seemingly insurmountable obstacles to become extremely successful.[26]

"Fatima the Spinner and the Tent" tells a similar story. A wealthy girl was shipwrecked. She learned a profession and had established herself when she was again left destitute by disaster. After she had overcome this second misfortune, calamity again befell her and, as before, she had to learn a new way to make a living. After this, she was shipwrecked in a strange country. But here she found that she needed to meet the test of the Emperor. Her task involved making a tent, which required all the skills it had been necessary for her to learn as a result of her frequent bad luck. She fulfilled the task and was able to settle down to a peaceful, abundant life.[27] Both of these stories illustrate that it takes some disappointment, some failures, some "bad" luck, to lead to a successful, appreciated life.

"The Dam" moralizes that nothing can be accomplished when a group argues within itself. In this legend, brothers argued over whether or not a dam should be removed in order to irrigate their land. While they continued their dispute, a tyrant took the dam and their land as well.[28] Perhaps the theme of this legend is most easily summarized by ". . . that house divided against itself, that house cannot stand." [29]

One fable discusses the idea that simply because a person is different does not necessarily mean that he is wrong or insane. In this example, a group was told that their water would change and this new water would cause them to go mad. One member

---

[25] "The Gnat Namouss and the Elephant," *ibid.*, pp. 58–60.
[26] "The Wayward Princess," *ibid.*, pp. 63–65.
[27] "Fatima the Spinner and the Tent," *ibid.*, pp. 72–74.
[28] "The Dam," *ibid.*, pp. 100–102.
[29] Mark 3:25.

of the group saved up some of the old water. Thus, while the others went insane, he remained normal. However, those who had gone insane considered him to be mad merely because he was different. Eventually, the man, in desperation, also drank the new water and became "normal" by the standards of the others in the community.[30] Another idea illustrated by this is that man requires association with other men: he cannot survive in isolation. This man was with others; but because he was considered to be mad, he was unable to associate with them. In effect, he was living the life of a hermit despite the fact that he was surrounded by others. Therefore, to him it was necessary to conform to this society's standards in order to be accepted.

Whereas "When the Waters Were Changed" discusses the idea of conformity, "The Dervishes from the Other World" touches on individualism. It develops the idea that the needs of the individual vary. In the story three men who had returned from the "Other World" were asked what had helped them most during their life. Each had a different reply, which confused the people. However, each answer had been right in accordance with the needs of each.[31]

Today, we hear a great deal about individualism versus conformity. The two stories, "When the Waters Were Changed" and "The Dervishes from the Other World" indicate that this should not be a controversy revolving around the decision of one or the other, but, rather, in what proportions these two should be mixed. Indeed, the idea that "No man is an island" is readily accepted by most. "When the Waters Were Changed" showed that extreme individualism can lead to a life of social isolation that is as bad as, if not worse than, physical isolation. So, man must subordinate his individuality to social conformity if he is to live in society. On the other hand, individualism should not be completely forgotten. Each person is an individual with different needs and desires. As shown by "The Dervishes from the Other World," what works for one may not work for another. If we were all exactly alike, the world would be an exceedingly dull place. If, that is, the world were existing at all. After all, if

[30] "When the Waters Were Changed," in *Tales of the Dervishes*, pp. 21–22.
[31] "The Dervishes from the Other World," in *Reflections*, p. 40.

there were no individualism, there would be no variety of interests and no diversification of occupations. Everyone would do the same things. Man could not exist under such circumstances. Therefore, it is obvious that you cannot have only individualism or conformity. It seems, according to Shah, that man must conform his individualism to the point that he can successfully interact with other men to form a society.

It takes all the small pieces to make the working whole: this is the idea examined in "The Chariot." In this analogy, the author compares the basic features of man with the basic features of a chariot.[32] The conclusion was that although they may function separately with some success, the parts must work cooperatively in order to achieve maximum potential. It also discusses the idea that these various aspects of man must be in correct proportion in order for man as a whole to be efficient.

The legend "In the Land of Fools" tells of wise men going on a visit to other lands in order to broaden their knowledge. However, when they came upon a strange object (a minaret), they tried to define it in terms of their own, rather limited, background. One thought it was a giant plant; one thought it had been built on its side and hoisted up in some manner; the third determined that it had been built by giants. Therefore, they spent the rest of the trip alert for giants.[33] Here was an ideal opportunity to increase their understanding of something entirely new to them. Yet, instead of seeking out someone and asking him about this in order to learn, they depended on their own experience. Often, people state their purpose as trying to increase their knowledge when, in reality, they are looking for an opportunity to demonstrate their own intelligence. The result in this legend was that the "wise" men defeated their purpose. In everyday events such an attitude of knowing all can lead to embarrassment and ridicule as well.

"Trapped Rat" discusses a situation in which a rat, having no other alternative but to die, was able to kill a dog.[34] We have often heard that necessity (often in the form of fear) will enable one to carry out superhuman tasks. In this instance, the rat be-

[32] "The Chariot," in *Tales of the Dervishes*, pp. 207–208.
[33] "In the Land of Fools," in *Reflections*, pp. 47–48.
[34] "Trapped Rat," *ibid.*, p. 32.

came a hero though his actions had been inspired by a sense of desperation, not because of any desire to protect others. In the same sense, it is often said that the hero does not act bravely to help others but, rather, because he really has no other choice. This story bears out this idea. Some go a step further and say that there have never been any heroes in the true sense of the word. According to these theorists, those men considered heroes do their "heroic" deeds in their own self-interest, such as the desire for survival or glory. Whether one agrees with this idea or not, most will agree that necessity results in the successful completion of dangerous deeds that would not have been attempted under ordinary circumstances.

"Three Wishes" tells a story very familiar to people of the Western world who have read *The Arabian Nights*. This legend relates the story of a man given three wishes. The first two wishes made his life so miserable that his third wish was that his life be returned to normal and that he should forget all his unhappy experiences.[35] This has been the theme of a number of stories, particularly in juvenile literature, although the moral can be readily applied to adults. One of the basic ideas of the story is that a person should be satisfied with his lot in life. Another theme could be that one does not really appreciate something when he obtains it too easily. Often, most of the fun in wanting something is in the desire itself, not the attainment of the desire. Thus, this story advises the reader to work toward realistic goals that fit into his way of life. Wealth come by too quickly or too easily can often cause the "lucky" one more anguish than pleasure.

A very interesting thought expressed by Shah is: "Please, not again what you studied, how long you spent at it, how many books you wrote, what people thought of you—but: *what did you learn?*"[36] Often a person puts so much emphasis on what he has to do to reach a goal that he loses sight of the goal itself. He may or may not reach it. Evidently it is of little real importance; or perhaps the goal is not as glorious to tell about as the effort involved in reaching it. After all, it is much more exciting to describe in detail the effort it took to climb a mountain than to say merely, "I climbed a mountain" even though the reaction

[35] "Three Wishes," *ibid.*, p. 45.
[36] "What Did You Learn?" *ibid.*, p. 45.

of the listener may be about the same to both accounts. Nevertheless, Shah advises that it is the goal that is important, particularly
in the learning process. No matter what one endures, or what
he does, or what others think about him, he has accomplished
nothing if he does not learn something from his experiences.

Another reflective thought of Shah's is: "If you believe
everything, you are not a believer in anything at all." So it is in
this world that a person can only believe a relatively few things
strongly. If he tries to believe everything, he will find himself
in one instance believing one thing, and in another instance believing just the opposite. After wading through this sticky mess
of contradictions, he will find that really he has no beliefs at all.

Shah's writings are inspiring and thought-provoking. Even
the person who begins reading *Reflections* or *Tales of the Dervishes* with the intention of being amused will soon find himself
in a state of deep thought and self-analysis. Most of these stories
have a moral that is quite evident—in the same manner as in
children's stories. Others entice the reader to cast about for a
meaning. In either case, these books are very entertaining.

It is interesting to note how closely many of these stories
resemble some of the Western legends. It is not just that the
themes are the same. Any culture is bound to have stories moral-
izing about greed, dishonesty, and other such topics. What is
surprising is that the events in the stories related are so similar.
One would think, in many cases, that the same event had been
witnessed by someone from the East and someone from the West
and recorded by both. Anyone who reads such examples as "The
Rich Man Who Was a Beggar" or "Bayazid and the Selfish Man"
will be struck by this fact.

After I read Idries Shah's writings, I found that religious and
philosophic sayings and teaching stories in the Orient seem to
have the same tradition although they are written in different
languages and by different nationalities. Those sayings and teaching stories have exercised a great influence over people's minds
throughout history in the Orient. It is not the purpose of this
paper to make a comparison of the sayings and teaching stories
by the religious founders, philosophers, and the saints. However,
it is certain that the religious beliefs and philosophies in the
Orient can be traced in a similar pattern. For example, Lao Tzu,

the Chinese philosopher who was born in 604 B.C., said almost the same thing as stated in the New Testament of the Bible: "My yoke is easy and my burden is light." [37] In Taoism, the wording of this idea is: "My teachings are very easy to understand and very easy to practice." [38] It is also true that the nature of Sufi sayings and teaching stories may be found in the Bible, Chinese classics, and other Oriental religious teachings.

[37] Matthew 11:30.

[38] Holmes Welch, *The Parting of the Way; Lao Tzu and the Taoist Movement* (London: Methuen & Co., 1958); Frederick Henry Balfour, *Taoist Texts, Ethical, Political and Speculative* (London: Trubner & Co., 1884); *Tao Te Ching* (Taoist Texts) 70.

VI

A MESSAGE
AND METHOD OF LOVE,
HARMONY,
AND BROTHERHOOD
by
Professor Nasrollah S. Fatemi

> *The Sufi law of life requires:*
> *Kindness to the young*
> *Generosity to the poor*
> *Good counsel to friends*
> *Forbearance with enemies*
> *Indifference to fools*
> *Respect to the learned*
> —IDRIES SHAH, THE SUFIS

1.

Many of the great spiritual movements in history have begun at moments of stress and strife. Confucius, Buddha, the Prophets of Israel, Zoroaster, Socrates, Plato, Jesus, Mohammed, Gandhi, and other thinkers, philosophers, and religious leaders spoke up amid trials and discord. In their times, the world was much like our own: states were at war, and people suffered disillusion, frustration, mistrust—a spiritual and moral anarchy.

Among the writers and thinkers who played a great role in the history of the Muslim world during its periods of stress were the Sufis. Their movement was expressed in outward form as a protest against the formalism of orthodoxy in Islam, and gradually developed into a rebellion against the decadence, corruption, and tyranny of a sick, materialist society. Sufism was the antithesis of arrogance, intolerance, demagogism, hypocrisy and inhumanity. The Sufis' purpose was to create a renaissance of man's spirit, through which he might live a simple, innocent, happy, and harmonious life. They hoped to open man's eyes, that he might see how egoism, greed, pride, and strife are folly and that the universe is spiritual, and that men are the sons of God. The Sufis agreed with St. Paul that "the fruit of the spirit is love, joy, peace, long suffering, gentleness, goodness, faith, meekness, and temperance."

Few terms in the dictionary of Islam are as impressive as the term "Sufi" or "Sufism." Its very mention often provokes debate about its meaning, its evaluation, and its purpose. To some orthodox and traditionalist Muslims it can stand for qualities deeply distrusted and despised. To others, it connotes humanitarianism, tolerance, harmony, defiance of the superficial rituals, love of mankind, and the attempt to achieve spiritual fellowship. To a few, the Sufis are dreamers, rebels, and meddlers who interfere with the serious rituals of the church and the business of the state. To many, they are the conscience of society and the antennae of the community, who exhibit in their activities a pronounced concern for humanity and a deep interest in and knowledge of the values at the core of society. They oppose the civil and religious leaders who, for the sake of selfish interests, create conflict and division in their communities. In the words of Bayazid Bastami: "A Sufi belongs to the sect of God."

"Being a man of timelessness and placelessness," states Idries Shah "the Sufi brings his experience into operation within the culture, the country, and the climate in which he is living."

While the church and civil powers in the ninth and tenth centuries tended to be absorbed in the pursuit of material and personal power, the Sufis felt the need to resist that cruel, tyrannical, and arrogant society, to ridicule the corrupt rich and the merciless mighty, to exalt the low and to help the helpless. They turned their eyes to the huge masses of simple, poor, ignorant people. For during this so-called golden age of Baghdad civilization, a minority of rich people ruled an immense empire of millions of poor peasants and slaves. These people accepted poverty, hunger, ill-treatment, disease, and suffering with tranquil resignation. They accepted the whip of the agents of the caliphs and the empty words of the church as a preordained fate. They accepted their Hell as did Milton's Satan:

> So farewell hope and with the hope, farewell fear,
> Farewell remorse, all good to me is lost;
> Evil be thou my good.

The Sufis considered this situation reprehensible, and risked imprisonment and even met death, protesting against the materialism, indifference, extravagance, and inhumanity of the society. They tried to attack the hypocritical pretension of the bigoted religionists and to introduce people into the realms of "inner thoughts and values." The questions they repeatedly asked were, "Is God the object of formal worship, or of love? Is the purpose of religion to unite, to comfort, to improve and to bring all races and peoples of the world together in love and brotherhood, or to divide, to tyrannize, to shed the blood of the innocent in futile wars, to mesmerize, to commit all kinds of crime in the name of Allah and to exploit our fellowmen?" The God of Islam is supposed to be compassionate, all-loving, all-merciful. He tells us, "Do not despair of my mercy." "Despairing of love and mercy is a greater fault than your sin."[1] Everything in this world—folly and wisdom, power and impotence, wealth and poverty, happiness and sadness, glory and humiliation—is only empty and transitory without love and involvement. Everything in this life is mortal, except God and good deeds.

[1] Koran 39:54.

No village law, no law of market town,
Law of a single house is this—
Of all the world and all the worlds of gods
This only is the law, that all things are impermanent.

Unquestionably, these divine injunctions for love and brotherhood were nowhere, at the time, so well heeded and practiced
as among the Sufis.

2.

Sufi ideas throughout the centuries have been the source of
inspiration to poets, the fountain of ideas to many thinkers, and
the treasure of wisdom to the sages and savants of the East. The
message is harmony, brotherhood, peace, and friendship. Its
realm is the whole universe. It goes beyond religion, ideology,
color, creed or race. "It follows the religion of love."

The Sufis, in the words of Hakim Sanai, are looking for the
ocean of love and they do not bother with the rivers and canals
of conflict and prejudice.

Their mission is to bring unity, brotherhood, hope, and
happiness to the family of man. Their purpose is to help any generation that is suffering from the ills of mistrust, materialism,
prejudice, and conflict.

Idries Shah, by expounding the Sufi tradition, has given the
troubled Western world an opportunity to find joy and peace
of mind in the teaching of Sufi leaders.

In his book *The Sufis* (1964), Shah gives us a historical
account of the rise and the impact of Sufi ideas on the world.
He prefaces his work with a statement by the Sufi master Sanai:
"Humanity is asleep, concerned only with what is useless, living
in a wrong world. Believing that one can excel, this is only habit
and usage, not religion. This 'religion' is inept. Man is wrapping
his net around himself. A Sufi bursts his cage asunder."

In a second book, *The Way of the Sufi* (1968), and elsewhere, Idries Shah speaks of the great contribution of Sufism to
world culture. He has translated many of the relevant Sufi poems
and prose into English.

He deals with various attitudes and teachings of the Sufis and with the evidence of their absorption into medieval Christianity, Hinduism, Judaism, and the ideas of modern philosophers of the West.

The greater part of *The Way of the Sufi* explains many aspects of Sufi activity and practice that are relevant to the contemporary world. He invites his readers to understand Sufism— the cult of love, meditation, and world fraternity.

Idries Shah's books are designed to present, in a very clear fashion, "Sufi ideas, actions, perceptions and contributions to the world of ideas: not for the microscope or as museum pieces, but in their relevance to a current community of nations—what we call the contemporary world."

These contributions and ideas, completely presented by Idries Shah in his books, will be discussed in the following pages.[2]

3.

The early publicly known Sufis were ascetics and quietists rather than mystics. However, in the beginning of the ninth century they developed an ecumenical doctrine linked with the ideas of Zoroastrianism, Buddhism, Judaism, Christianity, Neoplatonism, and Islam. Sufism thus showed that it regarded all religions as more or less "perfect shadowings forth of the great central truth which it seeks fully to comprehend, and consequently it recognizes all of them as good in proportion to the measure of truth which they contain." The practical aim was to escape from the subjective self and until this lesson was learned, no advances toward Truth could be made. Even today Sufis regard God as identical with pure Being. Sufism, therefore, is considered to be an idealistic pantheism: everything represents God. A Sufi may be

---

[2] It is important to understand that ordinary scholars, however profound, whether they be in the East or West, may not be able to understand Persian and other Sufi literature without a proper Sufi background. Sufis have written most of the great literature of Persia, and much of it is written in a very specialized manner. It has more than one meaning. Many mistakes have been made both in translation and in trying to explain Sufi ideas by people who do not understand this multiple-meaning characteristic of Sufi literature. That is why Idries Shah's works are so important and deserve careful study by scholars and intellectuals.

described as one who conceives of religion as an experience of eternity—one who holds that the soul, even in this life, can unite itself with the Divine. He calls himself Ahl al-Haq, the man of the Truth.

It was the Egyptian philosopher, Dhul Nun (d. 861), who publicly introduced the idea of gnosis (*Marifa*) into Sufi doctrine. Though born of a Nubian slave, Dhul Nun became the model of a renaissance man. He was well versed in philosophy, law, literature, alchemy, ancient Egyptian history, and hieroglyphics. His writings show a knowledge of hermetic wisdom. Dhul Nun is considered to be the first Sufi *Qutb* (the pillar of the universe) and the first historical exponent of its theosophy. He is to Sufism what St. Paul was to Christianity. He emphasized the idea that the true knowledge of God is attained by means of ecstasy (*Wajd*).

Dhul Nun states that gnosis (*Marifa*) is "God's providential communications of the spiritual light to our inmost hearts. He who belongs to God and to whom God belongs is not connected with anything in the universe." [3] The following prayer of Dhul Nun is a good indication of his pantheistic formulation:

O God, I never hearken to the voices of the beasts or the rustle of the trees, the splashing of waters or of the songs of birds, the whistling of the wind or the rumble of thunder, but I sense in them a testimony to thy unity [*Wahdanyya*], and a proof of thy Incomparableness; that thou are the all-prevailing, the all-knowing, the all-wise, the all-just, the all-true, and in Thee is neither overthought nor ignorance nor folly nor injustice nor lying. O God, I acknowledge Thee in the proof of Thy handiwork and in evidence of Thy acts; grant me, O God, to seek Thy satisfaction with my satisfaction, and the Delight of a Father in His child, remembering Thee in my love for Thee, with serene tranquility and firm resolve! [4]

In his poetry Dhul Nun uses the language of the devoted lover, as Rabia of Basra had spoken before him:

[3] *Hujwiri*, p. 382, trans. Gustave E. von Grunebaum, in *Medieval Islam* (2d ed.; Chicago: University of Chicago Press), p. 238.
[4] Abu Naim, *Hily IX*, trans. A. J. Arberry, p. 342.

I die, and yet not dies in me,
The ardour of my love for Thee,
Nor hath Thy love, my only goal,
Assuaged the fever of my soul.

To Thee alone my spirit cries;
In Thee my whole ambition lies,
And still Thy wealth is far above
The poverty of my small love.

I turn to Thee in my request,
And seek in Thee my final rest;
To Thee my loud lament is brought,
Thou dwellest in my secret thought.

To Thee alone is manifest
The heavy labour of my breast,
Else never kin or neighbours know
The brimming measure of my woe.

Guidest Thou not upon the road
The rider wearied by his load,
Delivering from the steeps of death
The traveller as he wandereth?

O then to me Thy favour give
That, so attended, I may live,
And overwhelm with ease from Thee
The rigour of my poverty.[5]

Dhul Nun was once asked to expound the qualities of the gnostics. He answered:

The gnostics see without knowledge, without information, without description, without unveiling, and without veil. They see God in everything. They move as God causes them to move; their words are the words of God; their sight is the sight of God. God through his prophet tells us: "When I love a servant, I the Lord am his ears so that he hears by Me; his eyes, so that he sees by Me; his tongue, so that he speaks by Me, and his hands so that he takes by Me."

[5] *Ibid.*, pp. 53–54.

Dhul Nun once asked a woman what was the end of love. "Thou fool!" she replied, "Love had no end, because the Beloved is eternal." [6]

Mahmud Shabastari (A.D. 1250–1325), a celebrated Sufi doctor in his book *Gulshani Raz* (The Mystic Rose Garden), explains the Sufi theory of pantheism. But his pantheism is "an amplification rather than a definition of the idea of the Divinity, infinite, omnipresent and omnipotent." The following verses express Shabastari's theory of pantheism and union:

> *Verily "I am the truth" is a revelation of absolute*
> *Mystery, save "the truth," who can say "I am the truth?"*
> *If you desire that its meaning may be clear to you,*
> *Then read the text, "There is naught but praiseth Allah."* [7]
> *When you have carded "self" as cotton,*
> *You like Mansur, "The wool carder," will raise this cry,*
> *Take out the cotton of your illusion from your ears,*
> *Hearken to the call of the one, the Almighty.* [8]
> *This call is ever coming to you from "The Truth."*
> *Why are you tarrying for the last day?*
> *Come into the "Valley of Peace," for straightway*
> *The bush will say to you, "verily I am Allah."* [9]
> *The saying, "I am the Truth" was lawful for the bush*
> *Why is it unlawful in the mouth of a good man?*
> *Every man whose heart is pure from doubt,*
> *Knows for a surety that there is no being but one.*
> *Saying "I am" belongs only to "The Truth,"*
> *For essence is absent, and illusive appearance is absent.*
> *The glory of "The Truth" admits no duality,*
> *In that glory is no "I" or "we" or "Thou."*
> *"I," "we," "Thou" and "He" are all one thing,*
> *For in unity there is no distinction of persons.*
> *Every man who as a void is empty of self,*
> *Re-echoes within him the cry "I am the Truth";*
> *He takes his eternal side, "other" perishes,*

[6] *Fariduddin Attar, Tadhkiratual Auliya* (Biographies of the Saints) (Teheran, 1915), pp. 20–26.

[7] Koran 18:46.

[8] "With Whom Shall Be the Power on That Day? The one, the Almighty." Koran 20:14.

[9] The Story of the Burning Bush comes from the Koran in reference to Moses when God spoke to him.

Travelling, travel, and traveller all become one.
Incarnation and communion spring from "other,"
But very unity comes from the mystic journey.[10]

Furthermore, Shabastari states:

That man attains to the secret of unity
Who is not detained at the stages on the road.
But the knower is he that knows very Being,
He that witnesses Absolute Being,
And being such as his own he gambles clean away.
Your being is naught but thorns and weeds,
Cast it all clean away from you.
Go sweep out the chamber of your heart,
Make it ready to be the dwelling place of the Beloved.
When you depart out, He will enter in,
In you, void of yourself, will He display His beauty.[11]

Bayazid of Bistam (d. 875) is regarded by many as one of
the founders of the pantheistic school. He was the grandson of a
noted Zoroastrian, and his Sufi teacher was Abu Ali of Sind. In
all his teachings, Bayazid identified himself with pantheism. He
stated in public: "Beneath this cloak of mine there is nothing but
God." He embarrassed his Sufi brethren and scandalized the
orthodox by exlaiming: "Glory to me! How great is my majesty!
Verily I am God: There is no God beside me, so worship me." [12]

On another occasion Bayazid declared that the gnostic's lowest rank is this: that the attributes of God are in him. A single
atom of the sweetness of love and knowledge of God in a man's
heart is better than a thousand palaces in paradise. Knowledge
without love and service is useless.

In expressing his mystical experience, Bayazid declared: "Once
He raised me up and stationed me before Him, and said to me,

---

[10] Mahmud Shabastari, *Gulshani Raz*, trans. E. H. Whinfield (The
Mystic Rose Garden) (London: Trubner & Co., 1880), pp. 45–46. Cf.
Mahmud Shabastari, *The Secret Garden*, trans. Johnson Pasha (London:
Octagon Press Ltd., 1969), with an Introduction on Sufi thought by
Imam el-Arifin Sheikh Imdad Hussein el-Qadiri.

[11] *Ibid.*, p. 41.

[12] John A. Subhan, *Sufism, Its Saints and Shrines* (Lucknow, India,
1939), p. 21.

O Abu Yazid, truly my creation desires to see Thee, I said,
'Adorn me in Thy unity, and clothe me in Thy self Lord, and
raise me up to Thy oneness, so that when Thy creation see me
they will say, We have seen Thee: and Thou wilt be That, and
and I shall not be there at all.' " [13]

This very statement was the source of the doctrine of *Fana
Fellah* (self-absorption in God), which, from Bayazid's time onward, assumed a central position in the structure of published
Sufi theory. All talk, turmoil, rite, ritual, convention, custom,
noise, and desire accordingly is outside the unity with God; remove the veil of dualism and one will find joy, silence, beauty,
calm, and rest. When one is united with his Beloved there is
neither command nor prohibition. The statement was a modification of the Sufi doctrine of negation (that all else but God is
nothing) to the theory that when self as well as material world
had been cast aside the perfect man would unite with God.[14] "I,
we, Thou, He are all one thing, for in unity is no duality." According to Bayazid, all that exists is learned in two ways, by
abandoning self-interest and by following God's command to
love your fellowmen. Bayazid, like many other Sufis, never followed formal religious rites and rituals. Someone asked him why
he did not attend prayer services in the mosque. He answered,
"I have no leisure to pray, I am roaming the spiritual world and
whenever I see anyone fallen and in need of my service, I do my
best to help him." Once Bayazid was on his way to Mecca. A
man met him on the road and asked where he was going. Bayazid
told him his destination. The man asked him how much money he
would spend. "Two hundred dirhams," was Bayazid's estimate.
The stranger told him that he had a wife and children and no
income to support them. Then he suggested that Bayazid should
pay him the two hundred dirhams and instead of walking seven
times round the black stone of Kaaba, he should walk round him
and this would complete his pilgrimage. Bayazid accepted the
offer, paid the money to the stranger, and returned home.

The analogy with Buddhism is found in the work of Ibrahm
Ebn Adham, prince of Balkh (d. 777). The son of the Viceroy of

---

[13] Sarraj, *Kitab Al Luma*, trans. A. J. Arberry (1947), pp. 380–391.
[14] Fariduddin Attar, *op. cit.*, pp. 60–71.

Khorassan, he spent his early life in luxury and laziness. Like Buddha, one day when he was hunting a fox he heard a voice behind him saying, "It was not for this thou wert created; it was not this thou wert charged to do." When he continued his chase, he heard another voice clearer than before, "O Ibrahim! It was not for this thou were created. It was not this thou were charged to do!" He considered this a warning, returned home, abandoned his horse and joined his father's shepherds in the mountains. Later he left Khorassan, roaming from place to place seeking peace of mind. Finally in Syria he came in contact with some monks from whom he learned how to make peace with himself and his creator.

When a friend asked Adham for a definition of service he replied: "The beginning of service is meditation and silence, then follows remembering (*Dikhr*) and service to your fellowman." When one of his disciples told him that he was merely studying rhetoric, he commented, "You are in greater need of studying silence." His favorite prayer was: "O God, Thou knowest that paradise weighs not with me so much as the wing of a gnat. If Thou befriendest me by thy recollection, and sustainest me with thy love, and makest it easy for me to obey Thee, then give Thou paradise to whomsoever Thou wilt."

The similarity of the views propounded by the Sufis to Neoplatonic philosophy proved attractive to the Persian Sufis, among whom there was a strong gnostic element. These Iranians, bored with the dry formalism of a rigid theology and a stiffened ritual, discovered in Sufism the philosophy they were seeking. The hard and fast system of *Shariah* (Islamic Law) and the clear-cut dogmas of the clergy and the finality of their doctrine and law had always been alien to the minds of the Persians. Inevitably the Sufis and the Persians found great difficulty in trying to reconcile their rebellious, imaginative doctrine with the orthodoxy of the Islamic clergy. The latter represented Allah as having created the world for all, and then He removed Himself to His seat in the highest heaven, leaving His creatures to work out their own salvation or condemnation by their own free will, according to the light given them by the prophets. But the Sufis, in sharp contrast, represented Him as the sublime Being, immanent and ever-working in His creatures, the sum of all existence, the fullness of life, whereby all things move and exist, not only predestinating but originating all actions dwelling in and terminating with each individual soul. The Sufi believed that he would see his God face to face in everything and in seeing Him, would become one with Him. His God was his friend.

Baba Kuhi of Shiraz (d. 1050), a contemporary of Abu Said, another great Sufi teacher, explained Sufi pantheistic beliefs in the unity with God in the following verses:

> In the market, in the cloister—only God I saw.
> In the valley and on the mountain—only God I saw.
> Him I have seen beside me oft in tribulation;
> In favour and in fortune—only God I saw.
> In prayer and fasting, in praise and contemplation,
> In the religion of the prophet—only God I saw.
> Qualities nor causes—only God I saw.
> I opened mine eyes and by the light of His face around me
> In all the eye discovered—only God I saw.
> Like a candle I was melting in his fire:
> Amidst the flames outflashing—only God I saw
> Myself with mine own eyes I saw most clearly,
> But when I looked with God's eyes—only God I saw.
> I passed away into nothingness, I vanished.
> And lo, I was the all-living—only God I saw.

Mansur al-Hallaj (d. 922) spoke in a similar fashion. Mansur declared that when man is completely absorbed in his divine Beloved, he abandons self and becomes conscious only of his God. In this state he is one with God.

> Swift for Thy sake, I sped over land and sea
> And clove a way through world and steep, heartfree,
> And turned aside from all I met, until
> I found the shrine where I am one with Thee.[15]

Hallaj, walking through the streets of Baghdad, told his audience to stop wasting their time and money by attending services in the mosques or making pilgrimages to Mecca in search of God. He admonished the citizens for their financial and business dishonesty. He accused the authorities and businessmen of robbing

[15] Attar, *op. cit.*, trans. Reynold A. Nicholson, p. 186.

orphans and old women. He asked them to spend their money on the poor and the sick and look for God in their hearts.

"Cleanse your heart! Dedicate yourselves to the service of your people!" he exclaimed, "and there you will find truth and tranquillity!" When Hallaj was brought before the Inquisitor and he was commanded to repent, his answer was: "I am He whom I love, and He whom I love is I. We are two spirits dwelling in one body. If thou seest me, thou seest Him and if thou seest Him, thou seest us both." [16]

In 922 Hallaj was crucified for claiming identity with God and thereafter Sufism became more and more openly and frankly identified with pantheism and gnosticism. The legend of his death attributes to him a nobility and magnanimity similar to that found in the story of the crucifixion.

> When he was brought to be crucified and saw the cross and the nails, he turned to the people and uttered a prayer ending with the words: "And these Thy servants who are gathered to slay me, in zeal for Thy religion and in desire to win Thy favour, forgive them, O Lord, and have mercy upon them; for verily if Thou hadst revealed to them that which Thou hast revealed to me, they would not have done what they have done; and if Thou hadst not hidden from me that which Thou hast hidden from them I should not have suffered this tribulation quite gladly." [17]

4.

The aim of all Sufis was to achieve perfect union with the divinity. Like Plotinus, they assumed the supremacy of the supernatural over the material world. Sufis divided the works of God into two kinds—the perceived world and the conceived world. The former was the material visible world, familiar to man; the latter the invisible, spiritual world. The Sufis tried to show that in the relation existing between them could be found the means whereby man might ascend to perfection. The one watchword in

[16] Reynold A. Nicholson, *The Idea of Personality in Sufism* (Cambridge, 1923), p. 30.

[17] Reynold A. Nicholson, *Legacy of Islam* (London: Oxford University Press, 1931-1968), pp. 210 ff.

his philosophy is continuity or evolution. "There shall be no impassable gulf dividing God from man, spirit from matter: 'They shall be the first and last links of a single chain.' " [18] The first things that issued forth were the primal elements, called by some the objects of primary intellect. In this way also, intelligence, souls, elements, the heavens, and the stars come forth. Then from these simple elements started forth the vegetable, animal, and mineral kingdoms. The final end and aim of all is man, who by a process of evolution is at last achieved.[19]

Jalaluddin Rumi (d. 1273) in his immortal book, the *Masnawi*, gives a clear account of a Sufi's ideas of evolution:

> *I died as inanimate matter and arose a plant.*
> *I died as a plant and arose again as an animal.*
> *I died as an animal and arose a man,*
> *Why then should I fear to become less by dying*
> *I shall die once again as a man,*
> *To rise an angel perfect from head to foot.*
> *Again when I suffer dissolution as an angel,*
> *I shall become what passes the conception of man!*
> *Let me, then, become non-existent, for non-existence*
> *Sings to me in loudest tones: To Him we shall return.*

Shabastari, in a similar passage, describes man's journey from the lowest point, through the vegetable, animal, and human grades up to the highest point of obliteration of all secondary consciousness and to a total perception of the external phenomenal world:

> *Know first how the perfect man is produced*
> *From the time he is first engendered.*
> *He is produced at first as inanimate matter.*
> *Next by the added spirit he is made sentient,*
> *And acquires the motive powers from the Almighty.*
> *Next he is made lord of will by "The Truth."*
> *There is no other final cause beyond man*
> *It is disclosed in man's own self.*[20]

[18] G. E. Sell, *Essays on Islam* (Madras: S.P.C.K. Depot, 1901), p. 10.
[19] *Ibid.*
[20] Shabastari, *Gulshani Raz*, p. 33.

Robert Browning, as if following the Sufis' ideas, states:

Thus He dwells in all,
From life's minute beginning, up at last
To man—the communication of this scheme
Of being, the completion of this sphere of life.

Man is complete only when he has gained intelligence. This is the beginning and the end. And it makes the mystic circle complete. From God is the origin and to God is the return.[21]

Rumi, referring to the aim and object of our life says: "From realms of formlessness, existence doth take form, and fades again therein." The heart of the Sufi is inevitably bodied forth as the mirror of the universe.

In order to know the truth or to know God, man must look into his own heart, as Rumi wrote:

All the earth I wandered over, seeking still the beacon bright, never tarried in the daytime, never sought repose at night, till I heard a reverend preacher all the mystery declare, then I looked within my own bosom, and 'twas shining brightly there.

Nasir Khosrow, the famous Persian poet (1004–1088) referring to the knowledge of one's real self, states:

Know thyself, for knowing truly thine own heart
Thou knowest that good and ill in thee are part.
Discern the worth of thine own being, and then
Walk with pride amidst the common run of men.
Know thyself, and the whole world thus discover,
Then from all ill shall thyself deliver,
Thou knowest not thyself for thou art lowly,
Thou shouldst behold God if thou thyself could see,
Be a man! Care naught for viands or for sleep;
For viands and sleep solely concern the brutes,
Whereas thy soul in thought and spirit hath its roots
Arouse thyself! How long more wilt thou slumber?
See thyself, full of marvels without number.
Quick, break the chain, bear away that treasure care.
Have one care only, and that—to cast out care.

[21] Sell, *op. cit.*, p. 12.

5.

The introduction of the idea of gnosis into Islam is the result of Sufi doctrine. The Sufi distinguished three organs of communication: the heart (*Dil*), which knows Allah; the spirit (*Ruh*), which loves him; and the inmost ground of the soul (*Sirr*), which contemplates Him. The nature of heart, however, is considered perceptive rather than emotional or intellectual; for whereas the intellect cannot gain real knowledge of God, the heart is capable of knowing the essence of all things, and, when illumined by faith and knowledge, the heart reflects the whole content of the divine mind. God said, "My earth and my Heavens contain me not, but the heart of my faithful servant contains me." "Look in your own heart," says Sadi, "for God is within you." He who truly knows himself knows God (*Man Arafah Nafseh Arrafa Rabbeh*).[22]

Although ordinary knowledge (*Ilm*) is obtained by study and hard work, mystic knowledge, *Marifat* (Gnosis) according to the Sufis, is based on revelation or apocalyptic vision. *Marifat* is not the result of any mental process but depends on the influence of the divine upon the human, which brings about its realization. The resulting influence is called *Faiz* or grace. This flows down from God each moment, calling upon the soul and attracting it to Himself. Union, then, is the receiving of these emanations into oneself by being "drawn" more and more, as for example, according to the order expressed by Rumi:

> *The motion of every atom is towards its origin,*
> *A man comes to be the thing on which he is bent,*
> *The soul and the heart by the attraction of wish and desire*
> *Assume the qualities of the Beloved."* [23]

Those who seek truth, according to Sufis, are of three kinds: (1) the worshipers, who believe that God makes Himself known by means of reward. They worship him in the hope of winning

[22] Reynold A. Nicholson, *The Mysticism of Islam* (London: Routledge, 1914), pp. 70–71.

[23] Rumi, *Divan Shamsi Tabriz*, trans. R. A. Nicholson (Cambridge University Press), p. 210.

paradise; (2) the philosophers and scholastic theologians, who assert God makes himself known by means of glory. Yet since they can never find the glorious God whom they seek, they assert that his essence is unknowable; and (3) the gnostics, to whom God makes Himself known by means of ecstasy. They are possessed and controlled by a rapture that deprives them of the consciousness of individual existence.

The gnostic therefore performs only such acts of worship as are in accordance with his vision of God, though in so doing he will necessarily disobey the religious law that was made for the vulgar. His inward feeling must decide how valid the external forms of religion are, nor need he be dismayed if his inner experience conflicts with the religious law. Religion sees things from the aspect of plurality, but gnosis regards the all-embracing unity.[24]

Man is complete when he has gained gnosis, but gnosis is also the primal element; so it is the beginning and the end, the first and the last, and thus the mystic circle is perfect. Rumi, referring to the supreme cycle, states: "From realms of formlessness, existence doth take form,/And fades again therein. To him we must return." [25]

Sufis believe that man has the privilege of possessing the divine attributes. According to the Koran, God proposed a deposit of divine attributes to the heavens and to the earth and to the mountains between them, but they refused and so He entrusted them to man. So it is that the universe is the mirror of God, as the heart of man is the mirror of the universe. The man who is seeking God or the truth must look into his heart.

Jami gives a Sufi interpretation of gnosis and God's manifestation in the human heart in the following verses: [26]

*From all eternity the beloved unveiled this beauty
in the solitude of the unseen,*

*He held up the mirror to His own face, He displayed His
loveliness to Himself.*

[24] Niffari, *Treatise on Speculative Mysticism,* quoted by Nicholson, *ibid.,* pp. 71-72.
[25] Rumi, *Masnawi,* Book 1, Tale 5, trans. G. E. Sell, p. 364.
[26] Jami, *Lawaih,* trans. E. H. Whinfield (London, 1906).

*He was both the spectator and the spectacle, no eye
but His had surveyed the universe.*

*All was one, there was no duality, no pretence of
"mine" or "thine."*

*The vast orb of Heaven, with its myriad incomings and
outgoings, was concealed in a single point.*

*The creation lay cradled in the sleep of non-existence,
like a child ere it has breathed.*

*The love of the Beloved, seeing what was not, regarded
nonentity as existent.*

*Although He beheld His attributes and qualities as a
perfect whole in His own essence,*

*Yet He desired that they should be displayed to Him
in another mirror,*

*And that each one of His eternal attributes should become
manifest accordingly in a diverse form.*

*Therefore, He created the verdant fields of time and
space and the life-giving gardens of the world,*

*That every branch and leaf and fruit might show forth
His various perfection.*

*The cypress gave a hint of His comely stature, the rose
gave tidings of His beauteous countenance.*

*Wherever beauty peeped out, love appeared beside it,
whenever beauty shone in a rosy cheek, love lit his torch
from the flame.*

*Whenever beauty dwelt in dark tresses, love came and found
a heart entangled in their coils.*

*Beauty and love are as body and soul, beauty is the
mine and love the precious stone.*

*They have always been together from the very first
never have they travelled but in each other's company.*

Man is the crown and final cause of the universe.

*Though last in order of creation man is first in the
process of divine thought,*

For the essential part of him is the primal intelligence
of universal reason which emanates immediately from
the god-head.

The gnostic man is a "copy made in the image of God."
Gnosis, therefore, is unification, realization of the fact that one
has achieved the last stages of a mystical journey and has become
the "man of God."
To Rumi:

The man of God is made wise by the truth,
The man of God is not learned from the book,
The man of God is beyond infidelity and faith,
To the man of God right and wrong are alike.[27]

6.

The stages of the Mystical Journey are eight: service, love,
abstraction, knowledge, ecstasy, the truth, union, and self-nega-
tion. It is very difficult to analyze all the words of the Sufi poets
or to say to which stages of gnosis they refer, but these stages are
invariably there, though not necessarily in any narrowly systematic order. Generally speaking, however, it is the stage of
love that is the most popular subject of the Sufi poets, who
endlessly delight in singing of God and man as the Beloved and
the Lover. This fact alone helps to explain much Sufi thought.
For example, Ibn al-Arabi declares that no religion is more supreme than the religion of love. Love is the source and the
essence of all creeds:

My heart has become capable of every form: It is a pasture for
gazelles and a convent for Christian monks. Temple for idols, and
the pilgrim's *kaaba*, and the tables of Tora and the Book of the
Koran. I follow the religion of love, whichever way his camels
take. My religion and my faith is the true religion. We have a
pattern in Bishr, the lover of Hind and her sister, and in Qays
and Lubna, and in Mayya and Qhaylan.[28]

[27] Rumi, *Divan Shamsi Tabriz*, p. 28.
[28] Ibn al-Arabi, *A Collection of Mystical Odes*, trans. R. A. Nicholson
(London, 1911), p. 67.

Furthermore, Ibn al-Arabi declares:

The believer praises the God who is in his form of belief and with
whom he has connected himself. He praises none but himself for
his God is made by himself, and to praise the work is to praise
the maker of it; its excellence or imperfection belongs to its
maker. For this reason he blames the belief of others, which he
would not do if he were just. Beyond doubt the worshipper of
this particular God shows ignorance when he criticizes others on
account of their beliefs. If he understood the saying of Junaid,
"The colour of the water is the colour of the vessel containing it,"
he would not interfere with the beliefs of others, but would perceive God in every form and in every belief. He has opinion, not
knowledge; therefore, God said, "I am in my servant's opinion of
Me," i.e., "I do not manifest myself to him save in the form of his
belief." The God of religious belief is subject to limitations, for
he is the God who is contained in the heart of his servant. But the
non-religious God is not contained by anything for he is the
Being of all things and the Being of Himself, and a thing is not
said either to contain itself or not to contain itself.[29]

Therefore, all the evil thoughts which breed dislike, hatred, and
religious division and prejudice must be cast aside and replaced
by love.

"Love," says Rumi, "is the remedy of our pride and self-
conceit, the physician of all our infirmities. Only he whose gar-
ment is rent by love becomes entirely unselfish."

The Sufis, in their poetic utterances, have not specified
whether their language of love refers to heavenly or earthly love,
perhaps because: "Whether it be of this world or that,/Thy love
will lead thee yonder at the last."

Furthermore, they truly believe that pious words and the
love of God are naught without love of man and acts of charity:

> *Cheer one sad heart, thy loving deed will be*
> *More than a thousand temples raised by thee.*
> *One free man whom thy kindness hath enslaved*
> *Outweighs by far a thousand slaves set free.*

[29] R. A. Nicholson, *Trans. Eastern Poetry and Prose* (Cambridge,
1922).

The seventeenth-century hermetic mystic Henry Vaughan expresses well the Sufi presentation of religion as an experience of eternity, based on a union of man and God as lover and beloved:

> *I saw eternity the other night,*
> *Like a great ring of pure and endless light,*
> *All calm, as it was bright,*
> *And round beneath it, Time in hours, days, years,*
> *Driven by spheres.*
> *Like a vast shadow moved in which the world*
> *And all her train were hurl'd.*[30]

"This ring," Vaughan concludes, "the Bridegroom did for none provide but for his bride."

The Sufis believe that the ordinary orthodox theologian who has made a church and an institution out of his faith and religion and who flourishes on religious struggle and strife can never enter the "Empyrean Heaven" of mysticism. He will forever be a slave to his dogma, forever doomed to wander. No religious institution can grasp the full meaning of humanity. Inevitably, the Sufis resented the interference of the Muslim church in the personal affairs of individuals. The great Hafiz of Shiraz, for example, elegantly tells the clergy to mind their own business:

> *Blame not us wild rogues and gay*
> *As if our score thou must pay*
> *Saint or sinner, everyone*
> *Reaps at last what he hath sown,*
> *Am I given to wine or prayer?*
> *Pardon that, that is my affair.*
> *If I from virtue fell to vice,*
> *My father lost a paradise.*
> *Thou who bidd'st me hopeless be*
> *Of God's predestined charity,*
> *Dost thou know behind the veil*
> *Who laughs in bliss, who weeps in bale?*
> *Drunk or dry, the world entire*
> *Hath one object of desire.*

[30] Edmund G. Gardner, *Dante and the Mystics* (New York: Octagon Books, 1968).

Whether to mosque or church we come,
Love is everywhere at home.
On the tavern's lintel now
Resteth my devoted brow.
Kneel thou too, O critic dull,
And knock some wits into thy skull!
Cup in hand let Hafiz die,
Straight to Eden he will fly.

When mysticism is fully realized, it leads the Sufi to the annihilation of self in the absolute truth; he becomes a friend of God, a servant to His people, and a perfect man:

When preaching unity with unitarian pen,
Blot out and cancel every page that tells of
Spirits and of men.[31]

Jami, the Sufi mentor, refers in this verse to the first stage of enlightenment:

Wouldst thou thyself from selfhood disembroil,
To banish vain desire must be thy toil,
Empty thy hand of all it closes on,
And suffer many a blow and not recoil.

7.

The Sufi argues that the ordinary theologian of any creed is in the bondage of vested interests and enslaved by the dogmas of his religion, believing blindly what the establishment requires him to believe. In contrast, the Sufi has no other interest but his love of God and a world brotherhood; he gains his knowledge and his strength by direct and personal communication with his creator:

Dismiss care and be clean of heart,
Like the face of mirror on which there is no reflection
When it becomes clear of images, all images are contained in it.

[31] Hafiz, *Divan*, quoted by Sell, *Masnawi*, p. 18.

Indifference to all religious differences is a cardinal Sufi dogma:

> *While my loved phantom dwells in pagoda's bounds*
> *'Twere mortal sin, should I the Kaba compass round,*
> *The Kaba is but a church, if there His trace be lost;*
> *The church my only Kaba, while He there is found.*[32]

Omar Khayyam, describing this universalism:

> *In cell and cloister, monastery and synagogue, one lies*
> *In dread of Hell, one dreams of paradise.*
> *But none that know the secrets of the Lord*
> *Have sown their hearts with suchlike fantasies.*

Hafiz, the poetic genius of Shiraz, was excommunicated for saying:

> *Between the love of cloister and that of the tavern*
> *There is no difference,*
> *For wherever love is,*
> *There is the face of the beloved.*
> *Wherever the pious works of the Muslim hermitage display*
> *Their beauty,*
> *There are the bells of the Christian convent*
> *And the name of the cross.*

When the clergy of Shiraz reprimanded Hafiz, his answer was:

> *Despise not the Sufi*
> *Whose throne is the ground*
> *The emperor swordless,*
> *The monarch uncrowned!*

> *Beware! When high bloweth*
> *The wind of disdain,*
> *Whole stacks of obeisance*
> *Are worth not a grain!*

[32] Rumi, *Divan Shamsi Tabriz*, p. 238.

Even idol worship was explained by the Sufis. Mahmud Shabastari, the great Sufi poet, in his book *Gulshani Raz*, states:

> *Since all things are the manifestation of being,*
> *One amongst them must be an idol.*
> *If the Musalman but knew what is faith,*
> *That faith is idol worship.*
> *If the polytheist only knew what an idol was*
> *How could he go astray in his religion.*

Abu Said Ibn Abul Khair (967–1049) is described by his biographers as the first master of theosophic verse, the first to popularize and to make quatrains, "The focus of all mystic pantheistic teachings." The following quatrains are a good example of what is meant:

> *Said I, "to whom belongs thy beauty!"*
> *He replied, "since I alone exist to Me;*
> *Lover, Beloved and Love am I in one,*
> *Beauty, and Mirror, and the Eyes which see!*

> *"Those men who lavish on me titles fair*
> *Know not my heart, nor what is hidden there;*
> *But, if they once could turn me inside out,*
> *They'd doom me to the burning, that I'll swear.*

> *"The gnostic, who hath known the mystery,*
> *Is one with God, and from his self-hood free:*
> *Affirm God's being and deny thine own:*
> *This is the meaning of 'no God but He.'*

> *"My countenance is blanched of Islam hue;*
> *More honour to infidels' dog is due!*
> *So black with shame's my visage that of me*
> *Hell is ashamed, and Hell's despairing crew."*

> *When me at length thy love's embrace shall claim*
> *To glance at paradise I'd deem it shame,*
> *While to a Thee-less Heaven were I called,*
> *Such Heaven and Hell to me would seem the same.*

> *To gladden one poor heart of man is more,*
> *Be sure, than fares a thousand to restore:*
> *And one free man by kindness to enslave*
> *Is better than to free of slaves a score.*

Till mosque and seminary fall beneath ruin's ban
And doubt and faith be interchanged in man,
How can the order of the Sufi
Prevail, and raise up one true Musalman? [33]

Rumi states that love is the guide and uniting force of Sufism from the start to the goal.

"Cross and Christian, from end to end
I surveyed, He was not on the cross.
I went to the idol temple, to the ancient pagoda
No trace was visible there.
I bent the reins of search to the Kaaba,
He was not in that resort of old and young,
I gazed into my own heart;
There I saw him, he was nowhere else.
In the whirl of its transport my spirit was tossed,
Till each atom of separate being I lost."
"Say not that all these creeds are false,
The false ones capture hearts by the scent of truth
Say not, they are all erroneous thoughts,
There is thought in the world void of reality.
He who says everything is true is a fool,
He who says all is false is a knave."

Because the Sufi may abandon the mere external forms and rituals of religion and sings the praises of a universal Truth that is within the reach of everybody regardless of creed, color, or nationality, Sufism has become a religion that is both international and universal. Its literature and ideas, thanks to Idries Shah's books and teachings have a wide audience in North Africa, Persia, Pakistan, India, Malaya, China, Indonesia, Europe, and even the United States.

In long devotion to forms that cheat
Thou hast suffered the days of thy life to fleet:
But outward forms are still passing away,
Changing their fashion from day to day.

[33] Edward G. Browne, *A History of Persian Literature*, Vol. II (London: Fisher Unwin), pp. 261–267.

Tread not ever on stones that are rough to thy feet;
Nor shift from one branch to another thy seat.
Seek high o'er the sphere of the world thy rest;
In the world of reality make thee a nest.
If Truth be thine object, form-worshippers shun;
For form is manifold, Truth is one.
In number trouble and error lie.
To unity then for sure refuge fly.
If the might of the foeman oppress thee sore,
Fly to the fortress and fear no more.[34]
Learn from your orient shell to love thy foe,
And store with pearls the hand, that brings thee woe;
Free, like yon rock, from base vindictive pride,
Imblaze with gems the wrist, that rends thy side:
Mark, where yon tree rewards the stony show'r,
With fruit nectareous, or the balmy flower:
All nature calls aloud: "Shall man do less
Than heal the smiter, and the railer bless?" [35]

8.

To summarize, the Sufis (as did those with Neoplatonic ideas) attributed reality to God alone. Man's participation in reality only depended on his identification with God. Spiritual perfection leads to the gnosis of the divine unity and to the bridging of the gap between God and man when the latter's soul transcends the confines of personality by losing the conditioned self in the intuition of the one. The attribution of Being to any entity besides God is polytheism. "The finite soul views the infinite with love." "Love implies longing and longing makes man renounce the world for the beautiful vision in which no distinction is felt any more between himself and the Most High, in whom the individual mind has become completely absorbed." [36]

Junaid states that the love of God is the center of our soul, the resting-place of our desires and the sphere of our love.

I will seek my love straightway
Over yon hills, down where yon streamlets flow.

[34] Jami, trans. T. H. Griffith, quoted in *The Sufi Path of Love*, p. 101.
[35] Hafiz, trans. Sir William Jones, *ibid.*, p. 107.
[36] Gustave E. von Grunebaum, *Medieval Islam*, p. 133.

To pluck no flowers I'll stay;
No fear of beasts I'll know,
Past mighty men o'er frontier-grounds I'll go.

Jalaluddin Rumi, apostle of the Sufi doctrine, describes the idea of love in the following verses:

Hail to thee, O love, our sweet melancholy,
Thou physician of all our ills,
Thou purge of our pride and conceit.
Thou art our Plato and our Galen.
Our earthly body, through love, is raised to the skies,
Mountains take to dancing and to nimbleness.
Love became the soul of Sinai, lover!
Sinai was intoxicated and Moses fell swooning!
Its secret is hidden 'twixt topmost treble and lowest bass,
Were I to reveal it, I'd shatter the world.
But, were I close to my confidant's lips,
I would, like the reed-pipe, say all my say,
He that is far from men that speak his tongue
Is speechless, though he have a hundred voices.
When the rose is gone and rose-garden fallen to ruin,
Whence wilt thou seek the roses' scent? From rosewater?
The All is the beloved and the lover a veil,
The living is the beloved and the lover a thing dead.
When love no more has this attraction,
It remains like a bird without power of flight.

Forever associated with the supreme values of love and gnosis is the doctrine of *Fana* (self-effacement). There are three stages, according to Rumi, for the cleansing of the soul: abandoning of the evil qualities, concentration on good deeds, and contemplation of the divine. Here one detects the analogue of Plotinus: "The soul thus cleansed is all idea and reason, wholly free of body, intellective, entirely of that divine order from which the wellspring of beauty rises and all the race of Beauty."

The Sufis also introduced the idea of union (*wasl*) with God. This is the stage of satisfaction because the Sufi submits himself to the will of God. At this stage he decides to serve God as his divine Beloved and to devote his life to the service of mankind. It is in this last stage that the Sufi claims to experience

meditation, nearness to God, love, hope, longing, service, intimacy, tranquillity, and contemplation. The Sufis believed that
"states" descend from God into the heart and thus the seeker
experiences only those "states" that God chooses to bestow upon
him. After completing each "stage" of the "path," the Sufi is
transformed from "seeker" to "knower" and reaches a new plane
of consciousness that the Sufis term *gnosis*. This is a stage of
mutual understanding of the divine knowledge of God.[37] Gnosis
leads man to *wasl*—union with God. At this stage, Sufis like
Mansur al-Hallaj [38] exclaim: "I am he whom I love, he whom I
love is I; we are two souls, endwelling in one body. If thou seest
me, thou seest Him and if thou seest Him, thou seest me."

9.

Finally, through Idries Shah and his works, there is presented
to this disturbed and distressed world, torn between materialism,
nationalism, and tribalism, a message of hope and harmony and
love for humanity:

*Humanity rages like a tempest, but I sigh in silence for
I know the storm must pass away while a sigh goes to God.*

*Human kind clings to earthly things, but I seek ever to
embrace the torch of love so it will purify me by its
fire and sear inhumanity from my heart.*

*Substantial things deaden a man without suffering;
love awakens him with enlivening pains.*

[37] Subhan, *op. cit.*, pp. 68–73.
[38] Mansur al-Hallaj was a Sufi saint who was judicially murdered for
his defiance of orthodox Muslims in Baghdad in 922.

VII

TRAVEL, TEACHING, AND LIVING IN THE EAST
by
Professor A. K. Julius Germanus

I had hardly finished reading *Caravan of Dreams* by Idries Shah when my mind imperceptibly slipped away from the capital of Hungary with its allurements of modern civilization, locomotion, electricity, and jarring noises that are the inevitable concomitant of our present life. My thoughts glided away into far-off India where I had lectured for years on the history of Islamic culture.

Prepared through well-founded knowledge of the subject gained from the greatest European Orientalists, I delivered my lectures after sunset in the open air at the University of Santiniketan, under the guiding spirit of Rabindranath Tagore. The students, boys and girls, after their *upashana* meditations, gathered in the terrace of the Library and squatted on the ground. All eagerly listened to my objective exposition of the advance of

Islamic learning in the Middle Ages, together with the bloody feuds of antagonistic parties and the misdemeanors of caliphs and ministers. The lofty palm trees beside the Library rendered the scene poetic with the rustling of their leaves when a benevolent breeze soothed the hot atmosphere.

Week after week I continued my lectures, introducing my Indian students to the European critical science that delves into the innermost secrets of manuscripts, weighs witnesses with the help of juridical methods, and builds up a scientific edifice seemingly above all possible doubts. I analyzed the historical sources, proved the plausibility of some and showed the fallacy of certain others. The whole shining construction lay before us in all its details, like the bricks of a demolished building. We could ponder each item and its adjacents, but we missed the soul, the spirit of the living *whole*. The more the number of my students grew, the deeper did I sink into a spiritual vacuum, vexed by the experience that the inner culture of an Islamic or a Hindu community cannot be comprehended by the analytical methods of European scholarship of this type. As a result of long, sleepless nights, I even acquired the conviction that the formal logic of the sciences cannot be applied to biology; and since the history of mankind is a biological process, it cannot be applied to it either. There is a deeper, a more intrinsic, motive of human consciousness than that which mechanical forces dominate, which originates in mystical sources: those discovered only by inspirational experience.

Islamic doctrine has wisely ordained the behavior of man through all the vicissitudes of his life. It has prescribed his attitude toward God and toward his fellowmen, as laid down in the religious law of the *Shari'at*. This is a strict ordinance: it punishes the culprit for his misdeeds and rewards the pious for his laudable actions. It seems that man as a Muslim attained a rational understanding of the universe, where there are strict laws and statutes based on knowledge.

But when God's benevolent eyes glanced at the shapeless dust, and the warm current of His breath raised it from nonexistence into life, the dust and blood assumed a form that harbored the spirit of God. This form, enshrining the divine essence, was the pulsating heart with its infinite yearning for its Creator. This yearning, this fervent desire and the throbbing, is the germ that whispers in the fragrance of plants when they turn their colorful buds toward heaven, and that searches for God in the most deeply hidden shrine of human sentiments.

Life itself, forced to writhe in the shackles of matter, dreams of its divine origin and strives to return where it essentially belongs. It seeks to liberate itself from the bondage of the mortal clay, it endeavors to purify itself from the illusive luster of pain and joy alike, and tries to rebound into the sole reality from which it was hurled into phenomenal unreality.

This craving is not simply an individual peculiarity of certain peoples or nations. It permeates those of every color, language, and religion and separates out as a golden conviction that beyond the finite knowledge and matter and above all temporary human institutions there is an eternal truth in which all appearances and conflicts dissolve and harmonize.

This is the feeling of the Sufis at all times and all over the world, without temporal or local bounds. Idries Shah's writings about the mystic Jalaluddin Rumi (d. 1273) carried my thoughts back into bygone days when I lived in Konia and admired the sanctuary of the Mewlewi dervishes. Rumi, in whose name the order was founded, sleeps under the wonderful blue dome, but his ideas are still alive. Rumi, who perceived inwardly what science has only proven after many centuries:

"First you were mineral, then vegetable, then man. You will be an angel, and you will pass beyond that too."

"To the ignorant, a pearl is a stone." [1]

"The infinitive universe lies beyond this world."

"The moment you entered this world of form, an escape-ladder was put out for you."

The *Caravan* goes on, while many dogs are barking. Who needs to heed the barks, when there is so much of greater value to attend to? Idries Shah moves in Oriental wisdom and presents it to his readers in his *Table Talk;* including the parables to be found in Persian and Arabic tales and even in practical jokes. I think it a guidebook in the turmoil of our present days' hasty

[1] Idries Shah, *Caravan of Dreams* (London: Octagon Press, 1969; New York: Penguin Books, 1972), p. 80 ff.

civilization, which devours our bodies and souls and leads us into lunacies.

Shah's *Red Sea Journey* (1957) and subsequent *Pilgrimage to Mecca* evoke thrilling memories. I had gone the same way and trodden the same path when, as a humble sheikh of the Azhar mosque, I performed my pilgrimage to the holy cities of Mecca and Medina in 1934. The same feelings, the same inebriating felicity, which Sufis experience at the sight of a symbol that hides the innermost secrets of the human soul, have overcome me as those indicated by my Sufi brother Idries Shah. It seems to me now, when I compare his pages with those of my *Allah Akbar* (Berlin, 1938), that we both stood together, hand in hand, before the Black Stone of the Kaaba in the Hejaz.

Shah's *Tales of the Dervishes* (1967) is a comprehensive series of authoritative stories, assembled from the hidden wisdom of the East. Life, with its endless pains, sorrows, and joys, has manifested itself in the keen mentality of the Oriental man who, by a strange coincidence of capacity, is also a sentient and a reasonable human being. This double nature of balance has its explanation in the rise of all prophets in the East. Knowledge and vision were born in the same source from which they emanate together, in the form of tales with an overt, a symbolic, and a still deeper meaning.

Idries Shah has undoubtedly excelled in this collection, most of whose items are known only to research workers in Oriental lore. It reflects a complete range of modalities of life and thought, the history of mankind even, with its constant colorful pebbles that display continually changing shapes. Princes and fishermen, superhuman beings and angels, visit the earth, villains arise as heroes, witches appear as saints, wise men fool the mob and the mob fools wise men, all in their turn. Treachery and sincerity alternate in the pandemonium of earthly life, but the Sufis' acquiescence hovers over the crazy dance with its silent motto: "Forever never, never forever!"

It is hard to condense, or even to employ customary scholarly methods to describe, the voluminous and important book *The Sufis;* [2] embellished with an Introduction by Robert Graves. One

[2] London: Jonathan Cape, 1969.

of the purposes of a Sufi book is to provoke certain reactions in the student; hence it should be read for experience as well as for content.

Out of the wealth of material I can only extract some passages that lend themselves to comment, particularly relevant to contacts made during my own life in the East. Nasreddin is here represented, as far as I know for the first time as a Sufi, and indeed his pungent anecdotes, related in the simple witty style characteristic of Turkish expression, have a real esoteric meaning. Out of the awkward positions and inexpedient situations that surround the ridiculed and ridiculing Nasreddin, they show the leading actors of society in their complete ignorance, and worldly vanity; and reveal the utter insufficiency of the ruling order. The jocularity of the tales hides a philosophic suggestion about the futility of worldly ambitions, because there is no real truth in the here-below. Nasreddin's tomb at Akshehir is still shown to curious travelers who are fooled into believing in its veracity.

Rumi holds a noble place in Idries Shah's *The Sufis*, which gives the perceptive reader a perfect insight into the secrets of Sufism. Reading this again and again, a visionary picture rises before my eyes: It was in Konia, in the garden of Rumi's sanctuary, where I sat at the feet of the dervish Dede Hajji Khan, in 1903. I eagerly listened to the words that fell from his lips like dew upon arid leaves.

> The Sufis are travellers on a journey from their earthly abode to the spiritual world. The stages between them and their destination are seven. Until the traveller rids himself of animal passions and passes safely through those seven stages, he cannot hope to lose himself in the ocean of Union, nor slake his thirst for immortality in the unexampled wine of Love. He must conquer aspiration by patience and must cleanse his mind from all selfish desire. Other-worldliness should alone absorb his thoughts, and to that end the gates of both friendship and enmity should be closed against the people of the world. Only thus can he find his way into the heart of the realm, where every traveller is a lover of the True Beloved. And thenceforward the traveller, his heart aglow with the sacred fire of Love, tears aside the curtain of earthly appearances. Seeing with clearer eyes, he is now quick to discern wisdom in apparent ignorance and even justice within

oppression. After traversing the realm of knowledge, the traveller enters the first City of Union, and drinks deep from the cup of its spirit. The next thing he does is to enter the chamber of the True Beloved. As all the sheen of the sea and its shade as well are reflected in the heart of a single pearl, so now the infinite splendour is manifested within the traveller's soul.

Looking around him with the eyes of Unity, he recognises his true identity in that of his host, and reads the name of the Beloved in his own name. He is now as a pearl in the sea of infinite splendour: poor in the things created, but rich in the things that are spiritual and pure. The renunciation of self is the essence of the Sufi doctrine. The lover must turn into the Beloved and thus gain admittance into the chamber of Love.

Dede Hajji Khan wound up his words, to which I listened enraptured, with a precious parable of a lover who knocked at the door of his beloved: "Who are thou?" the Beloved asked, whereat the voice replied: "I am thyself" and the door was opened to him.

The sun slowly set, aglow with fire on the horizon, the birds twittered softly in the bushes and looked about their nests in the sanctuary—while I still sat amazed, deeply thrilled by Dede Hajji Khan's mystic words. I thank Saiyid Idries Shah for flashing on my mind the means to evoke such memories.

Similar memories arise when one reads Idries Shah on the reality of Omar Khayyam. Shah heads a chapter on this subject with a quotation from the early female mystic Rabi'a al-'Adawiya, who died in 801: "True devotion is for itself—not to desire heaven, nor to fear hell." She declared: "I exist in God and am altogether His."

With Rabi'a's name is associated a basic enunciation of the doctrine of divine love. This emphasized the side of Sufi teaching that protested against the unadulterated worldliness prevalent in high places, and more than hinted at the futility of fame and riches.

This last endeavor gave the inspiration to Omar who, by vocation an astronomer, wandered with his searching eyes among the stars and saw the corruption and immorality reigning on earth. His ideal was Ibn Sina, the physician and philosopher, whose poetry of inner purport sank almost into oblivion, while Omar's quatrains have become immortal.

Was he indeed a Sufi, or only a despondent man, disillusioned with the values of human existence? In his lifetime he hardly gained any notoriety. His scattered Quatrains were collected and intermixed with the poems of predecessors and others into a motley of contradictory meanings; but a single sense of the futility of exact science and of the vanity of existence permeates his lines. Was he the poetic exponent of the moral doctrine prevalent in the thirteenth century all over the Islamic world?

In the West he was discovered by Emerson who in his *English Traits* (1853) prophesied that it would become the household work of every English home. Fitzgerald's poetic versions were edited and published again and again. I myself enjoyed the honor of preparing the centenary edition published by Harrap in London with the beautiful watercolor illustrations of my countryman Willy Pogány. This edition superseded the more elaborate and scholarly rendering of E. H. Whinfield and captivated great English literati like Algernon Swinburne, John Payne, George Meredith—and millions of people seeking a way of thinking outside the conventions within which they felt themselves imprisoned.

Further important work by Idries Shah is contained in his considerations of the dervishes. Islam forbids the idea of the total seclusion of monasticism. Still, men of an ascetic trend of mind gathered around a "guide" who inspired them with his transcendental behavior or teaching; and pious people who despaired of the actions and hidebound thought of their fellowmen (or dissented from the rigidity of orthodoxy and its limiting influence) bestowed endowments on these congregations, which soon enjoyed great respect and even adoration.

In the twelfth century, several dervish orders came into being, like those associated with the names of Abdul Qádir Jiláni (d. 1166), Abdullah Rifá'i, Shadhili, and Haji Bektash. The Bektashis gained recognition by the Ottoman Sultans of Turkey as brethren of the military janissaries, and the Grand Sheikh of the Mewlewi Order girded the Sultan with the Sword of Osman, founder of the dynasty.

I had the privilege of associating both with the Mewlewi and the Bektashi dervishes. I frequently visited their sanctuaries, now dissolved, in Istanbul and Cairo, and have written about their mystic trance states.[3]

The deep, authoritative, and penetrating analyses and expositions of Idries Shah, presented in his books and other materials, are valuable contributions to Sufism. For the general reader, their content provides a counterbalance to our present-day atmosphere of crude materialism, and emotional imbalance, which so many people mistake for spirituality.

[3] *Allah Akbar* (Berlin: Holle & Co., 1938); *Sulle orme di Maometto*, ed. Garzanti (Milano, 1938).

VIII

HISTORICO-LITERARY
ASPECTS
OF THE WORK
OF
IDRIES SHAH
by
Dr. Saleh Hamarneh

Two developments made it inevitable that Eastern thought and traditions should become better known in the West: (1) the post-imperial emergence of Eastern countries and their peoples into the wider areas of culture, education, commerce, and international life; and (2) the vast increase in the restless investigative spirit of the Western cultures in the physical and social sciences.

The first development, together with the growth of a generation innocent of the traditional patronizing attitudes toward ancient civilizations, provided a readership and an audience of younger people. Many of them became seduced by absurd cults, but quite a number of steadier spirits remained.

The second development took the cultivation of Eastern letters and traditions out of the hands of the few "specialists" who had, unconsciously, sought to monopolize them. This brought into the field a number of fresh minds and, consequently, a far truer range of understanding than had been possible in the "undermanned" situation of the past.

These factors naturally enabled more and more Eastern people of a wide culture to enter into contact with the West.

The moral and material achievements of the East in the past quarter of a century have also redressed the balance so that Eastern ideas are listened to with greater respect. As an example, if you look at the Western newspapers of today and compare them with the files of the same periodicals a generation ago, you will at once see that sneers at the Eastern people (along the lines of "if they knew so much, why are they in such a mess?") are now confined almost exclusively to provincial papers or to the ideologically committed, and they are preaching mainly to the converted.

Thus the stage was set for the emergence of Eastern thinkers and men of letters, of science, and of other branches of learning to address themselves to a world audience.

Yet there remained, and to some extent still remains, a barrier to the free communication of the Eastern heritage to the West. This barrier may be analyzed in the following parts: (1) a vestigial fear of the East, which plainly dates from the ancient battle between East and West for trade routes and Mediterranean hegemony, complicated by religious and cultural factors; (2) political programs, mainly or largely dedicated to representing certain Eastern nations as backward, untrustworthy, and undesirable: in a word, trying to invoke and strengthen the vestigial memory of past disasters; and (3) "cultural uncertainty," in which the self-questioning West constantly asks itself what it is doing and why.

The climate engendered by these factors may often tend to distort the real and objective attempts by Eastern workers to share their culture with others.

There is one living Eastern thinker whose writings have been accepted in the East and West alike as of high value and great promise in philosophical, social, and even scientific areas: Idries Shah.

This is not to say that his reception is likely to be immune from the factors of opposition to which reference has just been made. On the contrary, we should expect, just as much as acceptance and understanding of his work, opposition and jealousy. For this reason it is as well to dispose of this matter before proceeding to any consideration of his life and work.

There is the risk, for instance, that a narrower type of specialist might see in Shah's writings, successful and widely discussed as they are, a threat to his own monopoly of the field that he has (often with great sacrifices) made his own. There is a possibility that, in a preponderantly Western society, chauvinistic or xenophobic elements, which probably lurk in all communities, might feel that Idries Shah is an "outsider." There is the risk that emotional and sensationalist practitioners in mass communications, in need of a story, might decide to represent him as a would-be "spiritual mentor" in the manner of charlatan adventurers of the past who have attracted much attention and many converts among easily influenced women and others of an uncritical and credulous cast of mind.

It is possible to outline some of the requirements that an Eastern thinker would have to fulfill in order to escape the worst of the possible opposition based on malice and misunderstanding. First, for preference, he should be from a background that is respected and accepted in the East. He should be, that is to say, a respectable and responsible individual, known to people of caliber in the East, and vouched for by them. This Idries Shah undoubtedly is. He is no person of unknown antecedents, springing up from nowhere. He and his family have been intimately known for generations as people of the highest character and attainments.

Second, to escape the charge of being a national propagandist, or even of having a bias in favor of one cultural area, such an individual should not be associated too exclusively with the Arab, the Persian, the Indian or any other grouping. Hence the background of Idries Shah, with his Indian, Afghan, Arab, and Persian relationships, makes him an ideal choice. For too long the "specialists," tied to a linguistic basis, have been unable to recognize the inner identity of the thinking of the peoples of the East, and the consequence has been the clash between Arab and

Ajami (non-Arabs), and even the curious Persian conceit of ex-
clusivity, which is a recurrent feature of a few smaller minds in
Iran.

Third, such an individual should not be labeled with any
marked ideological commitment that would cause suspicion
that it colors his thinking. Idries Shah has, in contrast, been able
to emphasize the unifying factors in the various cultures, rather
than the divisive ones.

Fourth, the individual should have the ability to communicate,
to mutual satisfaction, with the thinking and creative people of
the culture that he is addressing. The cordial and interested
reception of Idries Shah's work by writers, critics, and men of
letters in the West is already demonstration enough that he has
this ability.

So Shah has the credentials, the background, and the ability.
What of his work?

An examination of his writings by an individual with an
Eastern background first of all conveys the conviction that Shah
has succeeded as few others have done in transposing the Eastern
"flavor" into Western languages and idioms. This has seldom
been successfully achieved by writers of either culture. The
Westerner has very often seen the Sufic tradition through the
filter of his own bias, and extant works on the subject are ample
witness to this tendency. The Easterner, in his turn, has often
been quite unable to explain his ideas in a manner sufficiently
intelligible to people in the West. In many cases when he has
been successful, his success has been due to his adoption of
Western modes of thought to such an extent that he radically
changes the message on which he is working. Even if it were to
be held that translation is mechanical, it would remain true that
this kind of mechanical process is far too crude to transmit the
meanings of Sufi thought.

The second achievement of Idries Shah is his blending of
the different nuances of Sufi thought—of the Persian, Arabian,
Turkic, and Central Asian cultural areas. Most scholars have
failed here because their orientation is perceptibly biased in
favor of one or two authors, or one or other culture, or one of

the several languages that are used in Sufism. But it is the very diversity of languages and other modes of expression that enables the Sufi student to appreciate correctly the materials available, and therefore a knowledge of the subtleties of more than one language is almost to be regarded as a necessity.

Shah's third fundamentally important contribution has been his emphasis upon the social importance of the discoveries, knowledge, and operation of the Sufi thinkers and sages. Due to the inevitable sentimentalization and deterioration of Sufic studies among specialists and masses alike, conditioned to emotional fervor, there has for centuries been a powerful tendency to imagine that Sufism is nothing other than a "spiritual way," a branch of mysticism, and a proper study for those who are obsessed by religiosity and may be self-centered enough to think of Sufism as a personal panacea. This tendency has gone so far that you may search through many encyclopedias and standard textbooks without realizing that the Sufis, of today and yesterday alike, are and were people of the most practical kind and that they have contributed powerfully to the human heritage of knowledge, particularly in social science, psychology, and the study of behavior, as well as in experimental fields. The emotional aspect has been overstressed: only because it is the most obvious.

Idries Shah has published a mass of facts and records that highlight Sufi achievements. Numerous Western authorities, after examining this material and checking it with other historical, cultural, and literary sources, have been surprised to find that unconscious chauvinism and biased assumptions had prevented earlier recognition of these vast riches of research, tradition, and exposition.

Shah's insistence that Sufi thought is something of value to the present day has been seized upon with considerable interest in many countries; especially where research is continuing into "new" methods of enlarging human consciousness and improving learning capacity. Especially relevant recently was his quoting, on television, certain American psychological experiments into behavior. These showed that even animals could learn in one-twentieth of the normal time, not by training, but by observation of (and association with) other animals that already possessed their knowledge. Shah emphasized, with examples, how this method of "rapid learning" was a Sufi technique, and could be applied to human beings, as the British journal *New Scientist* had suggested.

People who formerly said that Sufism contained nothing of importance, while acknowledging that Sufism may once have had something to teach, still maintain that mankind must surely by this time have caught up with the knowledge possessed by the Sufis of the past. That this is demonstrably not the case may be observed in the effects of Shah's own work. As an instance, his book *The Book of the Book*,[1] although described at first by one critic as "buffoonery," has been discovered by scientists to be of such importance that it is used in advanced university psychological work. Many theses upheld by Sufi scholars of the past are now being reinvestigated with astonishing effect; and much research work on these lines, almost all of it prompted by Idries Shah's books, has been undertaken by scholars and scientists throughout the world.

Some of Shah's admittedly trenchant phrases, though they may cause affront to the more dogmatic and hidebound minds, appear to explain so clearly the disparity between the traditionalistic externals of Sufism and the penetrating insights revealed in its literature that we must accept them as the probable explanation for this dichotomy. As an example, although for the outsider and layman the Sufi appears (through textbooks and other secondary sources, and even by superficial inspection of certain Sufi groups in the field) to be merely a mystic and emotional devotee, there can be little doubt that this condition, if well-founded, results from the deterioration or misinterpretation of Sufism. Fruit cannot be judged by looking at rotten apples. In Shah's work there is found the seed from which fresh apples can grow. These are quite different from the rotten apples that are occasionally found.

It is only to be expected, of course, that if we have been wrong for so very long, we shall be less inclined to admit the truth than if we did not already have a vested interest in error. Many of us might even be tempted to try to oppose Shah's

[1] London: The Octagon Press, 1969.

diagnosis as the easiest way out of the impasse. But that would not be in the real tradition of scholarship, and could not have a lasting effect. Shah's work may be unique at the moment, but he has opened a door to the real interpretation of Sufism that is now unlikely ever to be slammed shut again.

IX

PSYCHOLOGY
OF
THE SUFI WAY
TO
INDIVIDUATION

by

Professor A. Reza Arasteh

1. INTRODUCTION

In the West, Islamic Sufism was the exclusive domain of scholars for almost two centuries. Through the desire of early missionaries to understand Muslim mysticism and through the efforts of various European Orientalists to edit, translate, and interpret Sufism, a way was gradually opened by which the soul-searching man of the twentieth century might enter this hitherto unknown realm. In fact, as man has intensified his anxious search for a universal answer to his emerging situation, he has probed more and more deeply into the world's cultural heritage. Traditionally, the West has turned to such men in history as Meister Eckhart; more recently, humanists like Albert Schweitzer came to realize that the last consequence of rationalism is mysticism—the same conclusion reached by Al-Ghazzali and Rumi, who lived at the end of the rational period of Islamic culture in the twelfth and thirteenth centuries. In our own time such men as the late Thomas Merton finally reinterpreted the origins of Christianity, summed up so well in the phrase from St. John's Gospel, "You must be born again." Furthermore, a great deal of literature has already been written to introduce the ways of Zen to the West and to describe its affinity with Christian mysticism.

The profound humanism of past Islamic culture is just beginning to attract the attention of modern scholars, who are eager to interpret it to the newly awakening, receptive audience of the West. By bringing to light the jewels of Islamic thought, our new men of wisdom may be able to enlighten our contemporary life, now darkened by unnecessary wars, sophistic conflicts or religio-ideological prejudices.

Idries Shah is one of the few men who have kindled the light for the English-speaking world. Whether it is in *The Sufis*, *Tales of the Dervishes*, *The Way of the Sufi*, or in his masterful essay on "Special Problems in the Study of Sufi Ideas," he has ably presented Sufism to the West and has conveyed its deep sense of reality to modern man searching for a soul. Whether he is interpreting the stories of the lives of Sufis or is relating tales concerned with complex human situations, his message rings out loud and clear: life is "simple," but its essence is embedded in our complex forms, which we must find a way to unfold.

In my own writings, I have emphasized the significance of past cultural elements for strengthening man's psychological state today. To this end and to commend the work of Idries Shah, I humbly present this essay to the symposium honoring an eminent scholar of Sufism who has opened the gate of its palace to the public.

2. SUFISM: A HISTORICAL IDENTITY

We must first of all realize that although a good analyst is one who can make cultural symbols significant and at the same time intrinsically meaningless, systems of psychology are generally culture-bound. In a sense Sufism is no exception. It has its own history (going back over a thousand years), its own evolution and refinement through successive chains of Sufi thought that have provided continuity and have established a recognizable cultural identity both in Persia and elsewhere. The links in the chain of trueborn Sufis have been original men in every era: they have been influential social figures and have achieved material comforts, though this was not their aim; they have enjoyed fame, name, and even power. But at the right moment they adopted "intentional isolation" in order to purify their psyche, regain their original sensitivity and go through a process of individuation. Often, they made an art out of science, philosophy, and religion.

Sufi literature is extensive. Over a thousand treatises and books in various languages have been written by Sufis themselves, and at least an equal number by scholars interpreting them. At the same time Sufism has also served as an umbrella for the withdrawn, as a mechanism of escape for individuals out of power, or as a mere pastime for those in power. Yet Sufism has given inner support to the innocent, has humanized the cruel, and tamed the wild. It has enslaved powerful kings and has made kings out of slaves. While it has liberated man from external forces, it has also been misused by political demagogues as a means for controlling men. Thus you can see my task is not an easy one, but we must put aside the historical and social implications for the moment and deal with Sufism as a process of individuation. To understand this process requires a special psychological frame of reference.

A psychological frame of reference for Sufism. In general, the Western psychological frame of reference, a product of Western culture, is inadequate for interpreting Sufism, though analytical psychology explains it better than any other school. In fact, what is known as "scientific" psychology and Freudian psychoanalysis are useful only for interpreting the nature of fragmented man. The inadequacy of scientific psychology stems from its obsession with trying to be an "objective" science, while Freudian psychology suffers from its founder's limited concept of man. Further evidence for these inadequacies can be found by a historical analysis of various schools. Early psychologists started the scientific study of man from the wrong assumption; that is, instead of beginning from the basic difference that sets him apart from animals, man's ability for *creative vision*, psychology began with the common denominators of animal-human behavior. Later, Freud made a similar error: before having a clear concept of man he started with mental illness and its cure. Had Freud been a philosopher turning to the pursuit of medicine instead of being a physician turning to philosophy, his theories would have taken a different form. Similarly, had he become acquainted with other cultures he would have made fewer mistakes.[1]

As a result of these historical facts, some psychologists in the early twentieth century studied animal behavior and applied their findings to children. Then during the 1920s and 1930s some studied children and applied their findings to adults. Following World War II, social psychologists began to study the average man and related their findings to those in the state of *individuation;* and psychiatrists applied what they had learned from their study of the mentally ill to healthy individuals. Under such historical pressures, which still consume our energy, it is no surprise that Jung's contribution to the study of man has not received the recognition it deserves, especially in America and in Asia.

Thus, psychological truth, like all of science, is only partial. I have often used the analogy of comparing truth to a gigantic diamond that fell to the earth aeons of time ago and broke into pieces. When each piece fell in a particular corner of the earth, the natives there eventually found that piece and cried out that they had found the whole truth. So too with psychological truth; even if we were to bring all the pieces of the diamond of truth together, it would still be a fragmented diamond. Our criteria for bringing together these pieces of truth about man must encompass the range of man's development. We must take man's stages of growth as a blank sheet on which we can map all systems of psychology in their proper place. We must have a comprehensive chart that can give meaning from zero to plus and minus infinity of growth. When I ponder on the stages of life, I perceive a range running from purely biological unconscious evolution to that of final pure psychic cosmic unconsciousness. Therefore, I

[1] R. Arasteh, *Final Integration in the Adult Personality* (Leiden: E. J. Brill, 1965).

propose the following four successive stages of growth (which can serve as frames of reference for systems of psychology):

1) Psychobiology is used to study the very early stages of human growth, when the child's expression is dominated by biological forces, not in terms of an action-reaction chain, but in relation to the child's total expression. A holistic approach is most useful here.

2) The second stage appears as soon as socialization is rooted. We must realize that the biological force is manifested through psychocultural forces, thus calling for a new theory and technique —that of psychocultural analysis.

3) The third stage begins with the objectivization of the ego and the awareness of single reality, namely experiential analysis, emphasizing experience and insight. At its peak, this stage will be transformed into cosmopsychology.

4) At this stage the person's insight is harmonized with the pulsation of the universe. For example, the ordinary experience belongs to the stage of *I-ness* (ego world), which at the experiential level becomes *he-ness* and at a deeper perception arises from the world of *oneness*.

There is no time to discuss the various inclusive systems of stages of human growth, but it suffices to reiterate that the Sufi's path of individuation begins at the experiential level and its stage of individuation requires insight into cosmopsychology. In order to realize the significance of this point of view, we must repudiate the long-acknowledged belief that man is a social animal. We must recognize that man is a religio-psychological being who began life in the unconscious union with nature. In his process of evolution, he separated from nature, experienced pain, time, and space; or if you wish, he was cast from Paradise, and since then he has been seeking a new union. Psychologically, he is evolving in terms of innumerable phases of relatedness and unrelatedness, and cultural renaissances, and he will ultimately reunite with the cosmos in a conscious existence state. In other words, there is a *koan* (as in Taoism) that man tries to decipher, there is a treasure (as in Sufism) that man tries to discover, or there is a Messiah (as in Christianity) that man tries to emulate. There are innumerable degrees of awarenesses, each engulfing the one before it (just as when one throws a stone in a pool of water), until "not-being" reaches the shore of Being.

Thus, we can conclude that, in a sense, mental health is a constant ratio between the degree of awareness and the degree of assimilation of experience within that ring of culture. In other words, in the process of human evolution creative imagination preceded intellect, and myth anteceded religion and science. Secondly, we must realize that cosmological evolution is based on the creative unconscious serving as the inner memory of each individual's growth. Individuals of the same class are ruled by their collective unconscious (Jung), and there also exists a cultural unconscious that merely serves as an anchor of the ship of being until the individual is ready to transcend the cultural level. Furthermore, we must differentiate between the experience, which is the union of subject-object, and behavior as interpreted by Western psychologists. Undoubtedly, in healthy individuals experience and behavior overlap, and inner and outer expression are the same; but in many cases, behavior is the rationalization or inhibitor of experience—it is a cover. In its occurrence experience has an organic and illuminatory nature, whereas behavior is characterized by conditioning. It is experience, not behavior, that produces change, and at the same time strengthens one's sensitivity. It is said that all the conditioning of Pavlov's dog was undone by one night's flood in the cellar where the dog was kept. In fact, anyone who prepares to take the path of Sufism must first "uncondition" himself.

3. THE NATURE OF SUFISM

With the framework of psychocosmology at hand, we can refer to Sufism as an art of rebirth, a process of regaining one's naturalness, a way out of automation, and a vehicle for creative vision. It is the process of awareness of the world of multireality and the perception of single reality. It is loyalty to life and cosmic laws, harmonization with true nature. It is liberation from the cultural self (purification of self) and relatedness to the cosmic self. It is inactivation of the cultural unconscious and reactivation of the creative unconscious through communication with collective unconscious.

A great number of scholars have attempted to determine the meaning of the words *Sufi* and *Sufism*. Some have argued that the terms originate from *Safa*—referring to the Sufi's purity of heart; others claim that *saff* means of the first rank or vanguard; and still others insist that the term *Suf* refers to their wool garments. Furthermore, because some Sufis traveled and stayed in caves, they became known as *shikaftis* (meaning "of the cavern"), whereas those who subsisted on little food were called "paupers." Other Sufis were better known for their ardor, like some of our present-day hippies. Sometimes Sufis were called illuminati, intuitionists, or "sincere ones." However, it is apparent that these terms were merely names to designate a situation and a beholder. They may fit certain traits that characterized the Sufis, but they do not reveal their total individuation. Just as we are still handicapped today in the assessment of man, so too have been observers, especially laymen, in the past. All that one can say is that Sufism was an inner experience that led to identification with one's object of desire. Essential to this (as we shall see) has been the object of desire, the so-called beloved, or if you prefer, the ideal-ego. In the history of Sufism, the object of desire has passed through an evolutionary process. The early Sufis were seeking the true qualities of a Muslim as stated in the Koran, and they identified as their aim and objective the holy book's qualities and images. The Sufis of the ninth century, beginning with Ali Abu Mansur al-Hallaj (who was crucified because he claimed he was creative truth) and culminating with 'Attar, chose the image of *Allah* (One) as their object of desire. Still later, Sufis like Rumi and Hafiz identified with the process of creative unconscious (so identified as love). All of them may have taken past or present *Qutbs* as archetypes for their transfer.

The process of this identification was manifested in the I-thou relationship. "Thou" can be any object of desire and "I" can be any person at any stage who is incited by the proper object of desire. In the process of union of I and thou, the essential is the inner motivation of the seeker. The heart must be motivated from within. The thou, the subject of desire, must be worthy enough. In Sufi literature, the purity of heart, the most essential of all, and the intention are often compared to a clear mirror. If one's mirror, through socialization, competition, marriage, or professional recognition, has become cloudy, then the seeker needs more cleansing than even an illiterate but natural man. If one's state is alienated through anger, hate, greed, envy, jealousy, and cultural habituation, one needs greater effort to attain inner freedom than does an honest craftsman. If one has become embedded in various rigid cultural patterns, especially forms of religions, one must undergo a greater struggle within oneself than the one who accepts the experience of the founders of religion as more essential than the rules and regulations of the church.

In any case, when the seeker falls into the path, he notices his object of desire, and his bent is total concentration for union with the object of desire. This intensive effort is expressed in terms of the lover-beloved relationship; including a process by which the total effort of the seeker is directed toward bringing the lover to the state of *ghorb* (intimacy). Therefore it is initially necessary that he also becomes aware of the pitfalls along the way. The most serious pitfall of the I-thou relationship is that the I knowingly and unknowingly enters the process of union in order to obtain the object of desire for himself (the lover) rather than for its own sake. He wants to manipulate and utilize something. The experience of the I-thou relationship never proceeds in this way. The requirement is sincerity and further sincerity. The question arises, "How do we know that we are sincere in such a procedure and in such an act of devotion?" Although the act is its own proof, the Sufis also followed signs and symbols, and like watchdogs watched over the rise and fall of their desires, in addition they analyzed such desires and looked into motives, intentions, and adopted various exercises.

One of the most interesting mechanisms for drawing the total attention of the lover toward his beloved was a five-step dance that revealed the total outlook of Sufis toward the process of the I-thou relationship. It also shows the principal experiences in *An* that had to occur before union of object-subject could take place. The dance started with meditation, intense concentration on oneself so that one could empty himself, de-embed himself, resensitize himself, and gain his state of naturalness. However, this was not enough. The Sufis knew that the regaining of naturalness must occur through action. The dance served this purpose.

In dancing the seeker took steps and moved his closed palm toward his chest (first act); then he took a step again and opened his palm and moved his hand toward the ground, symbolizing that he was released from "self" (second act). In the second step he raised his hand toward heaven, symbolizing the nature of God, manifested in religion as everything coming from Him (the third act). In the fourth act the seeker moved his hands over his head in such a way that the palms faced the sky, symbolizing that man doesn't know the nature of God; and in the fifth act the seeker pointed his right-hand fingers toward his object of desire, symbolizing that all that exists is thou and thou. The seeker performed this dance with great concentration on his object of desire, often symbolized in the guide or perfect man, or his earthly beloved. This tendency can be interpreted as movement "away from the cultural self and movement toward the congenial self."

When I becomes thou, duality turns into unity, resulting in an *An*—a new state, new feeling, and a situation in which one becomes aware of one's previous states and can communicate symbolically, holistically, and through experiential media. But how? By thinking? No. By conversation? No. By instruction? No. Then what is the anatomy of this mechanism of the I-thou relationship? My insight into creative men of all fields tells me that this medium has its own fundamental qualities. It is a vehicle based upon the whole man, rather than upon sense perception, action-reaction, stimulus-response, thinking, or being logical. It has its own psychological dimension; its laws and psychical mechanism have merely been touched upon. Space does not allow further discussion, but basically, the Sufi had to go through three stages, designated as: (1) illumination of name (the cultural self), (2) illumination of qualities, and (3) illumination of essence, all of which together transcended into the state of *individuation*. However, before the novice qualified for these steps, he had to purify himself through a long period of exercises, both inner and outer, best described as a process of rebirth and the way to individuation.

4. THE WAY TO INDIVIDUATION

Sufism as a way of individuation can be summarized in two major psychological steps, both of which are interrelated: disintegration (*Fana*) from a self-intellect, partial soul, and a social self, and reintegration (*Baqa*) as the universal self, that is, activation of one's totality. The early seekers used the image of their guide or God as transfer, that which embraces all creation. This mechanism was related to the Sufi idea of man. According to the Sufis man has potentially inherited forces that can lower him to a bestial state or elevate him. In an evolutionary sense this contradiction arose with the development of reason.

At this stage, the faculty of reasoning finds itself challenged by man's animal tendencies; out of its contradictions man must either go beyond reason to attain the state of certainty (*nafs e mutma'ana*), or fall downward into impulses (*nafs e amareh*). Indeed, so contradictory is man's nature that he can rarely harmonize these discordant elements. Disharmony appears most often among the tendencies of (1) *nafs e amareh* (the force within us that commands regressive and evil acts) and reason; (2) between reason and *nafs e mutma'ana* (what confirms certainty); and (3) intuition and reason in the final state of personality growth. All the Sufis describe *nafs e amareh* or simply *nafs* as being artful, cunning, motivated by evil, and possessing a passion-producing nature. In the form of lust it robs the mind of intelligence, the heart of reverence. It is the mother-idol that compels man to seek material aims in life and deprives him of growth, or it may even create in the mind such idols as greed, lust, and love of power per se.

In a social sense *nafs* manifests itself in seekers of power: those who exchange their genuine human character for power and become slaves of wealth, etc. The power of *nafs* develops in the mind such a craving that a ruler willingly commits inhumane actions to satisfy it. The evil in man's nature, like a voracious crab, consumes all his humane qualities. Thus, to gain security the power-seekers strive to possess and use power at the expense of their fellowmen. They become a tool of power, wealth, and their carnal desires. Those who want to succeed must fully develop the art of guile and treachery and act in such a way as to secure more power.

In the conflict between reason and *nafs e amareh,* reason may triumph by satisfying *nafs,* by preoccupation in various fields or by gaining the power derived from a virtuous life and suppression of passion by certain strong religious beliefs. Relatively free of *nafs's* trap, reason becomes solely concerned with the human situation, the result of which is a partial (specialized) man, who busies himself in only one area of life while believing that he possesses the truth. Yet he ignores his own real self; as Rumi explains in one of his discourses:

> Scholars argue heatedly about their specialities while ignoring their own selves—that which affects them the most. The scholar judges on the legality of this and that, but in relation to his own self he knows nothing about its legality or purity.[2]

The individual tries to use logic in every human situation and relate himself to something that will bring harmony to the situation. But because this object of relationship is not genuine, the solution is temporary. Rumi describes this situation in *Fihi ma Fihi:*

> Everyone in this world has his own interest, whether women, wealth, knowledge or something else. Each believes that his comfort and joy rests in that one pursuit. Yet when he goes in search of that object he does not find satisfaction in it and returns. After a while he declares that he was not really seeking joy and mercy; he seeks anew but is disappointed again; so he continues on and on.[3]

Rumi further declares that the intellectual self, proud of its knowledge, tends to become self-conceited and thus deviates from the real self. Nevertheless, the Sufis appreciated man's great potentialities; they declared that man is a mighty volume within whom all things are recorded. If the individual lets reason grow, it makes him aware of his potentialities and helps him set the basic

[2] M. J. M. Rumi, *Fihi ma Fihi* (Discourses), ed. Firunzanfar (Tehran: University of Tehran Press, 1952).
[3] *Ibid.*

purpose of life, that is, union with all—a state of trust. Yet at this point he may realize that reason is insufficient for handling his existential problem. He may even perceive that a more integrated state exists while also recognizing that reason cannot achieve it.

In this state of perplexity a diversity arises between intellect and the real self, reason and intuition, I and not-I. Although the not-I exists in a very real sense, it first appears veiled to man. Some people find it self-evident, others obscure, some find it intimately a part of themselves, to others it is inaccessible. When the mind is receptive, it may appear suddenly without the individual's realization, only to disappear a moment later.

The extent to which the self-intellect resists the voice of the real self will vary from one individual to another. One may become ambivalent and retreat to self-intellect again, another may hear the voice but ignore it, while still another may attend to it and become aware of his own state of being. This stage, however, cannot be attained from knowledge gained in books or from listening to others. Each must be his own awakener, that is, no one can awaken another by the mere instruction of Sufism. He must himself receive the idea of self-seeking, experience it and hear it within himself. A secret voice (Hafiz's "real conscience") may tell him: "If you are a man come forth and pass on. Whatever else hinders you (name, fame, or desire) bypass it. Seek the truth." [4]

Having attained a state of awareness, the individual knows intuitively that what he is, is not what he can become. He has a glimpse of a better state of self-security, but the conventional veils deprive him of its advantages. While in this state he may become aware of tension, and this anxiety situation, lacking any existential basis, compels him to retreat. People frequently fall into such a state momentarily and are satisfied with just knowing about it, for in this state a dominant ego stands against a dim inner voice. A social self, nurtured by everyday society, can easily inhibit the rise of a universal self. Because the conventional self arises out of the interaction of man with a limited environment, the dim inner voice is easily extinguished. The same things occur if an individual is under the pressure of social forces con-

[4] R. Arasteh, "Succession of Identities: Outer and Inner Metamorphoses," unpublished manuscript presented as a lecture at the George Washington University, Department of Psychiatry, November, 1962, p. 16.

tradictory to the universal self, or if the seeker still associates with a group far removed from universality. But if lucky, he falls into a more favorable situation thereby increasing his psychological disharmony. The voice of his own true conscience can now challenge his social self. His real personality (that is, what he ought to become) stands against his I, questions it, and criticizes it. The individual begins to analyze himself, and he becomes more interested in ultimate certainty than in such temporary satisfactions as possessing wealth, fame, and social prestige. He realizes that his existential problem is of even greater importance. As a seeker of truth, he recognizes that he possesses one heart and is potentially one entity and is not able to split into several parts. Thus he falls into a state of quest, and the object of this search consists of becoming a real self, a thoroughly-born man, a perfect and universal man. It means union with all, becoming God-like, and being only the Truth. To become like God represents a beautiful creation more than submission to the authoritarian image of God; it means "becoming love and loving to save, not loving God to be saved."

Initially, the individual cannot perceive this state, because throughout his life, from childhood to the point of awareness, mental blocks have hindered this perception. An analysis of history in terms of human relatedness would undoubtedly reveal a similar state of circumstances. The Sufis picture man's grave task as one of removing these barriers and becoming a mirror of the universe. The seeker encounters a difficult mental path, and in every act of search and reflection he also faces the possibility of falling into an illusion, thus making new beliefs, and losing the proper mind-set.

Selecting a guide. So perilous is the task that the Sufis emphatically advise a seeker to first acquire a guide ("light of the path"), specifically, a *Pir* who has undergone the experiences and knows the road perfectly, because he is "the essence of the path." [5] Sufism asserts that this guide is necessary because no person possesses the real touchstone to measure his own behavior, actions, and feelings. On the other hand, every person reacts to

[5] *Ibid.;* R. A. Nicholson, *Studies in Islamic Mysticism* (Cambridge: Cambridge University Press, 1921); M. J. M. Rumi, *Mathnawi,* ed. and trans. R. A. Nicholson, 8 vols. (Cambridge: Cambridge University Press, 1925–1940).

passion, and in some way admires his own actions. The difficulty arises because he cannot objectively measure his own vices and undesirably acquired habits. Thus, for both behavioral and mental change he must have a constant associate who makes him aware of his status and guides him to transcend himself. The seeker must be grateful, rejoice, and correct his states.

Such a guide can appreciate and understand the novice's waves of thought and guide him symbolically. At this point the seeker infers the essential principle of experiencing mystical sects. Sufis believe that although discussion is necessary, association with the guide (one whose mystical experience is superior to that of the seeker) is essential for the seeker's progress.[6] Rumi advises the seekers not to turn away from the guide and never to travel alone: "Take refuge in the shadow of the guide that you may escape from the enemy [nafs] that opposes in secret."[7] In selecting the guide, the seeker should insist on evaluating the companion according to his purpose and objective, not on the basis of race or nationality:

> Do not look at his figure and colour; look at his purpose and
>   intention,
> If he is black (yet) he is in accord with you: call him white,
>   for his complexion is the same as yours.[8]

Regarding the master-novice relationship, Rumi declares that the selfless leader is his own light, whereas the Sufi should seek the light through the guide. Out of this situation mystical principles arise: that is, the master cannot teach through instruction but only set up a situation in which the inspired novice experiences what he should:

> Soul receives from soul that knowledge, therefore not by book
>   or from tongue,
> If knowledge of mysteries comes after emptiness of mind, that is
>   illumination of heart.[9]

[6] N. A. Jami, Lawai-ih (Flashes of Light: A Treatise on Sufism), trans. E. H. Whinfield and M. M. Kazwini (London: Royal Asiatic Society, 1928).
[7] M. J. M. Rumi, Mathnawi.
[8] Ibid.
[9] Ibid.

The third principle is again derived from the second, that is, the seeker can only experience those situations that come close to his mental state. Traditionally, the Sufi seekers traveled extensively on foot and visited various *khaneqas* in order to find their guide. It was also believed that at the sight of a master a heart-to-heart communication took place:

> *When Umar* (Pir) *found the stranger in appearance a friend;*
> *He found his soul seeking (to learn the divine) mysteries.*
> *The Shayk* (Umar) *was adept and disciple eager: the man was*
>   *quick and the beast belonged to the royal court.*
> *That spiritual guide* (Umar) *perceived that he* (the seeker)
>   *possessed the capacity for receiving guidance: he sowed the*
>   *good seed in the good soil.*[10]

Authorities also related how Bayazid Bastami, a great Persian Sufi of the ninth century, met his master. His father, after giving him a basic education, wished him to study further in *feqh* (jurisprudence). While still a boy, he was taken to every notable theologian, but Bayazid did not approve of any until the father and son visited Junaid (a famous Sufi of that era), whom Bayazid immediately perceived as the master who could teach him. Although this master-novice relationship outwardly suggests formality and authoritarianism in its behavioral aspects, in mystical reality it is not so at all.[11] Two souls are constantly communicating: one gives and directs, the other receives and makes progress. It is not that the novice is obedient to an order but that he is receptive to evolutionary changes. The more the seeker transcends the less guidance he needs from the guide. This guidance promotes a rebirth, and the guide serves only as a transfer in this path.

The nature of mystical experience also explains the receptive relationship between the master's soul and that of the seeker. The water flows from a spring to a dry source as a one-way current. Among Sufis of similar rank the mystical experience may become a two-way traffic. In such a situation, the master can perceive the invisible current of events, comparable to a receptive radio with

[10] *Ibid.*
[11] R. and J. Arasteh, *Man and Society in Iran* (Leiden: E. J. Brill, 1964).

a strong antenna, whereas the novice, like a small radio with a limited range of receptivity, must keep his perception within narrow bounds and never concentrate on what is beyond his actual capacity. When a guide accepts a seeker, the latter must surrender himself and never question his leader. He must not criticize or by mistake infer the guide's action from his own deeds. He must not be weakhearted or enraged by every blow (discernment) that actually helps polish the mirror of his heart.[12]

Now, however, the question arises: What happens after one has decided to go through the art of rebirth? Traditionally, the individual had to pass through several behavioral stages (*moqams*) and a parallel set of reflexive internal modes (*hals*). The *moqam* is a required discipline achieved through exercise and daily practice, whereas the *hal* is a subjective state of mind, dependent on sensations and not under the control of volition. It is revealed to the novice (*salek*) and is understood in a different way. Like James's "stream of consciousness" the *hal* is not static or rigid. It is analogous to the flash of lightning that appears and disappears, or like snowflakes that fall on a river and vanish in a moment, becoming a part of the current.

In traditional Sufism the behavioral stages begin with "awareness," that is, a final rebirth, or the beginning of a new sign of living. Such a feeling may come to a person suddenly, or it may develop within him as a result of some experience. Yet the awareness is not enough; the seeker must cease unsuitable past behavior through repentance (*tubeh*), then make a decision to reform, and finally cleanse the self of enmity and cruelty. The aspirant is now in a position to select for himself a "pole" or leader, who is sometimes called *dalil-e-rah* (the light of the path), for such individuals have attained their ultimate identity. After repentance there appears a stage of avoiding doubtful and uncertain acts (*vara*). It is followed by piety (*zohd*) in which the novice concentrates on certain values and internal serenity. The next stage relates to patience (*sabr*) and is considered half the task and the key to joy. At every turn and at every level, the aspirant is faced with a situation, either favorable or unfavorable;

[12] H. Ritter, *Das Meer der Seele* (Leiden: E. J. Brill, 1955); M. J. M. Rumi, *Fihi ma Fihi*; M. J. M. Rumi, *Divan e Shams e Tabriz* (Tehran: Amir Kabir Press, 1957).

but in either case patience is demanded. The stage of trust (*tavakul*) is difficult to attain, for the individual must have trust without recourse to prayer or a request from God. Satisfaction (*reza*) is the final stage, a culmination of all the past stages; it is characterized as all positive and all tranquil.

Accompanying these stages are somewhat parallel modes (*hals*) relating to the state of mind. One of these conditions (*hal e moraqebe*) implies that one should measure his behavior according to the object of search. The other *hals* include: the state of nearness (*hal e qurb*), which suggests that one is making progress toward his goal; the state of love; the state of fear and hope; the state of intimacy; the state of certainty (*etminan*), where no doubt remains; and finally the state of unification and assurance.[13]

In summarizing these steps the Sufis assert that a seeker faces two major tasks: to dissolve his present status (*Fana*), then reintegrate again. "Unless you are first disintegrated, how can I reintegrate you again?"[14] Disintegration here refers to the passing away of the conventional self; reintegration means rebirth in the cosmic self. *Fana* is the removal of the "I"; *Baqa* the process of becoming "I." Instead of being related to the partial self-intellect, reintegration means bringing to light the secrets of the total personality. In a practical sense it means cleansing one's own consciousness of what Rumi calls fictions, idols, and untruths, and purifying the heart of greed, envy, jealousy, grief, and anger so that it regains its original quality of becoming mirrorlike to reflect the reality within it.[15] *Fana* means, in fact, a liberation from self-intellect, and *Baqa* is affirmation of truth and love.[16] In the process of rebirth the leaders recognized the existence of individual differences.

The situation of the novices differed just as their previous experiences differed. A man who had been a pious man had less difficulty in getting through the process than one who lacked concern for purity in action. According to Sufism, the former individual had a touchstone against which to measure his behavior

[13] R. and J. Arasteh, *op. cit.*; R. Arasteh, *"Succession of Identities."*

[14] R. A. Nicholson, *op. cit.*; M. J. M. Rumi, *Divan*.

[15] Mahmud Shabistari, *Gulshani Raz* (The Mystic Rose Garden), trans. E. H. Whinfield (London: Trubner & Co., 1880).

[16] R. A. Nicholson, *op. cit.*

whereas the latter lacked such a measure and perhaps followed his *nafs*. A man who had been engaged in disputation experienced more strain than one who had lived a pure life. Purity in action means living genuinely and depends on values that underlie the nature of universal man. It is therefore obvious that the guide had to begin at the point where the seeker was. He suggested to the individual seeker the above-mentioned behavioral and mental steps.

Through these behavioral and mental steps, the Sufis probed beneath possession per se to uncover the passion that drives man to seek added wealth and power, that is, where he is more concerned with the motive of action than with the action itself. Thus, they emphasized removing undesirable thoughts in consciousness and controlling the passions arising out of *nafs*. As a first step in this direction the guide told the seeker to concentrate more and more on every single act and his internal motives for that action. In contrast to those who saw only the goal, the seeker of the path of self-realization had to look into the origin of action: "Behold the image of the end in the mirror of the beginning." [17] The origin of action required meditation, which in turn produced a more transcendental state of mind and made the individual ready for the experience of union. *Sam'a* (whirling dances) were adopted to actualize these peak experiences.

The more serious seekers, under the close supervision of their guides, then sought to remove the objects of perception from their minds by applying various methods for emptying their consciousnesses of unreal materials. Secluding themselves, the seekers resorted to introspection in order to observe the contents of their psyches, watch over every mental state, analyze each experience, and perceive its imperfection. In this phase, the guide was regularly available to communicate with the seekers. This intense mental concentration usually produced psychic tension (contraction), or more specifically, rapture. The more able Sufis also adopted intentional alienation, that is, their method was entirely opposite to that of developing "I." [18] They customarily left social life and traveled alone, visiting prominent Sufis. This detachment from society provided the seeker with an excellent

[17] M. J. M. Rumi, *Mathnawi*.
[18] Mahmud Shabistari, *op. cit.*

opportunity for making himself aware of what he had once thought perfect and of knowledge based on sense perception. At the same time, his immediate experiences enriched his being by activating his insight, fostering love, and developing in him discernment in his approach to the state of emptiness.[19]

In actuality, the professional Sufi gradually tore off the veils of consciousness one by one, and ultimately attained his final state—that of nothingness—a state that is explained in the following often-told story: At one of the great court banquets, where everyone sat according to his rank while awaiting the appearance of the king, a plain, shabbily dressed man entered the hall and took a seat above everyone else. His boldness angered the prime minister, who demanded that he identify himself and acknowledge if he were a vizier. The stranger replied that he ranked above a vizier. The astonished prime minister then asked if he were a prime minister. Again the man replied that he was above that position. When asked if he were the king himself, he answered that he ranked over that too. "Then you must be the Prophet," declared the prime minister, to which the man again asserted that he was above that position. Angrily, the prime minister shouted, "Are you then God?," to which the man calmly replied, "I am above that too." Contemptuously, the prime minister asserted, "There is nothing above God." In reply the man said, "Now you know my identity. That *nothing* is me." In other words, the Sufis sought to lose what they currently perceived as labels, knowledge, and concepts, and to become empty (nothing) and attain the state of "void"; to attain a zero point so that they could become related to any state of being and achieve "everythingness." Just as the discovery of zero in mathematics made the system possible, so too in the art of rebirth the discovery of a state of "nothingness" (the void or emptiness) makes final integration a possibility.[20]

Having unfolded his unconsciousness, the seeker now received direct knowledge. With ever increasing insight he furthered his knowledge of the life process. Every moment the world came anew, like the swift current of the sea. Like flashes of lightning, a succession of insights illuminated his mind and in-

[19] R. A. Nicholson, *op. cit.*
[20] R. and J. Arasteh, *op. cit.*

creased his vision. In such a state universal trust appeared; imagination, perplexity, fantasy, and suspicion disappeared entirely. He became the mirror of all. For the Sufi who had gained such illumination all that remained was to become "all truth." He grasped truth intuitively and so quickly that interpretation could not occur, thus giving the individual a direct relationship with evolutionary events. The illuminated one brushed aside the words, then the thoughts, that covered the surface of this intuitive current. There came a time when the illuminated one felt that the current had become too rapid; no care of any kind then lingered in his mind and words had no use for him. He was unconscious, although he experienced a dreamlike awareness:

> Even so a hundred thousand "states" came and went back to the Unseen, O trusted one.
> Every day's "state" is not like (that of) the day before: (they are passing) as a river that has no obstacle in its course.
> Each day's joy is a different kind, each day's thought makes a different impression.[21]

Dreams play an important role in the process of unification. Traditionally, Persian Sufis were always interested in sleep and dreams. Indeed, a number of well-known Sufis entered this path after repeatedly hearing a voice in their dreams. The inquiring nature of their psyches spurred them on to rebirth. Rumi views reality as a dreamlike world and it is in a dream that one leaves oneself and enters into another self, or in his words: "In sleep you go from yourself to yourself." The unconscious becomes active in dreams; the cosmic self fully awakens. Contrary to common thinking Rumi views conventional life as a state of sleeping:

> Your life in this world is like a sleeper who dreams he has gone to sleep.
> He thinks "Now I am asleep," unaware that he is already in a second sleep.
> Like a blind man afraid of falling into a pit, his self in sleep moves into the state of unconsciousness and thus reveals itself in dreams.[22]

[21] M. J. M. Rumi, Mathnawi.
[22] Ibid.

Rumi, however, distinguishes between men of truth and slaves of passion, in terms of both their conscious and their dream states. In this respect, true sleep becomes wakefulness when accompanied by wisdom. The dream of true sleep reveals the signs of the path and the selection of the guide. Due to this vision, the heart awakens and telepathic knowledge first appears between two hearts. Then every expression symbolizes a moment of life—an act of the state of union.[23]

Thus, the individual Sufi analyzes the filters of language, logic, and culture until he becomes aware of the reality of form and what exists beneath in order to attain oneness with all. By this reverse process the seeker undergoes an intense inner experience, and he discovers that the materialistic and mystical essences of creation are the same. He feels the state of nonindividuality and perceives that there is nothing but motion. This positive energy is responsible for the interaction between particles; it is the factor that has caused evolution to proceed from plant, to animal, then to human beings. In passing from one state to the next man has forgotten the previous ones, except that he has a feeling of relatedness toward them. It is this active force, namely "love," that interrelates the whole universe. Following this inner experience, the seeker, instead of putting evolution on the basis of conflict, perceives that the positive force of love caused evolution. He discovers that "lover and beloved come from love."

To reiterate, the individual, in undergoing this inner experience, goes from himself to himself, from oneness to oneness; he gains a configuration of the total situation. United with all, he then travels backward into time and reproduces his previous state whenever he is related to a similar situation. He has embraced all of life beyond good and evil. In a practical way he has experienced qualities of every type of life—ordinary human existence and intellectual life; he has felt himself variously as a famous man, an ambitious man, and a religious man, and has passed beyond all of them, finally deciphering his true self. He has become an image of his community, mankind, and the rest of the world. He accepts them all, feeling related to them. In essence he is all of them. He receives them, and he has experienced their state of

[23] R. and J. Arasteh, *op. cit.*

being; his associated state can appear in his perceptive mirrorlike being. Thus, he can predict and possibly read as telepathy the desires and thoughts of others, and he exhibits certain powers, which to the ordinary man seem extraordinary. Ultimately, as a humble universal man, who is creative and emancipated, he is the owner of *An*, the creative moment, the direct experience of life.

Some psychotherapeutical results. In brief, we can now claim that *An* is the moment of conception, the instant of birth and rebirth, and the experience of joy and originality, which the Sufi has gained in his state of individuation. Its mechanism of growth is a dynamic relation between subject and object, where initially the subject depends on the object of desire; then there is an instant of union, followed by the object's dependence on the subject; and finally the state where each experiences union independently within the universe.

In this sense, the nature and process of *An* is similar to human creativity, where a long period of mental effort, tension, patience, and struggle within the group precedes a relaxed state in which the individual innovates—creates something new. Such an original production in art, science, religion or politics, or whatever, is only possible if the creator first perceives the vision, becomes faithful to it, notices its distance from his own reality, and then, even in spite of adverse public opinion, makes an effort to materialize it through unification with it.

I personally believe that this is the true nature of man. The real state of the uncontaminated child, before socialization and before the civilization of primitive man, is based on such a psychological makeup. In other words, both in the child and in primitive man, the "creative image," the means of experiencing *An*, existed before *thinking* became the instrument of reason and judgment. *An* existed before *concept* was born. However, the course of human history has kept man from retaining this pure quality. Thus each of us is born, and only by assimilating the group's accumulated cultural experience and later leaving it is it possible to become creative and to experience *An* again. Therapy in a way becomes a new insight into our pure state of being. This concept can be utilized in education, child-rearing, creativity, and in therapy. However, its greatest contribution can be in terms of psychotherapeutical training, especially in terms of the master-disciple relationship, namely, the master's total commitment to "care" and the disciple's devotion. This relationship, based on human worth, is only possible if one has an intense "creative passion" for turning a potential but fragmented man into a whole man. In my opinion, no fee can bring about such a relationship, and it is still more difficult if it is done on an hourly basis. The majority of Freudian-derived concepts are inadequate, culture-bound, and reflect certain commercial values created by the marketing orientation of the late nineteenth and early twentieth centuries. Of course there are exceptions. Indeed, detrimental social conditions today reflect, in part, the consequences of other professional duties—legislative, legal, educational—if done on a purely monetary basis, they do not give fruitful results.

A further contribution of *An* philosophy to Western psychotherapy deals with the real assumption of human nature as an entity. Thus, any therapy must emphasize conditions that will contribute to the restoration of a unitary experience and result in a spontaneous cure. For instance, a preverbal child in the care of a mother who cannot understand his nonverbal signs becomes irritable and perhaps neurotic, but as soon as he learns to speak a spontaneous cure is possible, and it would appear that many neurotic symptoms disappear. However, this judgment is based on only a few cases of mothers of children between the ages of ten to twenty-two months.

Consequently, we can conclude that with the acceptance of the principle of *An*, therapy as a technique takes on a new form. It is seen as a continual experiential exchange between therapist and patient until the situation is ripe for the spontaneous experience of cure. In such a relationship both therapist and patient are active, the major difference being that the therapist notices the succession of signs, interprets them, and enlightens the course of events, whereas the patient remains unaware of this situation. On the basis of this assumption, the *An* experience and spontaneous therapy derived from it contradict several traditional Freudian analytical approaches: it makes a passive analyst active; it encourages a patient to become expressive rather than talkative; it transcends the symptom-cure; and leads the analyst toward experience and an understanding of the origin of the attitude as the real measure for developing a healthy character. Rather than make the patient self-conscious and aware of the negative aspect of the unconscious, the therapist will direct him to a new state, a new disintegration of a new integration, a new separation or relatedness directed toward a decrease of past tradition, good and bad, and the rise of naturalness, sensitivity, receptivity, understanding the utilitarian service of thought, reason, and concept, and differentiating this quality from the prevailing dominant role of impulse and ego in modern man.

Furthermore, according to the experiential philosophy of *An*, no cure can result from becoming conscious of the neurosis of our time. In fact, it is a hindrance to man. In order to regain our original unitary status, we must either create a new force that can encounter and defeat the childhood experience and social experiences and create a synthesis, or assist us to forget and, if possible, to erase it entirely from our psyche, rather than to become aware of it. In fact, the division of the psyche in terms of id, ego, and superego deviates from the experiential psychotherapy of *An*. Actually, what is essential is our *totality*, on the one hand, and real experience, on the other. The therapist-patient relationship must follow a design (each according to his situation) so that these two qualities become active again. According to my system of thought, the direct path to the reestablishment of such a relationship offers the greatest benefit through various nonverbal mechanisms, such as creative experience, songs, music, writing, crafts, art, and relating these products to the emotional experience of the patient by the therapist in such a way that the chain of events creates a new experience of awareness for the patient and leads to a deeper realization of man as a totality. The Sufis were activists and their minds always developed new symbols. They advise us that the best remedy for a restless mind is to concentrate on physical activity for regaining bodily grace, and when the body is restless we must emphasize meditation. In other words, the control of the response to the demand of the psyche of the body is essential for cure.

Finally, the Sufis would accept the idea of transference in modern psychotherapy, but not as a projection of the parent-child relationship; rather they perceive it as a holistic approach for the identification with a realistic state of the master in order for the seeker to receive the grace and blessing of the next state.

In this sense the experiential therapy of *An* is forward looking rather than stressing past relations. In this light, Ernest G. Schachtel's meaningful essay on amnesia in childhood [24] deserves further interpretation. Indeed, the role of amnesia is of great importance in experiential therapy; great Eastern sages have often failed to record their childhood experiences, because they consider it unimportant to them. To them the significance concerns the *end*, the beloved, and this should be seen in the mirror of the being so that one's motive and effort match the goal.

[24] Ernest G. Schachtel, *Metamorphosis* (New York: Basic Books, 1959).

X

SPIRITUALITY, SCIENCE, AND PSYCHOLOGY IN THE SUFI WAY

by

Professor Mohamed Yahia Haschmi

In my work in the natural sciences, and particularly in chemistry and mineralogy, I originally took little interest in the Sufi mysticism of Islam. But through my interest in poetry I was able to find the solution of certain personal psychological problems. In this direction I had studied the *Divan* of "Umar ibn el-Farid, the 'Sultan of Lovers,'" (Lovers being the technical term for Lovers of God); but I had neglected the deeper aspects. This is contained in the material called *Nazm as-Suluk*, the great *Ta'iyeh*, which deals with the higher activities: metaphysical relationships and the spiritual journey according to Sufic methodology.

At the beginning of the year 1939, I lost my father the Sheikh, and became more attentive to Sufi thought. I made a study of the book *Islamic-Arabic Sufism* by Abdul-Latif Tibawi

(Beirut, 1928); and this study consoled me in the loss of my father. By the year 1953 I had, in the study of Sufism, realized that therein were contained ideas that harmonized with a contemporary outlook. The personal trial that resulted from the loss of my mother at this time was ameliorated by these studies, and I was also able to develop the theme in academic lectures in Germany, later published in abstract as *Islamische Mystik und moderne Weltanschauung* (Islamic Mysticism and Modern World-Outlook) in the German review *Universitas* (Stuttgart, July, 1956), and the Swiss journal *Die Tat* (Zürich, October 7, 1956).

In my present stage of spiritual activity I welcome the important works in which Idries Shah has been unfolding essential projections of the Sufi reality of Islam. Mysticism and Sufism together touched the deepest chord of the soul. It is important to note here the statement of the philosopher Bergson, in *The Two Sources of Religion and Ethics* [1] when he says: "Religion was none other than mysticism hotly poured into the human soul and subsequently cooled in steps until it became regularly crystallized."

Some students may make the mistake of supposing that it is either possible or valuable to distinguish between the end of mythology and the beginning of mysticism. This leads them into the error of imagining that they can be treated as are other subjects; or that the relationships between Buddhism, say, or Platonism, gnostic perceptions, and so on, are historically influential, one upon the other.

According to Muhammad Hamidullah: "All the Sufi schools of thought, like the Chishtiyah, Qadriyah and the Suhrawardiyah, receive their authority from the Prophet through Ali directly without any other intermediary." [2] Sufi ideas can, however, be perceived, as in any other analogical procedure, by reference to other constructs of thought. Indeed, if this were not so, the very large number of non-Muslims among Western scholars and Hindu thinkers would have been unable to accept or to approve

[1] Henri Bergson, in an Arabic translation by Sami ad-Drubi and Abdu'llah Abdu'd Dayem (Cairo, 1971), p. 254.

[2] Muhammad Hamidullah, *The Qur'anic Conception of State, the Qur'anic World*, p. 23, note. See also 'Abbas Mahmoud el 'Aqqad, *Geniality of Imam Ali* (Arabic) (Cairo, 1952), p. 30.

of Sufism or of Sufis. Some theologically centered observers cannot grasp this fact, with the consequence that they imagine that people who relate non-Islamic systems to Sufi thought are departing from Sufism and/or from Islam.

One of the great authorities of the Sufis is Idries Shah. This personage was born into the noble family of Sardhana, in northern India, which is also the Afghan Saiyid family of Paghman in Afghanistan. The present generation of this family is still highly regarded among the Afghans, as witness the notarized Declaration of the Sirdar Faiz Mohammed Khan Zikria, Afghan scholar and former Minister of Education of Afghanistan and Afghan Ambassador and Foreign Minister, when he recently desired to place upon historical record for the scholars of the world something of the standing of the family:

> The Musavi Saiyids of Afghanistan and Khans of Paghman are recognized as the descendants of the Prophet—May peace be upon him.
>
> They are recognized to be of the most noble descent of Islam and are respected as Sufi teachers and erudite scholars.
>
> Saiyid Idries Shah, son of the late Saiyid Ikbal Ali Shah, is personally known to me as an honourable man whose rank, titles and descent are attested and known by repute.[3]

Idries Shah's deep understanding of Sufism and his religious feeling of an enlightened kind may be inherited from his grandfather, the Nawab Saiyid Amjad Ali Shah. This legacy is like that of Max Planck, derived from his grandfather and great-grandfather. In Islamic history such a feeling existed between Omar ibn Abdul-Aziz (717–720) of the Omayyad dynasty, and his grandfather Omar, the second Caliph of Islam, who died in 622.[4]

Thus far the Indian and Afghan connections. The family is not only descended from the major aristocratic house of Arabia through the Prophet, but also carries forward the last blood of the ancient Persian imperial line of the Sassanians. This stems from the marriage of Hadrat Hussain, grandson of the Prophet,

---

[3] Sworn statement of Sirdar Faiz Mohammed Zikria, October 7, 1970.
[4] See my *Max Planck, Great Physicist and Thinker* (Arabic) (Aleppo, 1966), p. 12; *cf. Islamic Thought, ibid.*, pp. 130–136.

with Bibi Shahrbanu, sole surviving issue of Ardashir of Persia. The family is a part of the history of Islam, and has always kept alive the Persian, Afghan, and Arabian connections, through a succession of distinguished scions, many of whom are numbered among the saints of the Islamic tradition.

While in Christianity Jesus dies as the tragedy of that religion,[5] the tragedy in Islamic history lies in the murder of Hussain, son of Fatima, daughter of the Prophet. The two main divisions of opinion in Islam, the Shia and the Sunni, related to the leadership of Islam. The former accepts the caliphate as being resident only in the Saiyids (Hashimites) and the latter regards the office as being through election, relying upon this passage in the Koran:

And whose affairs are a matter of Council.   (43:38)

and also:

O Mankind! Lo, we have created you male and female, and have made you nations and tribes that ye may know one another. Lo! The noblest of you, in the sight of Allah, is that of the best conduct. Lo! Allah is Knowing, Aware.   (49:13)

Genealogy, in this respect, does not play a great role: that is to say, as in the Western tradition of *noblesse oblige*, the Hashimite descent imposes upon a man duties and standards that are of the highest; and, although people may respect him for his descent, his concern is always for his duty.[6] The best Saiyids are those who accept the dictum: "Speak not about your origins or your fathers. The origins of man are in his contribution."

As inherited sense of duty is important, so is historical information about the man, for biographical purposes and to under-

---

[5] In Islam, Jesus is not crucified. The Koran (4:157–158) says: "And because of their saying 'We slew the Messiah Jesus son of Mary Allah's Messenger,' they slew him not nor crucified, but it appeared so unto them; and lo! Those who disagree concerning it are in doubt thereof; they have no knowledge thereof save pursuit of a conjecture they slew him not for certain. But Allah took him up unto Himself. Allah was ever Mighty, Wise."

[6] William Foster, "The Family of Hashim," *Contemporary Review* (London, May, 1960).

stand motivations. The employment of Hashimite history with any material implications is, in today's Arab world, fraught with transitory implications.

Although to the average Western scholar Sufism is represented only in books and in one or two interesting survivals (mainly of folklore value) visible in the East, people like Idries Shah, through their travels and activities, have consistently maintained contact with the living heart of the Sufi tradition through the real adepts. These people, though they seldom seek publicity and take little interest in promoting propaganda, are numerous, well informed, and extremely active.

Most people, even in Asia, would hardly suspect that cabinet ministers, men of commerce, members of formally religious congregations, people engaged in the arts, sciences, and professions—and peasants and workers—belong to the widespread and very alive community called the Sufis.

There are various reasons for this comparative anonymity. Traditionally, the Sufis are people who point out fallacies in current beliefs. Many of them have become intensely unpopular precisely because they have not always borne hypocrisy with patience.

Nevertheless the Sufis, especially in their current efforts to spread useful knowledge and help the trend of mankind's thinking, are undoubtedly going from strength to strength.

When reading the books of Idries Shah, as an Oriental familiar with the cultural background of Sufism, certain points immediately become apparent. Shah has made available a great quantity of new material, taken from living schools of Sufism throughout the world. This alone (with some five hundred teaching tales, many of which might otherwise never have seen the light of day) is a remarkable contribution to knowledge. But he has done more. An example is his attitude toward the Sufi effort. Instead of assuming that Sufism is something that has developed through the centuries and taken different forms according to the individual personality of the teacher, he has been the first writer to take the panoramic view.

Shah has, in fact, accepted the Sufi contention that Sufism is always the same, it is only the environment that causes Sufis to present it in different ways. By doing this, he has been able, in his monumental *The Sufis* and in *The Way of the Sufi*, to reveal an astonishing vitality, variety, and effectiveness in Sufi thought.

His other contribution has been to take the Sufis as a whole to illustrate their specific roles and effects as part of a unity. This is in startling contradistinction to the ordinary scholar's method. The latter have always imagined, for instance, that Ibn al-Arabi was very different from Haji Bektash. The one, so the theory goes, was a theoretician and writer of love poetry, the other an organizer and founder of an "order" (*Tariqa*). What Shah has succeeded in demonstrating is the Sufi claim that any format used by a Sufi (whether poetry, temporal organizations, exercises, etc.) is merely the instrument that the Sufi employs to exercise his effect upon society.

It is, of course, true that such great Sufis as Jalaluddin Rumi have actually said this in their published works. But from Jalal's death in 1273 until Shah's work in 1964, nobody seemed to want to take any notice of the significant connotation of this important idea.

In *Thinkers of the East* (1971) and his *Wisdom of the Idiots* (1969) Shah has given us insights into the actual teaching methods traditionally—and currently—applied in Sufi schools. This material helps us to understand the classics and their background and origins far better. It is not too much to say that, without such a guide, much of the Sufi poetry and recorded lectures of the masters would not be completely comprehensible.

A further remarkable effect is seen in *The Way of the Sufi*. In this book first published in 1968 Shah is able to trace the connections between the different Sufi schools from the eighth to the twentieth century, and to exhibit their internal coherence in a way that has never been done before. Indeed, this book renders almost all previous work on Sufism, for general or scholarly readership, relatively incomplete. In short, Shah has been able to bring together in one volume materials that in the past, both in the East and West, have been studied separately because nobody has seen how to relate them, and because most scholars have been hampered by being specialists in only one or two languages and by not moving beyond their specialties. This restriction, of course, has not applied to practicing Sufis; but they, until recently, have been content to reserve this synthesizing knowledge to themselves.

It is this ability to relate sermons, exercises (*wazifas*), jokes, and anecdotes, biographical materials, pieces of *abjad*-notation, and much more, to an essential whole, which more than anything shows Shah's fidelity to the Sufi tradition: and his mastery of its materials.

Although he may be best known to the world at large through his extensive literary activities, his real "power base" is undoubtedly the support he receives from practicing Sufis and scholars who are deeply familiar with the traditions, literature, and circles of Sufism. He is well shielded against irresponsible criticism because he refuses to engage in controversy, preferring to allow the constructive effect of his work to spread.

Above all, of course, to many thinking people in the West, this work is attractive because he shows how problems familiar to current societies have been observed, faced, and solved by Sufis in the past, both in the social and psychological areas. Many of his books emphasize this aspect of his work. Its increasing acceptance is seen in the steadily growing use of his books in the study of social science, in universities and elsewhere. Since many of his "Oriental" stories are now recognized as structures illustrating human, not time-centered or culturally linked, situations.

A survey of *The Way of the Sufi* yields much of interest. In the Introduction, he gives this definition, from Nuri Mojudi: "The Sufi is one who does what others do—when it is necessary. He is also one who does what others cannot do—when it is indicated."

He makes the important point that the reading of books by people who profess themselves bewildered by Sufi lore leads to the conclusion that they want to be bewildered. Similar subjective desires are diagnosed among those who oversimplify. Their "Sufism" is just a cult of love, or meditations, or something equally selective, like concentrating on the "orders," which are mimetic.

In the part on "The Study of Sufism in the West" there are references to the limited sources generally available to Western students. In his consideration of the influence of Sufism upon the West, Shah quotes from much literary work dealing with the effect of Sufism upon the thought of such figures as St. John of the Cross, St. Teresa of Avila, Roger Bacon, and Geber, the "Father of Western alchemy." [7]

There are relationships between Sufism and Vedantist teaching, which not only passed into the Western literature of magic and occultism but also suggested advanced psychological ideas and processes, sometimes thought of as recent discoveries. An example is the archetype of the Jungian theory found in the philosophy of Ibn al-Arabi.[8] Freud's interpretations were anticipated in al-Ghazzali's *Niche*, nine hundred years ago. The symbolism of the *Niche* is rooted in the Koran, 24:35:

> *Allah is the light of the heavens and the earth.*
> *The similitude of his light is a niche with a lamp within . . .*

to which Avicenna gives a philosophical interpretation also taken as Ismailitic by some.[9]

The prevalent ignorance in the West concerning some of the greatest thinkers of the East is exemplified by Bertrand Russell's book on the *Wisdom of the West* (1959) which omits all mention of the Sufis or their influence on the West, which elsewhere he acknowledges.[10]

[7] Cf. my article "Enträtselung der Alchimie" (Dissolution of the *Mystery of Alchemy*), *Chemiker Zeitung* (Heidelberg, August 5, 1966). See also my communication at the Tenth International Congress for the History of Sciences, Ithaca, New York, 1962, "Ion Exchange in Arabic Alchemy." For the times in which Jabir (Geber) lived, see my article "The Beginnings of Arab Alchemy," *Journal for the Study of Alchemy and Early Chemistry*, Vol. IX, No. 3 (October, 1961). See also my article "Die Anfänge der arabischen Alchimie," *Chemiker Zeitung*, No. 89, 1965. There is a great similarity between the ideas in the quotations from Jabir given in the *Nihayat* and those found in the Latin works of Geber. The *Nihayat* is a commentary by Jildaki (fourteenth century) on Abu'l Qasim al-'Iraqi's book known as the *Muktasab*, cf. E. J. Holmyard, "Alchemy in Medieval Islam," *Endeavour* (July, 1955), p. 125.

[8] *The Way of the Sufi*, p. 38, note 26. Jung sees in alchemy a mystical process for ennobling the human soul; see my article "Enträtselung der Alchimie," *ibid.*, and C. G. Jung, *Psychologie und Alchimie* (Zürich, 1952), pp. 46, 51–53.

[9] Ibn Sina, *Rasa'il fi'l Hikmah wa't-Tabi'a* (Cairo, 1908), p. 125 ff.

[10] In his treatise *Mysticism and Logic* (London: Pelican Books, 1952), p. 26, Russell quotes the Sufi Rumi: "Past and future are what veil God from our sight. Burn up both of them with fire! How long wilt thou be partitioned by these segments of Reed?"

Efforts have been made in the West to stress the links between Sufism and Christian mysticism. Some scholars believe that the Sufis are a kind of gnostic; others postulate an Indian or Greek influence on Sufism; still others hold that Sufism is different from the Indian philosophical theories.[11] Shah points out the theory that in the *Divan* of Hafiz [12] there are derivations from Platonism or Christianity, but notes that so many diverse identifications have been attempted that in the end almost every element in Western philosophy has at one time or another been linked with Sufism. Even so, it is undeniable that the influence of Sufism, both direct and indirect, on Western thinkers is great.

Sufi literature contains the idea of evolution, the conception of the atom, of a fourth dimension, of relativity, and even of space travel. Over seven centuries ago, Ibn al-Arabi stated that thinking man was forty thousand years old, while orthodox religionists were holding that his creation dated back only four to six thousand years. Shah mentions that modern research indicates that "modern man" dates back some thirty-five thousand years.[13] In fact, the history of an identifiable man extends to some six hundred thousand years, although the thinking processes associated with contemporary man may not be anything like as old as this. Shah provides material for the reader to think about these questions himself.[14]

He further makes clear that our customary methods of approaching knowledge make it difficult for us to understand Sufi ideas if we take the vehicle for the content. Ibn al-Farid (1181–1235) maintained that Sufism is behind and before system-

[11] *The Way of the Sufi*, p. 39, note 31; see E. G. Browne, *A Literary History of Persia* (London, 1909), p. 442 and other sources in this note. Cf. S. Radhakrishnan, *Indian Philosophy*, II (German translation) (Darmstadt, Baden-Baden, 1956), p. 506, note 80.

[12] Hafiz: "one who knows the Koran by heart." See my article "The Influence of Hafiz on the German Poet Goethe" (Arabic) Université Libanaise, *Étude Litteraire*, *Révue Trimestrielle*, 4ème Année, Tome I (Printemps, 1962).

[13] *The Way of the Sufi*, pp. 22 f, note 69, and see Professor Mohammed Ali Aini, trans. A. Rechild, *La Quintessence de la Philosophie de Ibn-i-Arabi* (Paris, 1926), pp. 66 f.

[14] See Richard Carrington, *Drei Milliarden Jahre, die Geschichte unserer Erde* (Munich, 1957). Original in English, *A Guide to Earth History*, trans. Kurt Wegenseil (London: Chatto and Windus, 1956).

atization, and that "our wine existed before what you call the grape and the vine" (the school and the system). He said:

> *We drank to the mention of the Friend*
> *Intoxicating ourselves, even before the creation of the vine.*[15]

This type of God-intoxication is found in Hallaj and other Sufis. The great Pakistani poet and spiritual guide Muhammad Iqbal takes it as his motto.[16]

Shah makes a most valid point in showing that Sufi projections should not be approached from a single standpoint. His *The Way of the Sufi* illustrates, for the general reader, something of the richness and range of Sufi ideas, while ensuring that these ideas are presented in a form applicable to contemporary culture.

In part two Shah deals with such classical authors as al-Ghazzali, Omar Khayyam, Attar of Nishapur, Ibn al-Arabi, and Saadi of Shiraz. Al-Ghazzali, acclaimed by orthodox Islam and particularly by the Sunnites, lived in the twelfth century, and insisted on purification of the soul as the beginning of spiritual progress. Al-Ghazzali quotes Mutanabbi's poem: "To the sick man, sweet water tastes bitter in the mouth." Eight hundred years before Pavlov, al-Ghazzali dealt with, and illustrated by vivid parables (sometimes in startlingly "modern" words), the problem of conditioning.

Al-Ghazzali's anticipation of modern scientific psychological discoveries, as shown in this book, is impressive, but it has not been given the attention it deserves because he specifically disclaims any use of scientific or logical methods in arriving at his conclusions.

Shah shows that the influence of al-Ghazzali on Western thought is enormous. In particular, the philosophers of medieval Christendom adopted many of his ideas.

Shah ranks Omar Khayyam among the Sufis. This is also

[15] This may be interpreted in terms of Jesus' miracle in turning water into wine at the marriage feast of Cana.

[16] See also A. Schimmel, *Gabriel's Wing. A Study into the Religious Ideas of Sir Muhammad Iqbal* (Leiden, 1963), pp. 340, 359, and her *Botschaft des Ostens* (*Paiam-i-Mashriq—Message of the East*) (Wiesbaden, 1963), p. 69 ff.

affirmed by Max Horten.[17] I have treated the theme in my Arabic article "Avicenna as Forerunner of Omar Khayyam." [18] It appears convincing because Khayyam is among those who seek spiritual enlightenment.

Attar, one of the great Sufi classical masters, lived in the twelfth and thirteenth centuries. He inspired other Sufis and wrote, in all, about one hundred and fourteen books, among which the most famous are the Sufic *Divine Book*, the *Parliament of the Birds*, and the *Book of Counsel*. His theme is the quest of the human soul for perfection as a pillar of the social fabric and ethical standard of Islam.

Mohiudin Ibn al-Arabi is one of the greatest Sufis of the Middle Ages, whose life and writing have been shown to have deeply penetrated the thought of East and West alike. His aim is the sublimation of love from earthly to divine love. Shah quotes from him (p. 80, The Face of Religion):

> *Now I am called the shepherd of the desert gazelles,*
> *Now a Christian monk,*
> *Now a Zoroastrian.*
> *The Beloved is Three, yet One:*
> *Just as three are in reality one.*[19]

On Saadi of Shiraz, Shah says: It is hard to find words to describe the achievement of the thirteenth-century classical author Saadi. Western critics are amazed that Saadi could write both *The Orchard* (Bostan) and *The Rose Garden* (Gulistan). Shah gives the quintessence of these two books; quoting some most interesting passages. I give the following:

---

[17] Max Horten, *Die Philosophie im Islam* (München, 1924), p. 190.

[18] Université Libanaise, section de langue et Literature Persans, *Étude Litéraires Révue Trimestrielle*, 5ème Année, Tomes 3 & 4 (Autonne, 1963/Hiver, 1964), p. 317.

[19] I know from Mohiudin Ibn al-Arabi the following poetry: "Formerly I denied my comrade,/If his religion does not draw him near to me./My heart is capable now of all forms./It is a pasture for the gazelles,/A convent for the Christian monks,/A temple for idols, the Ka'bah of pilgrims,/The Tables of Mosaic Law and the Book of the Koran./I am for myself, the religion of Love./Whichever way the camel of love may take,/My religion and faith are there." See also Émile Dermenghem, *Muhammad and the Islamic Tradition*, trans. J. W. Watt (London: Longman, 1958), p. 141.

JEWELS AND DUST

If a gem falls into mud it is still valuable.
If dust ascends to heaven it remains valueless.

THE ALCHEMIST AND THE FOOL

The Alchemist dies in pain and frustration—while the fool finds treasure in a ruin.

THE PEARL

A raindrop dripping from a cloud,
Was ashamed when it saw the sea.
"Who am I, where is a sea?" it said.
When it saw itself with the eye of humility,
A shell nurtured it in its embrace.[20]
The Sufi must have patience, and follow the proverb:
"If you cannot stand a sting, do not put your
finger in a scorpion's nest."
Don't complain of your pain but act:
"Throughout the long night a man wept
At the bedside of a sick man.
When day dawned the visitor was dead—
And the patient was alive."
One must use things in their own places:
"Fools burn lamps during the day. At night they
wonder why they have no light."
It is necessary to know the direction:
"I fear that you will not reach Mecca, O Nomad!
For the road which you are following leads to Turkestan." [21]

From Jami (1414–1492) it appears that this Sufi esoteric transmission link with the Asian masters was used by the Western mystical writers. He cites among teachers in the Sufi transmission such names as Plato, Hippocrates, Pythagoras, and Hermes Trismegistus.

The unity of being seems to be through love:

[20] Rumi said: "If a shell not be satisfied (with a raindrop) it cannot form a pearl." See *Khulasa'i Mathnawi*, Aga Bad'uz-Zaman Fairuz Anfar, with commentary (Tehran, 1321 A. H.), p. 1; in original (Pers.): "Ta sadaf qani' nashud pur durr mashud."

[21] In original: "Tarsam narasi ba Ka'bah, ay A'rabi!/kin rah ke tu mirawi be Turkistanast!"

Love becomes perfect only when it transcends itself—
Becoming One with its object;
Producing Unity of Being.

He knows also the sublimation of inclinations, which play a great role in modern psychology: "Ordinary human love is capable of raising man to the experience of real love."

Sinai, Shah notes, lived during the eleventh and twelfth centuries, and is esteemed among the earliest Afghan teachers to use the love motif in Sufism. Rumi acknowledges him as one of his masters. He uses the allegory of the human quest for higher enlightenment and his *Dervish Songs* represents lyrical expressions of Sufi experience.

Jalaluddin Rumi, from the thirteenth century, is one of the greatest Sufis. His major work, generally considered to be one of the world's greatest books, is his *Mathnawi-i-Manawi* (Couplets of Inner Meaning). Shah enumerates his known works and gives his essential ideas. The idea of evolution is very clear:

> Originally, you were clay. From being mineral, you became vegetable. From vegetable, you became animal, and from animal, man. During these periods man did not know where he was going, but he was being taken on a long journey nonetheless. And you have to go through a hundred different worlds yet.

The poem "I Am the Life of My Beloved" reveals him as a true searcher for truth. He described also "The Man of God," particularly he who is drunken without wine. Much may be written concerning this great Sufi; Shah tries to give the quintessence of Rumi's assertion that eternity lies in remembrance: "When we are dead, seek not our tomb in the earth, but find it in the heart of man."

Shah describes the four major orders: the Chishti, the Qadiri, the Suhrawardi, and the Naqshbandi. The eponymous founder of the first is known as Abu Ishaq from Syria, born early in the tenth century. This order made its strongest impact upon India. Characteristic of this order is love for music; for the past nine hundred years their musicians have been esteemed throughout the continent. The author gives interesting materials about this order.

On music the author mentions the following from Hadrat Muinudin Chishti:

> They know that we listen to music, and that we perceive certain secrets therein.
> So they play music and cast themselves into "states."
> Know that every learning must have all the requirements, not just music, thought, concentration.
> Remember:
> *Useless is a wonderful milk-yield*
> *From a cow which kicks the pail over.*

The second order is well known in Syria. It is named after Abdul-Qadir of Gilan, who was born at Nif, to the south of the Caspian Sea. He died in 1166 and used terminology very similar to that which was later employed by the Rosicrucians in Europe. Abdul-Qadir specialized in the induction of spiritual states, called the *Science of States*.

Shah quotes the tradition that this Sufi, like Jalaluddin Rumi, was supposed to have displayed marked supernormal capacities in his early childhood, and his hagiographies are full of accounts of these. Characteristic of him is "States and Jackals":

> The Jackal thinks that he has feasted well, when he has in fact only eaten the leavings of the lion.
> I transmit the science of producing "states." This, used alone, causes damage. He who uses it only will become famous, even powerful. He will lead men to worship "states," until they will almost be unable to return to the Sufi Path.

The third order is the Suhrawardi. The Sheikh after whom it is named is well known in Syria and especially in Aleppo, because he spent his last years in this city. But the order itself is not locally known. Suhrawardi lived in the twelfth and thirteenth centuries. He hailed from Persia and traveled widely. The materials for a study of his order seem merely legends or fictions, so that its prevalence is not clear, but Shah tells us that India, Persia, and Africa have all been influenced in their mystical activity by the methods and disciplines of the order, even though the Suhrawardis are among the most fragmented of Sufic groups.

Their practices vary from the production of mystical ecstasy to completely quiescent exercises for "perception of Reality."

The last order is the Naqshbandi. Perhaps not the founder, but certainly one of the greatest personages of this school, is Khwaja (master) Bahaudin Naqshband (d. 1389). Later it was known as the Naqshbandi Chain: "Designers" or "Masters of Design." Bahaudin spent seven years as a courtier, seven looking after animals, and seven in road building. He studied under the redoubtable Baba el-Samasi and is credited with having restored the original principles and practice of Sufism. The Sheikhs of this order alone are reputed to have the authority to initiate disciples into all the other orders of dervishes. It is difficult to reconstruct the history of this order, because its members never publicly adopted any distinctive dress, never carried on attention-attracting activities, and are thus difficult to identify. But the order spread in the Middle East and Central Asia, and its members have gained the repute of being mainly Muslim pietists, of which the following recital is typical:

> But this is an old tale you tell—they say.
> But surely this is a new tale you tell—some say.
> Tell it once again—they say;
> Or, do not tell it yet again—others say.
> But I have heard all this before—say some;
> Or, but this is not how it was told before—say the rest.
> And these, these are our people, Dervish Baba, this is man.

A notable passage is entitled "A Meeting with Khidr" who is styled in the Koran the spiritual guide of Moses, and has become a symbol for knowledge of secrets. In the Koran, it is said: "Then found they one of Our slaves, unto whom We had given mercy from Us, and had taught him knowledge from Our presence. Moses said unto him: May I follow thee, to the end that thou mayst teach me right conduct of that which thou hast been taught? He said: Lo! thou canst not bear with me . . ." (Koran 18:66–68). (Jung affirms that Khidr is a symbol for the Unconscious.[22]) Although sin against God is one thing; sinning against

---

[22] C. G. Jung, *Psychologie und Alchimie* (Zürich, 1952), p. 170. Jung quoted: Vollers, "Chidher," *Archiv für Religionswissenschaft*, XII (Leipzig, 1909), p. 235.

man is worse. There have been great Sufis who went into the heart of this doctrine like Rabia el-Adawiya who said: "I will not serve God like a labourer, in expectation of my wages." To illustrate this, Shah quotes Shibli, Junaid, and other Sufis. The story of Shibli's discipleship under Junaid, given here, comes from *The Revelation of the Veiled* (*Kashf el-Mahjub*).

Very moving is the story of Hallaj. When the crowd threw stones, which inflicted great wounds, he made no sign. One of his friends, a Sufi teacher, approached and struck him with a flower. Hallaj screamed as if being tortured. The meaning of this story is that a small hurt from a friend is worse than a severe injury from others.

In the story "Why the Dog Could Not Drink" Shibli, a great Sufi, learned from a dog:

> Shibli was asked: "Who guided you in the Path?"
>
> He said: "A dog. One day I saw him, almost dead with thirst, standing by the water's edge.
>
> "Every time he looked at his reflection in the water he was frightened, and withdrew, because he thought it was another dog.
>
> "Finally, such was his necessity, he cast away fear and leapt into the water; at which the 'other dog' vanished.
>
> "The dog found that the obstacle, which was himself, the barrier between him and what he sought, melted away.
>
> "In this same way my own obstacle vanished, when I knew that it was what I took to be my own self. And my Way was first shown to me by the behaviour of a dog."

The significance of this story is that we should see things clearly and not through our egoism. We must distinguish between real things and the mere reflection of self.

Only one thing must be worshiped. "But how can you, with one heart love two?" This point is also made in the Koran and the Bible.

The Sufis write love poems and people think they mean ordinary love, for, as the Prophet is said to have remarked: "God has hidden the men of greatest knowledge."

According to Rumi, mankind passes through three stages of worship: first he worships anything—man, woman, money, children, earth, and stones; then when he has progressed a little fur-

ther, he worships God; finally, he does not say, "I worship God";
or, "I do not worship God." He has passed from the first two
stages into the last.

For Unity with God Rumi gives the following:

> One went to the door of the Beloved and knocked: A voice
> asked: "Who is there?"
> He answered: "It is I."
> The voice said: "There is no room here for me and thee." The
> door was shut.
> After a year of solitude and deprivation this man returned to
> the door of the Beloved. He knocked.
> A voice from within asked: "Who is there?"
> The man said: "It is Thou."
> The door was opened for him.

Stories figure prominently in the book. The story of "Moses and
the Shepherd" is an example of "Speak to every man according to
his understanding." This, by tradition, is ascribed to Mohammed.
From the Sufi is the opinion "When a door shuts, a hundred may
open." "The Story of the Indian Bird," which Rumi tells in
Mathnawi, is a symbol of the soul's abode.

The chapter "Themes for Solitary Contemplation" sets out
the stages through which the Sufi must pass:

> *Until faith becomes rejection*
> *And rejection becomes belief*
> *There will be no true believer.*

Defining true worship, there is a striking quotation from
Rabia el-Adawiya:

> *O Lord!*
> *If I worship thee from fear of hell, cast me into hell.*
> *If I worship thee from desire for paradise, deny me paradise.*[23]

[23] We find this idea in Ma'arri, a poet-philosopher from the tenth century.
He said: "I adore God without hoping for profit;/A worship for dignity
and praise./I defend my religion from expecting payment./While people
adore Him for reward." See M. Y. Haschmi, *Lughz Abi'l 'Ala'* (The Mys-

Shah gives, from Junaid of Baghdad, eight qualities of the Sufi: (1) liberality as that of Abraham; (2) acceptance of his lot, as Ismael accepted; (3) patience, as possessed by Job; (4) capacity to communicate by symbolism, as in the case of Zacharias; (5) estrangement from his own people, which was the case with John; (6) woolen garb like the shepherd's mantle of Moses; (7) journeying like the traveling of Jesus; and (8) humility, as Mohammed's humility of spirit.

The final chapters, "Letters and Lectures," "Sufism and Islam," and "Deep Understanding," are equally noteworthy. In the first, the author affirms, the Sufi message in written form is regarded as being of limited effectiveness, both in depth and durability. It will be established because "that which is introduced into the domain of Time will fall victim to the revenge of Time." Consequently, as in the waves-of-the-sea metaphor which Sufis so often use, Sufism is constantly renewed by successive exemplar-teachers. This is expressed by Niazi Rauf Mazari: "Love is Action; Action is Knowledge; Knowledge is Truth; Truth is Love." Thus it is a circle, from love to love. From Bahaudin Naqshband comes: "Read therefore what has been prepared, for you may earn the blessing of eternal felicity."

In the dialogue between Sufism and Islam it is shown that they are not in contradiction. The Sufi's belief would be the most perfect of religious beliefs, inferior to none. Further, the difference between the prophets and the saints is thus defined: If they have religious faith, their faith is not equal. Their difference lies in their knowledge, not in their feelings. A king is the same as his subjects in having two eyes, a nose, and a mouth. He is different in character and in function. In the chapter on "Deep Understanding": "Religious vehicles have throughout history taken various names." Sufism embodies all thoughts; each has its usefulness. Nothing that is put into words is common to all Sufis and behind all the forms lies the reality. Not every man can understand the value of Sufism; just as a jewel is valued differently by a trained jeweler and by an ordinary shopkeeper.

tery of Ma'arri) (Arabic) (Saida-Libanon, 1968), p. 73, for a comparison between Ma'arri and Buddha. The same article in *Thaqafatu'l-Hind* (Indian Culture) (New Delhi, India, October, 1962).

CONCLUSION

After studying *The Way of the Sufi* and the other works of Idries Shah, we must conclude that Sufism is a manifestation within the soul. We cannot know its beginning and all its sources. Love is the leitmotif of this tendency. Therefore this can unite the whole world. Hakim Jami said:

> *Love becomes perfect only when it transcends itself—*
> *Becoming One with its object;*
> *Producing Unity of Being.*

In every creed there are new interpretations of this theme, which also hold good for creations like angels; they are, according to Ibn al-Arabi, the powers hidden in the faculties and organs of man.

The Sufis' approach must be flexible: "Speak to each in accordance with his understanding." Thus, all religions and world outlooks must be regarded with wide-hearted tolerance and understanding. The difference between religions is superficial but not essential. The same quintessence unites all. Sirdar Ali Shah quoted: "There are as many ways to God as souls of men."

Some Sufi materials reveal to us, as already noted, archetypes of Jung, and of many modern scientific theories, including psychological and psychotherapeutical discoveries. Included among the discoveries of the Sufis is the therapeutic use of music.

Sufism stands for freedom of the spirit and for the timeless, deep understanding of the human soul. Shah's works awaken the desire for further studies of this subject. Today we can learn very much from Sufism not necessarily for direct imitation, but for the cultivation of an understanding of the possibilities of our own development. I am sure that Sufism has a part to play in promoting world harmony, and for this reason, if for no other, we should welcome what Saiyid Idries Shah has done to present it in a form suited to the age in which we live.

XI

EXPERIENCE, BEHAVIOR, AND DOCTRINE IN THE QUEST OF MAN

by

Professor Rom Landau

Sufism is probably the most difficult subject to write about, and I feel that it is virtually impertinent of me to write about one of its exponents. If a man has lived through genuine Sufi experiences, it would amount to a sin against his innermost spirit to claim to be a Sufi. Sufism is a state of holiness, for it deals only and alone with a man's approach to, and identification with, the divine, and the exclusion of all other experiences, whether physical, emotional, or intellectual.

Idries Shah has written a good deal about Sufism, and I believe he strives to bring readers or pupils closer to it. If he succeeds in this, he will merit our fullest recognition. If he is a Sufi himself, such recognition will have as little meaning to him as if we were to present him with a gown of rough wool (*suf*).

He cannot, of course, "prescribe" a Sufi path—al-Ghazzali did not succeed in that, and even Ibn al-Arabi could do it only in philosophical terms, that is, in terms of rationality, a discipline fundamentally alien to Sufism—but he passes on Sufi truisms, and this merits consideration and approval.

Idries Shah opposes the creation of cults, whether of a personality (including himself) or any Sufi or other methodology or order. This is a very sound opposition, for the "cult" of a teacher or a doctrine inevitably sterilizes that doctrine. In that opposition Idries Shah does not stand alone. Almost half a century ago Krishnamurti opposed himself to cults of people or doctrines with an ardor amounting to passion. Treating a teacher or a doctrine as a cult easily suggests sheep running after the fashionable "ism" of the moment, be it Fascism, Expressionism, Zen-ism, or present-day Hippieism. In that shape, even Suf-ism becomes meaningless, for genuine Sufism is an intensely individual experience.

Idries Shah also warns against the prevailing tendency of raising a teacher to the status of a "true" teacher. This is salutary advice, for even during the present century we have seen the adulation of scores of teachers, whether in Europe, Asia, or Africa, most of whom were forgotten a few years later, like yesteryear's morning mist.

He is equally right in warning against the fashion of "instant illumination," against "magical powers of techniques without preparation," and "of all knowledge coming from the East." In plain English this seems to imply a warning against the fashionable would-be Zen, especially as practiced, in the fifties and early sixties, in California, before it found itself replaced by the equally Californian Hippieism. Though Los Angeles and Big Sur bore some responsibility for the practice of these gospels, their real progenitor and center was the otherwise far more sensible city of San Francisco.

For several years I had the enlightening experience of teaching (Islamics) quite close to one of the relevant decisive centers. So, day in and day out, I watched how men and women with a modicum of intellectual experience would plunge headlong into the Zen-revelation. Their "study" of Zen required no previous academic degrees or proofs of intellectual capacity; it called for no form of self-discipline; and preached plunging into the experience of the moment, identifying oneself with it, regardless of whether in the ordinarily accepted codes of morality the "experience of the moment" was acceptable or not. "Spontaneity" implied giving in to any impulses or urges, however good or evil these might be. Inevitably most "study" days ended in drunkenness, preceded as they were by a day of chain-smoking, and descending to behavior that even present-day would-be liberals would consider reprehensible. "Instant illumination" meant "do as you like." It was hardly surprising when one of the students, originally a nice, football-addicted American in his mid-twenties, went mad, and had to be removed to an asylum where he suffered, among other things, from "folie de grandeur."

Idries Shah would no doubt agree that self-discipline and the acquisition of the relevant technique are preconditions for any spiritual progress. Without these, no art can be mastered, whether it be music, poetry, painting, science, or Sufism. On one occasion, Michelangelo said that he must "have a perfect knowledge of anatomy," so as to be able to forget it in his work. Without self-discipline and "technique," life easily degenerates into immorality. Some Persian would-be Sufis of the eleventh century were indifferent to the commands of Islam, were in the habit of getting drunk, overeating, and leading preposterous lives. When reprimanded by their fellow Iranians, they would reply that to a "Sufi" these worldly indulgences were meaningless, for the only reality in a Sufi's life was his spiritual relationship with the divine. Less than a hundred years ago, there lived a very famous Sharif in northern Morocco, venerated by thousands as a saint. He had provided himself with an admirable English wife, but also liked to indulge in every type of wine and spirit. When questioned by his followers, he would reply that, as he was a saint, the whiskey or champagne, once inside his mouth, would become as innocuous as spring water.

I am not sure that I agree with Idries Shah in his objection to training by "emotional or intellectual means." To narrate "stories and sayings" (as is so often done by Zen teachers) might be quite useful. But man is rooted in emotional experiences and is incapable of not pursuing some sort of intellectual research. Neither of these can be eliminated by an act of will—unless he

has really become a Sufi. In the latter case, emotional or intellectual pursuits might completely disappear in a "substratum," as
has breathing or the digesting of food. In the ordinary person,
even the desire for "enlightenment" will be preceded by an
emotional impetus and by some sort of intellectual contemplation.
If the latter is completely absent, the aspirant will probably land
in the arms of some "occult" charlatan or spurious teacher.

Idries Shah is certainly right in maintaining that no one
"may be transformed into something greater or higher than the
ordinary man by any act of will from a teacher." Teachers are
all very well, but they possess neither the power nor the many-
sidedness of life itself. It is obviously life and the conditions with
which it surrounds us that shape our progress and our attainment
of a goal. No teacher can replace a man's inmost reaction to the
death of his child, to financial disaster, or to incurable cancer.
He might possibly modify these reactions, but only in a very
slight manner and would be incapable of bringing about a radical
change in them.

Idries Shah seems equally right in claiming that "practical
activity is preferable to quietism." Quietism is an admirable
"dynamo-charging" during an active life, but it cannot replace
it. The ideal type of life is obviously one of activity in a given
number of material areas, and intercessions of quietism or contemplation, not of material things but of what might be called
spiritual verities. It is these last that ultimately matter, but they
will be just a froth upon the imagination unless they are nourished
by material landmarks. Life without quietism turns a man into a
robot. For few of the average man's material activities bear any
spiritual significance or point toward spiritual aims. Most lives,
unfortunately, are divided into a spiritual and a material sphere,
and the two only seldom intertwine.

Evidently we all have to follow activities that will provide
the material necessities of life. I should doubt, however, whether
such activities in themselves are essential to a life genuinely aiming
at the "spiritual." For the true Sufi, activities or no activities
might seem equally important or nonimportant. Strangely enough,
the further we advance on a spiritual path, the more easily physical problems solve themselves and the less important they become
to us.

Idries Shah's opposition to "over-scholasticism" seems sound. Anything that is "over-" is wrong. But it would be dangerous to dismiss real learning from a would-be Sufi's curriculum.

Teachers may be of little use; yet they might be eminently helpful. Whether a Gurdjieff was really a helpful teacher is not for me to say. I know that he has had, and still has, shoals of devoted followers; but my personal contacts with him invariably left me in real doubt. His spiritual or "occult" knowledge, however genuinely founded and however profound, seemed to exist somehow apart from him. The two were not identical; in fact they existed on two very separate planes. His everyday technique with regard to his pupils, however revolutionary, however startling, often used to leave behind a sense of bewilderment, not to say, fear. I doubt whether the "technique" of any true Sufi ever provokes such a sense. Sound scholasticism is indispensable in a teacher. But if that scholasticism does not infuse his entire being, if a gap exists between it and the teacher's character, behavior, or intercourse with his followers, much of the value of the scholarship is lost. Ouspensky, on the other hand, was first and foremost a scholar, completely apersonal, completely manifesting his doctrine, and thus eminently helpful to *his* pupils. I worked with him for a considerable time and never had the faintest suspicion of charlatanism or striving for effect among his motives. A Rudolf Steiner, too, seemed to identify himself completely with the "doctrine" he propounded. Hence his enormous effectiveness and the sense of gratitude, sincerity, and devotion he inspired in his pupils.

Whom then might we consider as the ideal type of teacher? Obviously the person whose character and daily conduct constantly manifest the "superiority" of his doctrine. Teaching merely by words will hardly produce Sufis. Teaching that emanates from the teacher's character and his way of living has enormously persuasive powers. Krishnamurti could hardly be called an intellectually impressive teacher. He repeated himself again and again, and used a language that was neither very comprehensive nor very accurate. And yet he seldom failed to leave a profound impression upon his hearers. When, well over forty years ago, I first went to meet him (in the late Lady de la Warr's house), I was strongly prejudiced against him, and was ready to criticize whatever he might say. Yet after an hour's conversation, I left him with a sense of very profound sympathy and even affection. And throughout the following years these sentiments never altered. What then was the secret of his influence? It was his complete identification with his "doctrine," expressed as an almost overwhelming human warmth, absolute honesty, and a touching lovableness. You simply could not help loving him, no matter how critical you might be of his words.

That quality should certainly not be missing from a Sufi teacher's inner armory. For while his aim can be nothing but the recognition of, and the contact with, God, one of the faces with which God confronts us throughout our life is . . . man.

XII

IDRIES SHAH
AND
THE SUFIS
by
Sir John Glubb

We owe a great debt to Idries Shah, both in the external and in the internal fields. Let us first consider the external world, for which his writings regarding the Sufis seem to provide some relevant advice on modern trends.

One of the chief obstacles to the general comprehension of Sufism is the principle that no one can understand it except a Sufi, and that the would-be Sufi can only learn about it from a Sufi teacher. To put this statement in another form, Sufism cannot be defined in words, nor can it be comprehended by the human intellect. It can only be imperceptibly "caught" or imbibed by association with a Sufi master. Moreover the master will not teach it like a school subject, in a given number of lessons, definitions, or propositions, for much of the training consists of absorbing the spirit of the master.

These ideas are diametrically opposed to the trend of modern education, derived in itself, directly or indirectly, from the basic idea that nothing exists except that of which we obtain cognition through the human senses of sight, touch, smell, or hearing. By the use of these human senses, physical science has greatly expanded our knowledge of the material world, but we are not warranted in assuming that this world is the only one that exists. Great scientists are usually ready enough to admit that all the achievements of modern science are little more than a match struck at midnight in a dark forest.

In spite of all the, to us, miraculous discoveries of science, the universe and the mystery of life in it still completely baffle us. Indeed, as the first enthusiasm of scientific discovery tends to wane, the mystery becomes more, rather than less, insoluble. But although the limitations of physical science are now becoming gradually clearer, there is always a time lag in popular appreciation of new trends. The public in general is still under the influence of the impression, now superseded, that physical science can solve all human problems and that the human intellect can shape the future of mankind. Perhaps the simplest refutation of this optimism lies in the conceptions of time and space. We cannot grasp the idea of endless time, yet if time were to end, we cannot understand what would replace it. It would seem that this is one of the innumerable problems that the human mind is incapable of grasping.

In spite of the growing realization of the limitations of physical science, our teaching methods seem increasingly to reflect the belief that physical science is the only subject of any importance. The corollary is the belief that the acquisition of "facts," or information, is the object of education. The imparting of facts to the pupil more and more assumes the character of mass production, increasingly dehumanized. "Facts," for example, can be acquired almost without an instructor, by reading, by lectures delivered to classes so large as to be impersonal, by tape recorder, or by television. Whether or not the student has memorized these facts can be tested by public examination, or even by a quiz. This process of "cramming" facts into the human mind, it is to be noted, can be carried out without producing any effect on the "personality" or character of the student.

It is scarcely surprising, in view of these methods, that the Western democracies no longer produce leaders. Indeed the very idea of outstanding personalities is deprecated. The object of the system seems to be to produce as many human beings as possible who are exactly similar to one another. All children must be sent to similar schools, all must use the same syllabus and the same textbooks, under teachers who are themselves the products of the same standardized, mass-production system.

Yet, while we continuously expand standardized education of this kind, we cannot but be aware that "facts" are not the important things in life. Love, joy, peace, courage, loyalty, unselfishness, self-control, generosity—these are the considerations that make for healthy, happy, and peaceful living conditions. Yet we make little or no effort to inculcate them, nor can their existence be easily ascertained by public examinations, on which the subsequent career of the student largely depends. These false standards tend to undermine all our existing Western civilization and, if not rectified, will bring it down in ruins.

In view of these considerations, the Sufi methods, as explained by Idries Shah, assume urgent importance. First, that real education must be absorbed by the student from his teacher. The number of students to each teacher must be limited to a small group with whom he can live in intimacy, who can know him well and "catch" his spirit by infection, rather than by books, lessons, or precept. We must appreciate that words can never fully express human feelings or character, which consist of spirit. Physical science tends to disregard spirit, though we are all aware that it exists. We all say that we like this school or this community because it is inspired by such a wonderful spirit. We cannot exactly define what this spirit is, although we can sense it.

A second and no less important principle to which Idries Shah refers is that experience is as valid a part of knowledge as is academic learning. In some countries there are chairs for professors of government, which are filled by intellectuals who qualified for their positions by themselves passing examinations on the subject of government. Neither the professors nor the students has ever governed anyone. The same tendency is perceptible in every field. The old nanny who has looked after children for forty years is replaced by a young girl, who has passed academic examinations in child psychology. The gardener with fifty years' experience is looked down upon by the young botanist with a university degree.

It is not intended to suggest that academic knowledge is unnecessary, for it has transformed our lives, but the sole reliance on academic qualifications is apt to lead us astray. We are increasingly influenced by intellectuals, who produce theories that prove unsuccessful in their application to everyday life. The tendency of the academic mind, then, is to demand a modification of the facts of human life to fit the theory, rather than the reverse. A sentence employed by Idries Shah about Sufism might well be taken to apply to any subject affecting human life. "No investigation into the reality of Sufism can be made entirely from the outside, because Sufism includes participation, training, and experience." This principle could well be more frequently applied to academic interventions in politics. To understand the government of men, go down into the fields, the streets, and the factories. It is necessary to participate in order to understand. A phenomenon that we have experienced in our own persons carries a complete conviction, which cannot be acquired from academic studies.

The way of training, without the opportunity to acquire experience, suppresses and stills the intuition, says Idries Shah. "Humanity is turned into a conditioned animal by non-Sufi systems, while being told that he is free." So much for the external applications of the methods of the Sufis.

The second angle from which we can view their teaching is that of the interior life. Only a man who has been trained as a Sufi can understand Sufic thought, Idries Shah tells us. Evelyn Underhill, in the same manner, uses the simile of a man visiting a Gothic cathedral. From the outside, the windows look dull, gray, and dusty; but people inside the building find themselves bathed in brilliant colors projected by the sun shining through the colored glass. The difficulty about religion is that those who view it from the outside, without in any way participating in it, cannot acquire any conception of it.

Forming any idea of Sufism is rendered particularly difficult by the fact that it was originally passed down by a secret code. In the earliest period of Islam, from A.D. 630 to, perhaps, A.D. 900, there was no persecution in Muslim countries, and there was considerable latitude of belief. But in later, Turkish, times, Sufis or *batinis*—interior livers—came under suspicion. They were not, indeed, orthodox Muslims but tended to believe that there was something of truth in all religions. Although Sufism flourished from the seventh century onward in a Muslim environment, it was in reality as near to Christianity as to Islam. Sufis, indeed, were sometimes accused of being secret Christians.

Sufism was able to respect various religions that many people would believe to be irreconcilable. It did so by its belief (1) that there was something good and true in all the great religions, and (2) that the outward and superficial aspects of religion are of little or no importance. The majority of the human race regard religion as a matter of rules, dogma, and ritual that do, to some extent, differentiate between one religion and another, and even between one sect and another. These superficialities are to the Sufi of little importance, though admittedly useful to the general public.

To reach a higher understanding of the "real" world, the Sufi was required, first of all, to "renounce" the world, or at least to realize the small degree of importance to be attached to passing daily events. The next step, perhaps almost an automatic one, was humility. The more a man or woman appreciated the futility of mundane affairs and the vastness of creation, the more did he appreciate his own smallness, insignificance, and unworthiness.

Once the pupil had made some progress in detachment from the world, he began to realize that the motive force of Sufism was love. The achievement of these three qualities—detachment from the world, a realization of our own insignificance, and the adoption of love as the dynamic of living—cannot be taught in external scholastic lessons. A man may indeed listen to a mathematical lesson proving his own smallness in relation to the universe, the world, or the total number of the human race, but his character will not thereby be affected. World renunciation, humility, and love can only be "caught" by living in a group of people who themselves practice these qualities. "He who tastes, knows," as

Idries Shah tells us. These considerations show the reason for the previous statement that a man can only become a Sufi by living in contact with a Sufi master. The necessary qualities cannot be acquired by means of the intellect.

One of the most interesting aspects of these Sufi principles is that they are almost identical with those laid down by Christian mystics. Renunciation of the world, humility, and love are the basic preliminaries of Christian mysticism. Sufis and Christians alike believe that proficiency in these three can lead to the spiritual experience variously called ecstasy, the Vision of God or the Divine Union.

In one passage, if I understand it rightly, Idries Shah seems to say that, whereas other mystics are satisfied if they reach the stage of ecstasy, the Sufi knows that the ultimate objective is work. I venture to suggest, however, that Christian mystics were equally aware of this fact. A period of partial seclusion might be needed until renunciation of the world had been achieved and consolidated, but the final objective must be to return to the world to work. "To be in the world but not of the world," was the final objective, as a study of the lives of many of the great Christian mystics will show.

In his book *The Sufis* Idries Shah gives many interesting details regarding the secret Sufi codes, which were founded on the numerical values allotted to the letters of the alphabet, and on the similarity of sound between Arabic words. The manner in which he traces the Order of the Garter back to the Sufi source will interest most English people.

That numerous Arab customs and ways of thought entered Western Europe from Muslim Spain, Sicily, or southern Italy cannot be denied. We know that Dante, Thomas Aquinas, and other Christian writers derived many of their ideas from Sufi sources. "Albertus Magnus" (b. 1193), Idries Shah tells us, "was well versed in Saracenic and Sufi literature and philosophy. As Professor Browne notes, he exceeded the usual custom of Western Orientalists, for, 'dressed as an Arab, he expounded at Paris the teachings of Aristotle from the works of al-Farabi, ibn Sina (Avicenna) and al-Ghazzali.'"

We cannot understand how Sufis and Christian mystics could cooperate or learn from each other's works if we visualize religion as a system of commands and prohibitions, dogma and ritual, fixed by authority. But both the Sufis and the Christian mystics had transcended this rigid conception of religion by using humility and love as their watchwords.

There are so many ideas in the books of Idries Shah that it would be easy to fill another book in commenting on them. For the present, however, we must limit ourselves to the repetition of the first sentence of this brief essay. "We owe a great debt to Idries Shah."

XIII

IDRIES SHAH:
PHILOSOPHER, WRITER,
POET—AND
THE TRADITIONAL
TEACHERS

by

Dr. Zeki el-Mahassini

The Arabic poet Abu Tamam al-Ta'ii says, describing the great Prince Abi Dulaf al-Igli:

He is a Sea, from whichever side you enter it,
Kindness and generosity are its shores.

If Abu Tamam, who lived in the second century of the Hegira,[1] would allow me to change this verse, I could say, about Idries Shah:

He is a Sea, from whichever side you enter it,
Literature and knowledge are its shores.

[1] He died at the beginning of the ninth century of the Christian era.

Studying his works and influence, I have often found myself comparing him with Jamal'udin al-Afghani, the Reformer, who helped the East; changed bad to good, and ignorance to knowledge. Two distinguished Islamic thinkers were his pupils: the Sheikhs Mohammed Abdu and Rashid Rida, who carried a mission to the world of ideas, literature, and faith in all Islamic and Arabian lands.

Our Prophet Mohammed has said: "Souls are soldiers enrolled. Those who harmonize know one another and those who are not at one, conflict."

There is a distinct affinity between the work of Jamal'udin and of Idries Shah.

The Way of the Sufi (1968) is important and effective not only because of its content, but also because of the way that content is presented. It covers the entire gamut of the great thinkers of the Sufi tradition, al-Ghazzali, Ibn al-Arabi, Rumi, Attar, and many more, explaining the significance of their work by examples that allow the reader to follow the thought by inner contemplation and subconscious elaboration.

He provides valuable correctives to theories of Sufism held in the East and West. By showing the pitfalls and mistakes as well as the successes of other scholars, he converts, as I have already said, bad into good.

His method of approaching the problem of disseminating knowledge about Sufism is ingenious. He directs attention to the psychological outlook of the Sufis, explaining their ideas. Then he deals with the forms of Sufi activity, emphasizing the difficulty of understanding Sufi materials if they are approached purely from an outside viewpoint.

Very typical is the manner in which he appraises the contribution of al-Ghazzali to world thought. It is plain that he has mastered, and even elaborated, the Ghazzalian technique, which itself signaled a breakthrough in interpretative methods in the religious and philosophical fields, influencing profoundly even Christian thinkers who were bitterly opposed to Islamic approaches to life.

His treatment of Omar al-Khayyam is significant, both because he updates Western knowledge by bringing Sufi insights to bear on Khayyam and also because he is able to demonstrate, both directly and by implication, that the role of the Khayyamic corpus is stimulative, and not merely representative of Khayyam's shifting feelings, as so many critics have assumed.

His writings on Saadi, on Ibn al-Arabi, and upon Rumi are equally important.

As a Sufi, of course, and a teacher, Idries Shah is not concerned either to stuff his readers with facts, or to enter into controversy. His books, like all the best products of the Sufi technique, are designed to provoke experiences in the reader. Those who are hostile may well feel their hostility stimulated. It is then for them to recognize this typical effect, and do something about it.

After examining the significance of Rumi and quoting verses from this master of spiritual thought, Idries Shah reproduces the following interchange, taken from the records of the order of the great Bahau'din Naqshband of Bokhara:

> *Many questions, one answer.*
> *I came to a city, where people crowded around . . .*
> *They said: "Where are you from?"*
> *They said: "Where are you going?"*
> *They said: "In what company do you travel?"*
> *They said: "What is your bequest?"*
> *They said: "Whom do you understand?"*
> *They said: "What is your doctrine?"*
> *They said: "Who has the whole doctrine?"*
> *They said: "Who has no doctrine at all?"*
> *I said to them:*
> *"What seems to you to be many, is One;*
> *What seems to you simple is not;*
> *What seems to you complex is easy.*
> *The answer to you all is, 'The Sufis.'"*

Competent authorship, literary skill, and mastery over hitherto unfamiliar Sufi materials are exemplified in the teaching story about the King and the Wolf:

> A certain king decided to tame a wolf and make it a pet. His intention was based on ignorance and a wish to be approved and admired—a common cause of much trouble in the world. He had

a cub taken from its mother as soon as it was born and had it brought up among ordinary dogs. When the wolf was fully grown it was taken to the king, and for many days it behaved exactly like a dog. People who saw this astonishing sight marvelled and thought the king so wonderful that they made him their adviser in all things. The king himself believed that he had worked a near-miracle. But one day, when he was out hunting, the king heard a wolf-pack coming near. As they approached, the tame wolf ran off to join them. This story is the origin of the proverb: "A wolf-cub will always become a wolf, even if it is reared among the sons of men."

Of particular interest to both Eastern and Western students are the Questions and Answers that Saiyid Idries quotes from Sufi authorities. The interpretation on the psychological plane of Sufi thought in its reconciliation with Islam, as with all other forms of systematic thought, is illuminating. As an example:

Question: According to Muslim belief, it is blasphemous for the dervishes to say: "We do not fear Hell or covet Heaven."

Answer: They do not mean this. They mean that fear and covetousness are not the paths in which a man should be trained.

It is this level of explanation that shows how deeply the less thoughtful divines have misunderstood Sufism when they choose to believe that it—or any of its practitioners—are in conflict with the Shariat, the Law of Islam.

The book thus explains to both the people of the East and the West how Sufi thought accommodates the thinking of both.

Another book *The Sufis* (1964) illustrates the operation of the Sufic influence in many of the world's literatures and forms of human association.

This book, based not only upon already published materials, but also on traditional Sufi lore and Sufic interpretative methods, reveals a point hitherto obscured, which makes Sufism unique among spiritual undertakings. This is, there is no other system that has influenced so many other historical forms of thought. Shah quotes even easily accessible documentation to show how, uniquely, Sufism has infused Christian, Jewish, Hindu, and Islamic thought in a truly organic manner. Such an achievement, if it had been effectively recognized in the past, would long ago have established Sufism's primacy as an influence in world thought. The introduction by Robert Graves is valuable, both because of his known expertise in allegorical and intuitive interpretation and also because he discerns that this is a book written for those who can perceive its truth, and is not merely a work of information.

Sufis, the book indicates, consider that man can reach ultimate perfection through the development of consciousness and of new abilities, mental and inspirational. This thesis distinguishes Sufism from systems designed for indulgence, not for development—no matter what their adherents may believe about the matter.

"The natural Sufi," Graves remarks, "may be as common in the West as in the East, and may come dressed as a general, a merchant, a lawyer, a schoolmaster, a housewife, anything. To be in the world but not of it, free from ambition, greed, intellectual pride, blind obedience to custom, or awe of persons higher in rank: that is the Sufi's ideal."

The Sufis has thus filled a vacuum in the field of Western studies about Eastern subjects, and could, perhaps, only have been written by a man, well known and respected in the East, who can speak to the West in the West's own idiom. Further, it eschews the artificial divisions between "Arab and Ajam," Persia and Turkey, Central Asia and India, Europe and Asia—divisions that have limited the range of earlier writers.

Again and again I found a strong likeness between the methods of Idries Shah and al-Ghazzali. He follows a subject with a scientific determination, analyzing and presenting materials exactly like al-Ghazzali, who presented Sufism in coherent form instead of dealing only with the exercises that are its other dimensions. Transposition of practice into the equivalent realm of spiritual philosophy, "action philosophy" as Shah calls it, is an achievement that even today many less sensitive scholars would not be able to comprehend.

But I must crack a joke with Shah. The great poet Abu Ala al-Maari, about whom I wrote a book entitled *Abu Ala, Critic of Society*, laughed at Sufis who refused to be associated with *Suf* (wool), remarking: "We are cotton and you are *Suf* (wool); so protect me from Sufism, guard me."

But even he admired the great Sufi al-Hallaj, sympathizing with him for the hatred and humiliation that he endured.

A more recent book by Saiyid Idries Shah, *Thinkers of the East* (1971), shows that even after sixteen major works the author's storehouse of Sufi lore shows no sign of depletion. On the title page is inscribed: "The rights that others have over you —remember them. The rights which you have over others—forget them." This is a saying of Saidena Ali.

Wise principles are conveyed in formats that, like works of art, make it possible for the reader to "work with them." In the chapter entitled "The Book of Wisdom," Simab says:

> "I shall sell the Book of Wisdom for a hundred gold pieces, and some people will say it is cheap."
>
> Yunus Marmar said to him: "And I shall give away the key to understanding it, and almost none shall take it, even free of charge."

Another paragraph, entitled "If He Looks Good, He Is Good":

> A man went to Imam Zainulabidin and said: "I recognize you as my leader and teacher, and I beg to be allowed to learn from you."
>
> The Imam asked: "Why do you believe that I am a leader and teacher?"
>
> The newcomer answered: "I have searched all my life, and I have never found anyone with such a reputation for kindness and warmth and goodly appearance."
>
> The Imam wept and said: "Dear friend, how frail a thing is man, and in what danger! The very reputation and actions you attribute to me are shared with some of the worst people in the world. If all men judge only on appearances, every devil would be thought a saint, and every superior man would be made out to be an enemy of humanity."

Another book by Shah, *Wisdom of the Idiots* (1971), clearly shows the highly practical approach used by real thinkers in the East, as distinct from those who merely have a reputation as thinkers. A typical story entitled "The Fruit of Heaven" conveys a significant message.

There was once a woman who had heard of the Fruit of
Heaven. She coveted it. She asked a certain dervish, whom we
shall call Sabar: "How can I find this fruit, so that I may attain
to immediate knowledge?"

"You would be best advised to study with me," said the dervish.
"But if you will not do so, you will have to travel resolutely and
at times restlessly throughout the world."

She left him and sought another, Arif the Wise One, and then
found Hakim, then Majzub the Mad, then Alim the Scientist, and
many more. . . .

She passed thirty years in her search. Finally she came to a
garden. There stood the Tree of Heaven, and from its branches
hung the bright Fruit of Heaven.

Standing beside the tree was Sabar, the first dervish. "Why
did you not tell me when we first met that you were the Custo-
dian of the Fruit of Heaven?" she asked him.

"Because you would not then have believed me. Besides, the
Tree produces fruit only once in thirty years and thirty days."

I have said little about Shah himself; others have dealt with
that subject.

In these times, to be nobly born can be as much of a disad-
vantage as an asset. Idries Shah has overcome this problem, and I
salute him for it; offering my homage with the perfume of Al-
Gota, the green lands surrounding my home of Damascus from
East to West. May this scent waft to him, and even to Kabul in
Afghanistan, whose people are proud that he appeared among
their kith and kin, like a glowing star rising against the evening
dusk to light the world, with the wisdom of a brilliant mind.

XIV

DERVISH TALES
by
Professor James Kritzeck

No one seems to be able to establish conclusively an etymology for the word *dervish*, which is exactly as it should be, since dervishes have always cloaked themselves with mystery. Dervishes are Sufis (pronounced soo-fees): the Persian and Turkish adherents of a form of contemplative life called Sufism (after *suf*, the woolen garments they wore), which has dominated Islamic spirituality since the twelfth century. They have their confreres in the Arab and Indian fakirs and the African Marabouts. Included among their numbers, over the centuries, have been some of the most learned and respected scholars of Islam as well as many of its greatest charlatans, madmen, wits, and wags.

The Sufis started out as disaffected and high-minded ascetics, according to our best information. They were men (and quite a few women) who found it impossible to discover God in the triumphant caliphate, the Draconian law, the impenetrably complacent *pax islamica*, or even the literal words of the Koran. They set out on their own, availing themselves of "ancient wisdom" from the Greeks, the Hindus, and the Chinese, and some of them became saints and mystics. Their mediocre students became theorists and, over the centuries, organized themselves into religious orders that ultimately took the form of lodges, having little or nothing to do with the original spiritual ideals. That was the point at which they started to take drugs, pierce their flesh, and whirl. That was also the point at which they got their bad reputation and first became known in the West.

One thing common to Sufis, as a rule, was a form of teaching—as old as the human spirit—in parables. It mattered not at all where the basic stories came from. Sufis always had a lot to hide anyway, and as the generations went on, the wisdom locked in their parables grew more and more esoteric. Yet it would be silly to underestimate the educational value of the "illuminations" that these parables gave to centuries of dedicated Sufis. They are indeed our best way of discovering what Sufism is all about.

Idries Shah, an inveterate story chaser, has put together eighty-two stories from this inexhaustible treasury in *Tales of the Dervishes* (1970). It is really too bad that he did not provide an introductory essay to the collection; as the author of several good popular books on the subject, he could certainly have done that very well.

Perhaps the reader would not have to know a great deal about Sufi tales to enjoy them, but he would certainly enjoy them more if he understood them better in terms of origin, structure, and context.

When approaching these tales the reader should be forewarned that he is not going into the orderly realm of Zen paradox. It would be truer to say that he is going into a messy rooming house, where people specialize in forgetting and remembering, snooping and tattling, looking askance and stealing from closets. It is not a realm in which it is wise to seek, still less to pretend to, too much accuracy. For example, how can a story concerning Dhu-al-Nun be passed on by the Caliph Abu-Bakr and brought into Europe by Pope Sylvester II? The answer is simple: none of those people had anything to do with it. Idries Shah asserts that "Sufi tales passed into folklore." Oftener it was the other way around. They come from everywhere, including man's dimmest and darkest past, now "The Past Thousand Years." They come from ·wordplay and proverbs, from fairy tales, tall tales, Greek plays, Hindu epics, Tibetan jokes, infancy gospels, the Desert Fathers, and even common sense.

At any rate, there they are: the Magic Mirror, the Fountain of Life, the Insane Uncle, the Head of the World, and Snow White—the belly laughs of the bazaar and the anguished fictions of bedeviled monks. "They are full of wonders and strange ideas." Even the greatest Sufi compilers, al-Ghazzali, Attar, and Rumi, did more or less the same thing with the same stories. Their deft touches are still apparent in the present volume, which is beautifully translated.

If the great saints themselves did not disdain the vulgar jokes of "Mulla Nasreddin," why should we? It is, first and foremost, the use to which this material was put by the Sufi dervishes that makes it all so very fascinating. Every one of the stories, some more poignantly than others, can be and has been made to illustrate various points of Sufi doctrine. The clearest thing that comes through is that, by discipline and initiation, the many hidden meanings in everything can be discovered and passed along. Surely that qualifies for mysticism.

If this particular collection is too mixed a bag, and some of its exercises too literal-minded, remember that Sufism has equipped and still equips men and women to make good use of their lives. In some eclectic Sufi circles, such as the Naqshbandis, stories like Idries Shah's are supposed to be ingested in a certain order, like a special diet. In this book they are in no "literary" order, and they seem almost embarrassed that no Scheherazade has found a way of pulling them together.

Perhaps one should simply try one out and see what it teaches. This one is from a book called *Asrar-i-Khilwatia* (Secrets of Recluses) by Sheikh Qalandar Shah, of the Suhrawardi Order, who died in Lahore in 1832. It is called "The Founding of a Tradition."

Once upon a time there was a town composed of two parallel streets. A dervish passed through one street into the other, and as he reached the second one, the people there noticed that his eyes were streaming with tears. "Someone has died in the other street!" one cried, and soon all the children in the neighbourhood had taken up the cry.

What had really happened was that the dervish had been peeling onions.

Within a short space of time the cry had reached the first street; and the adults of both streets were so distressed and fearful (for each community was related to the other) that they dared not make complete inquiries as to the cause of the furore.

A wise man tried to reason with the people of both streets, asking why they did not question each other. Too confused to know what they meant, some said: "For all we know there is a deadly plague in the other street."

This rumour, too, spread like wildfire, until each street's populace thought that the other was doomed.

When some measure of order was restored, it was only enough for the two communities to decide to emigrate to save themselves. Thus it was that, from different sides of the town, both streets entirely evacuated their people.

Now centuries later, the town is still deserted; and not so far away are two villages. Each village has its own tradition of how it began as a settlement from a doomed town, through a fortunate flight, in remote times, from a nameless evil.

In several ways this tale is an unusual one. It is much shorter than usual; it is singularly lacking in geographic or folkloric anchors; it spills its secret right after the first paragraph, and as a comic line at that; and it toys around with what most Sufi tales avoid like the plague: an expressed moral. However, it enshrines a typically impacted Sufi technique. In the first paragraph alone it calls attention to the "parallel streets" implying orthodoxy and heterodoxy; it puts a dizzy dervish in the role of go-between; it connects tears, as a sign, with death, the ultimate; and it seriously indicts the opinions of children, i.e., neophytes.

In their psychological teaching, Sufis claim that ordinary transmission of knowledge is subject to so much deformation through editing and false memory that it cannot be taken as a substitute for direct perception of fact. This story, I take it, illustrates the subjectivity of the human brain. As a parable, it has its universal applicability. Think, for instance, of the hot line. After all, it remains a possibility that the United States and the Soviet Union, by misreading some dervish's tears and yielding to increasingly built-up mutual fears, might desert the town.

XV

IDRIES SHAH:
THE MAN, THE SUFI,
AND
THE GUIDING
TEACHER
by
Adnan Mardam Bey

In order to examine the views and contribution of Idries Shah, especially as represented in two significant works, let us first look at the view and setting of the Islamic Sufis living in the lands of Asia that became Muslim. As is widely known, Idries Shah is from the Islamic background of the Afghans; and the country of the Afghans became a part of the Islamic domain when it was conquered by the Governor of Basra, Abdul-Rahman ibn Samra, during the reign of the Caliph Usman ibn Affan, the Prophet's Companion. This name—Afghanistan—was acquired much more recently, in the middle of the eighteenth century of the Christian era.

During the hegemony of the Omayyad and Abbasid dynasties, the rule of the caliphs ("deputies" or successors of the

Prophet) extended over immense areas of Asia, considerable portions of Africa, and significant domains in Europe. The strength of the Islamic bond was in maintaining a unity among these diverse peoples under the caliph.

The non-Arab Muslim peoples (then, as today, a majority of the total of Muslims) regarded the learning of Arabic as necessary to understand the text of the holy book, the Koran. The Prophet Mohammed is reported to have said: "The Lord is One, the Source is One, and Arabism is not from parenthood"; that is to say, Arabs are those who know Arabic, not from descent.

Thus the Eastern nations were united through the bond of religion and the Arabic tongue, but found it necessary to liberate themselves from archaic psychological sediments by an evolution containing elements from the past. So it was that Islamic culture developed, drawing upon the civilizations of the Persians, the Byzantines, Indians, Greeks, and others. The role of Islam is brilliant, achieving a bonding of habits, customs, and heritages. And an Eastern wisdom emerged in this new culture language, with its own coloring, distinguishing it from European wisdom.

The man of the East is spiritual in the religious way, rather than materialistic, believing in the soul and a day of judgment. He believes, from experience, in what is taught by feeling and discards the rulings of the intellect.

IDRIES SHAH'S SOURCES

As an Eastern Muslim, it is natural for Shah to seek his spiritual source in the wisdom of the East, and to receive his inspiration from it. It is not strange that he should mention in his works the names of Rabia al-Adawiya, al-Hallaj, Jalaluddin Rumi, Saadi of Shiraz, and others prominent in the Sufism of Islam—and weave his examples from among these names. For the Eastern reader, of course, the evocative power of these names is powerful, recalling memories that are dear to his heart.

Two examples alone are sufficient to indicate this: Rabia and Saadi. When we hear the name of Rabia, we immediately see the picture of a great human being, who ascended through her perceptions to the sky, and who made from love a strong cause between God (may He be glorified!) and man; finding in godly love happiness and peace—for God is beauty, bounty, and perfection.

Religion, as far as Rabia is concerned, is not based on fear. It is grounded in safety from fear, in an ever-renewed longing, a constant passion, an unquenchable thirst. Rabia is celestial music repeated in the ear of the universe, and accentuated perfumes: for it is she who opened the boundaries of Sufi knowledge, and made for us, from love, a source of inspiration and revelation.

And, when we hear the name of Saadi of Shiraz, we think of his great work the *Gulistan* (Rose Garden), whose pages contain a call to compassion, justice, sincerity, and becoming wise through the examples set by time.

Saadi traveled throughout the world of Islam, in India and in Afghanistan, in the Hejaz, in Syria and Asia Minor. He used to travel in the humble garb of the dervish, and he associated with people rich and poor, learned and ignorant. We find him, in his *Gulistan* stories, a pilgrim following a caravan on foot, a teacher in Kashghar, a prisoner in the hands of the Crusaders in Syria, in an Indian temple, and as a recluse in the Omayyad mosque. He is the one who said: "If you cannot feel for other people, how can you call yourself a human being?"

I am unable, of course, in this space, to produce even a short introduction to every Sufi and notable person mentioned in Saiyid Idries Shah's *Thinkers of the East* (1971) and *The Dermis Probe* (1970), and so I must content myself with touching on Rabia and Saadi.

Idries Shah is a student, in the soul, of these Eastern notables. He has drunk from their spiritual spring, and has imbibed the meaning of the literature about them. Readers of these books who are receptive to the Sufi spirit will find it here, distilled from traditional sources and presented faultlessly in contemporary terms. The Western role of Idries Shah is especially striking in view of his consistently Afghan psychology. For the Afghan will not merely adopt or adapt something, he will harmonize with such of it as he can, and he will employ it for constructive, even innovatory, purposes. The Afghans, unlike other peoples, did not rebel against the Arabs as such. They absorbed Arab ideas, formed strong links with the Arabs, and elevated basic ideas to the heights of human and soul communication, which we find in the teachings of the many Afghan Sufis and other scientists, thus giving fresh possibilities to the new age, the new culture, which was that of Islam.

The concept of different levels in understanding is well illustrated by these books. People of every kind of religious and ideological background throughout the world have delighted in Shah's books, even though they are often ignorant of the technical terms, such as Baraka, Imam, and so on, that he constantly uses. And the person who has grown up steeped in this terminology, of course, finds a second level or range of appreciation. And, further, as with all Sufi work, there are psychological, spiritual, and other elements that correspondingly affect anyone who is familiar with, or who comes to understand, these levels.

THE EXPRESSIONS, WORDS, AND SIMILES OF IDRIES SHAH

There is hardly a tale in the body of work that we are examining that does not contain special terms saturated with the spirit of a Sufi human being, such as Shah undoubtedly is. In addition to their obvious connotation for Easterners and Islamologists, he constantly employs words, terms, and expressions in special senses that are effective in communicating *nuances* to the Sufi, if not to the superficial and the grammarian or philologue. This has always been Sufi practice, to such an extent that Sufis, masters of words as well as of thought, have often been criticized by literal thinkers as if they did not understand their own subject!

Especially valuable in these books are the references to Junaid, al-Ghazzali, and others, as well as those like Rabia the saintly woman Sufi whom we have already mentioned. Many of them, for such is the nature of the Sufis, were and are for some highly controversial figures, but to us they are the pathfinders and the guides.

In addition to people and spirit, of course, the Eastern settings, even the animals and birds, the deserts in their infinite dimensions, the places like Morocco, Turkestan, Baghdad, and Kandahar of the Afghans—all add their magic and their meaning. To derive the real and deepest advantage from these relationships and internal dimensions requires a knowledge of the East that very few people possess. The influence of such writers in Persian as Attar, Sanai, and Rumi is clearly visible in Shah's work; as indeed is his saturation in the spirit of the Koran. You may benefit greatly from reading Idries Shah, in English and other languages, without a deep knowledge of the Persian and Arabic literatures, but you will not perceive their greatest depths. There are even some scholars today who, although working in these literatures, do not understand him as well, or appreciate him as much, as some Westerners who do not know these languages! The reason is that "a little learning is a dangerous thing," so that insufficiently informed Eastern thinkers can well misunderstand the profoundness of this work.

Above all, the reader should have a Sufi heart, or he will miss so much that could be a treasure for him.

IDRIES SHAH'S RELATIONSHIP WITH PREVIOUS POETS

Idries Shah has studied the moralistic poets before him, such as Saadi of Shiraz. Saadi projected moral teachings through the short tale, aiming by this method at capturing the attention and feelings of his reader; for the human spirit responds to tales and stories.

But Saadi's style, as in the *Gulistan Raz*, was not of his own devising. This technique was used by the Indians, the Greeks, and the Persian poets. Rumi, in his *Mathnawi*, employed examples and tales. The *Mathnawi* is full of stories, including much psychological training (adapted sometimes from the Indian *Kalila and Dimna*), relevant to the situation and time of Rumi's audience.

Idries Shah, not unnaturally, has taken a road similar to that of his two predecessors in the books now being analyzed. As a Sufi poet and writer, as well as a teacher, he excels in elevating the inner perceptions and in maintaining the teaching function in a truly Sufi manner. La Fontaine and other Western authors have adopted a similar method, though they have, of course, not pretended to work selectively and purposefully, so they stop short at the point of entertaining and inculcating morals, rather than at the point of opening up new possibilities for man. The admiration that Idries Shah has received for his remarkable literary skill, in which major poets have joined, proves him a worthy successor to those Eastern Muslim writers and teachers already mentioned: this is to say a very great deal, since their work is respected and regarded as classical throughout the world.

Tolerance and humility, traditional Sufi hallmarks, overflow from Idries Shah's books, but not at the expense of reality and justice. If a man, by humility, allows injustice to be done, he commits a crime, and Shah is not shy (in this resembling Rumi and Jami, for example) in quoting appropriate instances of this. Shah evokes the saying attributed to the Prophet, that "A Muslim is one from whose hand and tongue people are safe." Could there be a greater tribute?

Idries Shah shares his symbolism with those Sufis, Arabs and non-Arabs, who preceded him, such as Hallaj in his work *Altawasin*, Ibn al-Arabi in his *Futuhat al-Makkia*, Attar in his *Conference of the Birds*, and many others of equal note.

THINGS THAT DISTINGUISH IDRIES SHAH FROM HIS PREDECESSORS

As a faithful student and follower of the earlier Sufis, including the greatest men of letters for over a thousand years, Idries Shah has absorbed both their content and also their methodologies. He may be seen as an extension of their work in a new milieu, a new area, a new formulation. In order to achieve this, he had to absorb their patterns and contact the underlying unity, just as they did before him. Every creative person must start off by being a student of someone else.

The *Futuhat al-Makkia* of the great Sufi Ibn al-Arabi, this work which is still considered the peak of Sufi production, did not appear without a previous example. He had read and absorbed the book of *Altawasin* of Hallaj, then Ibn al-Arabi brought out the amazing *Futuhat*, unmatched either by those who came before or after. Thus also, Rumi, the greatest Sufi poet, was suffused with the perceptions of Sanai and Attar, to whom he acknowledges his debt ("my eyes").

What Shah has done is not only to absorb the content and methods of his predecessors, he has actually introduced arrangement, whereby, through the use of words and interplay of different kinds of stories, anecdotes, and moods, he has produced literature that can play upon the perceptions of man as man can on an instrument. The only exceptions to this influence are those whose subjective bias is such that they seize one part or another to like or to dislike. Again, although Saadi took ordinary people, for the most part, as the illustrations of his teachings, Shah has been able to develop an additional dimension by taking the words and actions attributed to Sufi great ones further to enrich our experience of what he says and tries to provoke in us.

Shah's ability to develop his themes in a manner that takes into account modern discoveries of Western man in anthropology, science, sociology, and psychology is admired by observers in the West and in the East. He has undoubtedly been able to do this because he has thoroughly grasped the essential significance of the Sufi message, ideal, and origins. The Sufi sees the fire burning, but does not stop at the flame; he penetrates it, and beyond it, to its creator. Even holy places may be seen as nothing by the Sufi, when he attains understanding of the infinitely greater holiness of God. This sense of the barrier that secondary considerations, bias, and conditioned responses impose was known to the Sufis, as you will see in their works, centuries ago. Shah brings them, by way of Eastern models, into the present day, for all cultures—an almost unexcelled achievement.

XVI

THE
SUFI ATTITUDE
by
The Reverend Sidney Spencer

Sufis have sometimes repudiated the traditional observances of Islam. It is said of the tenth-century mystic of Persia, Abu Sa'id, that he forbade his disciples to make the pilgrimage to Mecca, which has been commonly regarded as an obligation laid upon every Muslim who is able to undertake it. "It is no great matter [he said] that thou shouldst tread under thy feet a thousand miles in order to visit a stone house." This attitude, however, is far from being typical of the Sufis: they have in general observed the customary rules and regulations of Islam, while transcending all externals in their spiritual attitude. It is this dual way of adherence to the tradition and inner freedom of spirit that is characteristic of Idries Shah.

In one of the most impressive chapters of his *Caravan of*

Dreams (1972), he describes his own experience of the pilgrimage to Mecca. Making his way to Mecca, along with tens of thousands of others, he felt "the need for communion with a mightier, vaster force than mankind." That, as he saw, was the compelling impulse that actuated the pilgrims. They did not come to worship the Kaaba or the Black Stone. They came to worship Allah in the place rendered holy by the revelation received by His Prophet. In the consciousness of that common purpose, the barriers that divided them were broken down. Prosperous businessmen shared the reactions of their "untutored servants." The pilgrims, says Idries Shah, were marked by an astonishing variety of appearance. "There seemed to be no two people who resembled one another." But as they moved on to Mecca, "all indications of rank or distinction . . . every trace of petty individuality, had vanished." The cry broke forth from them all, "Here we are, O Lord, in Thy presence." At the first glimpse of the holy city all were moved to join in the Islamic confession of faith, "There is no God but Allah, Mohammed is the prophet of Allah." As he walked toward the sanctuary, Idries Shah felt "the magical quality of mystery and otherworldly fascination" revealed in it. Like all the pilgrims, he kissed the Black Stone embedded in the sanctuary—"the only surviving relic which was touched by the prophet Mohammed."

The pilgrimage made a profound and enduring impression on the writer's mind. In taking part in it, he identified himself with his fellow Muslims in their reverence for Mohammed and their devotion to the God whom he served. At the same time he affirmed his participation in a wider tradition. The pilgrimage, as he points out, was "an established part of Arab religious duty long before Mohammed. . . . It seems probable that this place was intimately connected with fundamental happenings in Semitic religion in times of which we have no recorded history in the modern sense." Islam, as he sees it, does not proclaim a new or exclusive revelation: it was Mohammed's task to restore the monotheism revealed to mankind through a succession of prophets. Islamic devotion is therefore a reaffirmation of the inner unity of God and man, which this revelation implies. In this chapter Idries Shah makes it clear that, like the great majority of Sufis down the centuries, he attaches himself to the central tradition of Islam.

The distinctive expression of Idries Shah's genius lies in the telling of tales drawn from all manner of Muslim sources, written or oral. *Caravan of Dreams* and *Wisdom of the Idiots* (1971) consist chiefly of such tales. The meaning of these stories is often highly enigmatic; it does not by any means lie on the surface. As the author conceives it, the real purpose of the "teaching story" is "the assistance of the interior movement of the human mind." "Its action is upon the innermost part of the human being. . . . It establishes in him a means of communication with a nonverbalized truth beyond the customary limitations of our familiar dimensions." The teaching story, in other words, springs from, and makes its appeal to, the inner and greater self that lies, as the Sufis (like all mystics) maintain, beyond the normal and superficial self, which is blind to its own deeper being. The stories are calculated to bring into play, perhaps by their very strangeness and unexpectedness, the forces of the hidden life. One is reminded of the Buddhist koans—the obscure and baffling sayings of Zen masters, which are said to stab the spirit awake. Certainly the teaching story is apt to be highly enigmatic.

One of the most intriguing of such tales is "The Shrine," which goes back, as it is said, to Haji Bektash, the founder of a well-known order of dervishes. It concerns the famous teacher, Nasreddin. His father was the keeper of a shrine, supposed to be the burial place of a great teacher, that was a place of pilgrimage for many. Nasreddin would naturally have inherited his father's position, but instead of that he traveled far and wide, riding on the back of a donkey, in quest of divine knowledge. Among the mountains of Kashmir the donkey died. Nasreddin was overcome by grief at the loss of his beloved companion. He placed a simple mound over his grave, and remained long by the grave in silent meditation. Men traveling over the mountains, when they saw him remaining there, were led to believe that this was the grave of a holy man. A rich man ordered that a shrine should be built on the spot. In course of time the shrine became widely known. When Nasreddin's father heard of it, he came to the place, and Nasreddin informed him of what had happened. The old man was amazed: he told his son that the shrine of which he was the keeper had originated in exactly the same way when his donkey had died thirty years before. A commentator has described the story as "a profound allegory of man's capacity for self-deception." Another suggestion is that it shows the parallel between real religion and what is commonly understood by it. Dervishes have used the tale to cast ridicule upon themselves by suggesting that all shrines are hoaxes, and thus to discourage men from entering on the path of discipleship unless they are really called to it. These are all rational explanations, but what the story really means can only be discovered by an imaginative effort transcending intellectual understanding, which each man must make for himself.

It is the essence of Sufism, as Idries Shah portrays it, that it is the path that leads to the higher knowledge by the evocation of the inner powers of the soul. He quotes from John of Antioch's (who is said to have lived in the thirteenth century) account of his own experience. John, it seems, was converted to Sufism because he saw the inadequacy of other forms of faith since they failed to provide the means whereby men could practice the religious message. It was the distinctive quality of the Sufis that they "made themselves knowing mediums fully sensitized, so that a certain high power could move through them." Through the guidance they gave they helped men to help themselves. "These are the men who love man, and whose love enables him to find the road to his own home." It is thus the power working within us, working above all through the spirit of love, that is the true witness to divine Reality. Idries Shah refers elsewhere to the miraculous power sometimes attributed to Sufi teachers and to the emphasis often laid upon such power. He quotes approvingly the words of Master Ahrar, who is said to have performed miracles every day. Such things, Ahrar said, "impress the sensation-seeking self-esteem of the populace," but in truth "the man converted by being witness to a miracle is less than equal to a lowly dog on the Way." His belief is rooted in excitement rather than in real faith. "If you are sincere, you will perceive the quality of real men directly and instantly, and not through miracles and tales of miracles." It is the insight that sees the divine Life at work in the dedicated soul that alone makes a man a "traveler on the Way."

Beyond the world of time and space, the Sufi knows, there is "a higher realm," which is the world of real Being. What we call events, Idries Shah says, are similitudes of "real events," which belong to the higher world; and it is the virtue of religious tales that they contain elements from the higher order which bring us into contact with it. In *Wisdom of the Idiots* there is a story that tells of the "Valley of the Paradise of Song" once visited by Ahangar the swordsmith. The Valley, said the smith, "was exactly like the one in which we live. . . . The people are the same people. . . . We who are here, we are their twins, the likenesses and reflections of them." People shrink from such knowledge, the narrator says, and when it comes they lose their interest in life, they grow old and die, "they cannot understand that they have more selves than one, more hopes than one, more chances than one —up there in the Paradise of the Song of Ahangar the mighty smith."

In the higher world, the story implies, there is a reversal of the values prevalent in the world of our common experience. In many of the stories that he tells, and in many of the sayings that he records, Idries Shah displays a realistic recognition of the forces that shape human conduct. That is characteristic of the Sufis. While they emphasize the possibilities dormant in the soul of man by reason of the divine Light that shines in his inmost being, they see the actual power of the egoism by which men are largely ruled. And they see that in one way or another evil is bound to be dominant unless the narrow self is transformed. Therefore, they look beneath the altruistic disguise that egoism is apt to assume. In his story "The Saint and the Sinner," Idries Shah speaks of a dervish devotee who made it his task to reproach wrongdoers and to lead them to the right path. He once found a man given to excessive gambling. Whenever this man went to the gaming house, the dervish put a stone on a pile, and every time this happened he was moved by anger at the gambler's sin and by pleasure ("which he called godliness") at having recorded the sin. This went on for twenty years. Whenever he saw the dervish, the gambler wished he might understand goodness and so enter Paradise, as the dervish would. But when the two men came to die, the gambler was taken to Paradise because of his aspiration after goodness, while the dervish was sent to the lower regions because for twenty years he had indulged himself with feelings of superior virtue. He had put the stones on the pile for himself, not for the other man.

Idries Shah, as a true Sufi, has no illusions about human nature. He gives "a motto for the human race" which runs, "Tell me what to do; but it must be what I want you to tell me." He says, again, of man, "Kick him—he'll forgive you. Flatter him—and he may or may not see through you. But ignore him, and he'll hate you, even if he conceals it until he dies." Most people, he says, are far more concerned to attract attention than to gain information. Nine out of ten "dedicated" people are actually "socially conditioned individuals who attribute what has been done to them to the work of a higher power."

It is no accident that the target of Idries Shah's attack is often the attitude of scholars or "intellectuals." He quotes the Sufi Ajmal Hussein, who was constantly criticized by scholars, as saying that the very existence of the Sufis was "a threat to the pretended scholarship of tiny noisy ones." At his invitation, fifty scholars once sent him questionnaires about his beliefs. He answered them all in different words. When they met to discuss his answers, each one clung to the reply that he had received as the true statement of Ajmal's position, and so their conference led to a prolonged brawl. "What matters to each one most [Ajmal said] is his own opinion. They care nothing for truth. . . . The real motive of their activity is to vie with one another." The intellectual activity that can be so debased as to become a matter essentially of personal rivalry stands, as Idries Shah clearly sees, in complete antithesis to the attitude of the Sufis, who seek to become "knowing mediums fully sensitized"—to attain the inner knowledge of truth, not by the mere play of ideas, but by the quickening of the vision that transforms the soul.

XVII

SUFISM
IN THE ART OF
IDRIES SHAH
by
Dr. Aref Tamer

The "People of the House" are the major Arab family known in
the world of Islam for absolute sovereignty, for pure descent, and
for a chain of ancestry from the Prophet Mohammed. History
has recorded that this family, throughout the centuries, has produced outstanding men, men of prominence and genius, who have
played major roles in the theatre of life, being continuously in the
eyes and the memory of the people. It cannot escape any re-
searcher into the history of Islam that many of them have been
active in administration, establishing nations, kingdoms, and prin-
cipalities, and leading armies on the field; while others adopted
science as the pattern of their lives, and were unsurpassed in their
activity and contribution in this area.

It is my opinion that Idries Shah, who is of this family, is one

of their outstanding men. The life of Saiyid Idries may seem
mysterious to some in the Arab world; thus it is all the more
necessary for his works to be circulated there. This is a task of
scholarship. As for myself, I am one who has been, through various phases of life, a supporter of virtuosity and genius; proud of
it, I follow with attentive interest the products of the minds of
the individuals of the House of the Prophet. It may indeed be true
to say that, in the depth of my self, I feel a spiritual attraction to
this noble family to which Idries Shah belongs.

It has continually made sacrifices for the sake of the world
of Islam. In every single century, the House has given, willingly,
many hundreds of its members in testimony of their adherence
and steadfastness, and brought a light that has penetrated to every
corner of the world.

As a historian of Islam, I cannot forbear from saying that
whenever I have entered a library, anywhere in the Eastern world,
I have been attracted to every book or article dealing with the
subject of Sufism. This subject has for long occupied my closest
attention and has been continuously present in my thoughts. This
school of thought, which in Islam directed the controlling minds
of various periods, still magnetizes the thought of scholars and
remains the subject of intense discussion.

In particular I have been interested in the works of Muhiyuddin Ibn al-Arabi, Suhrawardi, Jalaluddin Rumi, al-Hallaj, Omar
al-Khayyam, Hafiz, and the other important Sufis. I cannot say
why it is that I have been fascinated, since early childhood, by the
greatest Sufi poet, Jalaluddin Rumi. In the many long pages that
I have written about him, I have tackled the story of his spiritual
attraction to the significant and beautiful personage Shams-i-
Tabriz, who was related to the Fatimites who ruled in North
Africa and Egypt.

The deep spirituality and love of God shown by Jalaluddin
and provoked by Shams-i-Tabriz, is seen in the *Mathnawi* and also
in the *Divan of Shamsi*, illustrating meanings—and meanings within
meanings, at different levels. The Sufi par excellence Jalaluddin
thus calls for the longing for God, and regards life as a constant
struggle in which the fighter should never relent, even for a single
hour: for pain is the road to pleasure, and weeping the cause of

laughter. How can the field smile if the rain does not weep upon it? How can a baby get milk if he does not cry?

Shams-i-Tabriz was able to convert Jalaluddin from a preacher into a teacher, from a scholar into an inducer of experience and understanding. In like manner, Idries Shah has clarified and converted Sufi materials, in books and in speech and in action, into a method of provoking capacities for learning that are unimagined by the pedestrian scholar.

Idries Shah shines in his quotations from Jalaluddin Rumi, and in his manipulation of Sufi thought; demonstrating his learning and his knowledge, as well as his abilities in research and his capacity to include the necessary and exclude the accretions, so that his work is a model of objectivity. Not that this is any secret, for Saiyid Idries is admired for this ability by students of Sufism of the world—and the Sufis who are themselves authorities on the subject.

The Sufi schools that flourished in Iran, Turkey, and Iraq in the fifth and sixth Islamic centuries and afterwards served to rivet the attention of the Islamic world, and to open the doors wide for ideological freedom and freedom of thought. This school, thanks to the real genius of its directors, was capable of establishing what we can truly call a "thinking method" that extended its influence and control over chosen educated men in Islamic society. Practicing this method without being indebted to any political power, they sought and established proofs through search and contention, so that the branches of their institution encountered no limits, and included not only all areas of the Saracen world but also all spheres of study, and embraced outstanding individuals in both science and literature. It is essential that we should neither ignore this signal contribution nor neglect the importance of this school, recognizing its value in a myriad of areas. We find many parts of this story simplified in Idries Shah's books about Sufism, where he stresses the importance of liberating mental processes, awakening a certain pattern of awareness of life, and receiving the right guidance.

Shah's work reminds one forcefully of the affirmation of Jalaluddin: "How can the nations cross this nothingness, one after another? One moment in darkness, and another moment in light."

Who adds: "The human being is like a flower which passes through the periods of childhood, youth and old age, ending eventually in death. This is like what happens to the tree in Autumn." And he directs us to look intently on this universe, alternating between a state of Spring and Autumn; and then he ends by saying that the Arranger of all this and the primary cause of it is the "Mind of all," which infuses all in this world, like the scent of the rose emanating from the rose, whose perfume one smells and wears without seeing, or like the ecstasy that overwhelms the drunkard without his knowing its cause or action.

I do not want to expand here on the literary treasures that Idries Shah has revealed, for they are a lasting heritage for thinkers who move toward the Real. They should be assembled and preserved as a body of higher literature and made available to all for research and study.

I bow in respect to Idries Shah, a man of learning who has worked so much for humanity, without bias and in sincerity, and who has rendered great services to society.

There is nothing either unprecedented or even unexpected about the emergence of a major interpreter of traditional thought from among the descendants of the Prophet Mohammed. Nothing remarkable or unexpected, but something of outstanding importance. In our tradition, the "empty Chair" of such an individual need not be filled publicly. He need not make an outstanding impression on people of a different culture from our own in order to qualify for the respect and admiration that he should receive; but he must be capable of such success. And anyone who can show such achievements as Idries Shah has shown—in many fields —becomes in our eyes, just as much as in those of Western authorities, worthy of close attention, for his potentiality as well as for his established proofs of capacity.

A reader of these lines living in the West might not immediately appreciate the relative rarity of the appearance of an individual who commands the respect of various persuasions of Islam. Yet Shah's capacity to demonstrate the underlying unity in fact, in spite of the apparent differences, even oppositions, of manifestation and formulation, is one that the Western reader, since the time of Jalaluddin Rumi, has been able to grasp with greater ease than some of the scholars of the East whose thinking is centered upon appearances rather than internal logic. If we point to the fact that contributors to this book include Arab and other Christians, a Hindu monk, Turks, Persians, and Africans, as well as many others, we shall be able to underline something of the unusual catalyzing power, at deeper levels of the perceptions, of Idries Shah. In the East, as in the West, there is a deep-seated and burning desire to find and follow a way of life that can achieve the increasingly difficult objective of retaining coherence while providing common ground for people of many persuasions in their spiritual as well as in their psychological and social orientation.

The drastic misunderstanding by many Western authors and even numerous Eastern thinkers about the quality, nature, and texture of minority thought in Islam has been partly due to the misguided simplifications of a few fossilized prelates. The essential and inner significance of the mystical doctrine undoubtedly meets other certitudes of Islam in the analytical revelations of Idries Shah. In a word, he works at a more profound and sophisticated level than most thinkers employ, and this has plainly led to his being able, through perception and not shallowness, to lay bare basic truths of human existence.

It is only an interpretative method such as this that can command the respect of people with a greater range of understanding than narrow theoreticians; and it is only such a mind as that of Idries Shah that can also render, on the lower level, indications of the truth of the unity of the human experience of the divine in a manner that can bridge the gap between more superficial thinkers, of whatever ideology.

But in order to see whether the work being done by Shah accords with tradition, we may briefly turn to something written in the London *Times* some years ago, which represents the unalloyed traditional belief about the nature and operation of the family of the Prophet:

> They do no preaching, but circulate their message in a special way unfamiliar to this age and not specified . . . Humanity had to perfect itself by welding together, under rare and secret auspices, the scattered elements that it inherited, as well as imbibing cer-

tain secrets which took shape only rarely and under difficult conditions. Some of the methods were conventional study. . . .[1]

The London *Times* has the slogan: "When the Times speaks, the world listens." The world, it seems, is certainly listening a great deal to Shah and the traditions that are now being released in greater volume than they have for centuries.

The doctrine of a source of knowledge, developed in a specialized manner and transmitted from a remote origin to a receiving culture, may seem bizarre, as some Western observers have noted. But it is not without significance that the concept, which, in the more-stilted days from which we have recently emerged, appeared improbable in the extreme, now finds far readier acceptance where it would hardly be expected. Taking this quotation from a newspaper with a daily readership of three million people, Walter Lang, in speaking of the work of Idries Shah, notes:

> It may indeed be true that the mere reading of such material will, in the long run, switch in new areas of the brain—areas which have hitherto been dormant, but which in "normal" humanity would be fully active. In which case it seems high time that official psychology took a close look at a remarkable foundling wh'ch has been deposited overnight on the Western doorstep.[2]

Some modern psychologists (who are today of less importance than formerly, since fresh insights have become available through sociological research) would have held with Freud, and would have once convinced virtually every reader, that this kind of idea is a wish fulfillment. That is to say, the person has a wish and fills it in by inventing something to assuage his desire. More modern thinkers are beginning to see, and to indicate, overtly or covertly, that, just as a man who is hungry may dream of food (which actually exists), a man in need of a certain kind of guidance may also dream of it when it does exist and contribute to the knowledge of its existence. A thing does not have to be imagi-

[1] *Times* (London), March 9, 1964, p. 12.
[2] *Evening News* (London), July 22, 1970, commenting upon Idries Shah's *The Dermis Probe*.

nary in order to be desired. Such might easily be the case with the kind of phenomenon to which we are referring here.

Well, if this is the tradition, does reality give any support to it? Indeed it does. If there is a body of persons who know how to communicate with people at large with consummate efficiency, in spite of the relative strangeness of the material and ideas communicated, it seems as if they would certainly do so, as and when it was possible. The possibility would depend upon the time and the people. And it is hard to resist the conclusion that Idries Shah is a man with the requisite communication capacity.

To someone rooted in Eastern analogical traditions of thought, and especially the Arabic language, the very name of the man becomes significant when he is thinking along the above lines. *Idries* means the "scholarly communicator." And Idris is the traditional link between higher powers and humanity in the personage of the prophetic Idris of our scriptures. *Shah*, though a Persian word, is customarily employed not only for descendants of the Prophet (Persian—*Shahim*, Arabic—*Sayedna*) but also conveys the sense of the succession of kingly capacity, which operates in a continual series of levels, from the highest rarefication to the lowest, terrestrial one.

I am aware that here I am writing in a vein and a language that may not be familiar to all my readers, especially those who are not accustomed to the traditional symbolic use of words. But this usage exists, and it is possible to note that it is being used increasingly in the West today. This in itself can be a justification for its continued employment.

In our tradition, the teacher will often dress himself in the clothes of the people with whom he is to interact, and among whom he will live. There is an interesting story about the custom of the great-grandfather of Idries Shah, the Jan-Fishan Khan, whose personal name was Mohammed Shah.

The quite astonishing finesse, wisdom, and consideration shown by Saiyid Mohammed Shah indicates how personal interactions can be employed to create effects that are perhaps improbable in societies more familiar to us today. When the Saiyid once went to visit someone in Damascus, he first went to stay in Basra. There he lived the same kind of life as the man whom he was about to see, to familiarize himself completely with the surroundings and outlook of his host. When he eventually presented himself at this man's house, he was, as was his custom, dressed in almost exactly the same style of clothes as the man he was visiting. This behavior contrasts with the cloud of retainers that other people of rank always took with them when visiting anyone at all—just in order to impress or to maintain a sense of their own dignity. In a vivid metaphor, Saiyid Mohammed Shah used to call this artificial behavior "changing the air," altering the atmosphere, and making things different from how they really should be. It is common practice among certain Saiyids to dress like the people they are seeing; known as "putting on the local clothes."

This kind of deliberate and measured action, based upon insight and experience, is a far cry from the hit-or-miss methods employed by gurus. It is equally remote from the dogmatic approach of the externalist theologian or religious leader working through insistence, indoctrination, and the inculcation of a particular belief. It posits a third manner of operating: from knowledge.

It is interesting to compare the behavior and capacity of the Afghan sage of a century ago with the current adaptation of the same tendency and ability in his great-grandson Idries Shah. It sheds light, too, on the nature of the observer when we turn to the pages of one of Britain's major literary journals, *The Spectator*, where a man of letters is seeking to account for Shah's remarkable experiences and power to enter any circle in the East:

> A nobly born Moslem . . . speaking a kind of Esperanto of sophistication, and able to meet on personal—not journalistic—terms almost anyone he cares to call on in the Middle East, describes a journey there . . . An intensely interesting book, both for its unusual subject and for the author's outlook—worldly, astringent, high-spirited.[3]

In the colonialist period, from which much of the East has only very recently emerged, such men as Shah were regarded by some as a potential threat, to the temporarily ruling power, to a degree that those who did not live through such times might now

---

[3] *The Spectator*, April 5, 1957, p. 450, review of first edition of Idries Shah's *Destination Mecca*.

find it hard to believe. The existence of an alternative system of thought, of an intact society within the imperial domains of the West, a society with its own hierarchies and chains of command, which transcended national and colonial borders, these were obvious drawbacks from the administering power's point of view.

For this reason, just as much as because of the recurrent cycles of local coercive societies, the work of the Saiyids has for generations been carried out with considerable discretion. Traveling as students, practicing the military arts, carrying on international trade, and fufilling religious obligations were the main fields that were open to them; and consequently we find them working in these fields, often in a more or less uneasy relationship with the administering elements, throughout the Eastern world, from the confines of China in the east to North Africa in the west.

The need was always to help to maintain the structures of thought and social organization in which certain objectives could be reached; to keep abreast of the current developments in the expanding world, and to adapt the methods of teaching to changing situations. This could only be done by knowing the inner meaning of the thought in which they dealt, and sometimes only at the risk of their motives being seriously misunderstood.

When it was necessary, they showed themselves; when it was necessary, they remained in obscurity. Often nominees of various kinds represented the outward face of the movement, which was designed to preserve and maintain the essential capacity for teaching.

Saiyid Ikbal Ali Shah, the father of Saiyid Idries, is a remarkable example of this process. Since his death in 1969, it has been possible to trace some of his many activities in the light of the program outlined above. It is possible only to record some of the highlights for which he was known in this present work. When the Third Afghan War was in progress, he was working in Britain, appealing for the restoration of the rights of the Afghan nation, and publishing his demands in such prestigious journals as *The Edinburgh Review* [4] and the *Journal of the Royal Central Asian Society*. Although still in his twenties, he was a member of the Royal Geographical Society and the Royal Asiatic Society

[4] Ikbal Ali Shah, "The Claims of Afghanistan," *The Edinburgh Review*, VII, No. 75293 (1920), pp. 3–18.

of London, and an acknowledged authority on Afghanistan and Central Asia.

In the 1920s when the independence of Afghanistan was attained, Saiyid Ikbal traveled, in the guise of a newspaper representative, to the Grand Moslem Conference in Mecca, as the representative of his community, to take part in the planning of the postwar Islamic strategy. In the 1930s he was to be found in Geneva working in collaboration with the League of Nations, supporting disarmament and struggling for the expansion of the ideals of Islamic unity.

More than sixteen works are listed under his name dealing with the problems and needs, as well as the background, of Afghanistan. King Nadir Shah rewarded him, and Ikbal Ali Shah's name is now a part of the history of the independence struggle of Afghanistan.

When Afghan independence was assured, he turned to the problems of India, where the family was established as Nawabs of Sardhana. He knew all the major figures of the period following World War I and leading to Indian independence. In the 1930s he worked closely with the late Agha Khan, who wrote a preface for one of his books on Oriental culture in 1937. Saiyid Ikbal also wrote a life of the Agha Khan (Sultan Mohammed Shah), *The Prince Aga Khan, An Authentic Biography*, which was published in London in 1933. Saiyid Idries was associated with his father's work, and became a favorite of the old Agha Khan.

These interests in the constitutional progress of India involved Ikbal Ali Shah to such an extent that after the achievement of independence, at the special request of the President, Dr. Zakir Hussain, he was appointed India's cultural representative in all of West Asia—responsible for a population of more than one hundred million people.

During the Indian national struggle, Ikbal Ali Shah had pointed out the value of an independent state for the Muslims, and this, too, came into being as Pakistan. The foresight of this most unusual man, kinsman of Saiyid Jamaluddin Afghani, inspirer of nationalism in the East, as reflected in the above facts, is amazing. Although Pakistan and Afghanistan were to have their differences, Ikbal Ali Shah contributed toward the basic welfare of both of them. Although Pakistan and India were unfriendly from time to time, Ikbal Ali Shah was able to benefit both of them. Although he had supported the call for the establishment of Pakistan, he was a man of such caliber that the Indian government, seeking a man to represent Indian culture in the Western Moslem world, chose—Ikbal Ali Shah.

Very little has yet been written about Saiyid Ikbal Ali Shah, probably because so little time has elapsed since his death. But historians are already collecting information. Not all of them have been able to descry the underlying unity, the service of the community, and the view of the ultimate good that was found in him. V. Gregorian, for instance, in *The Emergence of Modern Afghanistan* [5] has frequently mentioned the important work of Saiyid Ikbal Ali Shah. But he has not determined the thread of unity that underlies his service to the Afghan nation.

Such was the significance of the man that, years after the national abolition of titles of honor in India, Ikbal Ali Shah was still referred to in official documents and on his Indian republican passport by his titles, including his royal appellation. And documents issued by internationally recognized Islamic authorities acknowledge that this family possesses sovereignty and that its titles cannot be removed by any existing power, which is a unique situation.

Many observers have confessed themselves bewildered by two things about the Saiyids of this family. In the first place, they seem to be able to go anywhere and to do almost anything. In the second place, it is hard, at the time certainly, to know why they should have chosen to carry out a certain course of action.

But this pattern, according to those who realize that an internal logic lies behind such activities, is by definition hard to understand, because the perspective is not there for the observer to employ. It might be said that only in retrospect can the motivation be seen; and even then it is not always clear, because not all the facts are known. The activities of Idries Shah himself, though many of them are known to a wide public, undoubtedly cover a far wider scheme of things than can be captured in such an article as this, even if he should make the information avail-

[5] Palo Alto, Calif.: Stanford University Press, 1969.

able. And, in addition, too much information may prejudice an operation.

There is a tradition that the teaching of the Saadat, the Saiyids, is like shoots on a bush. Violent disputation and activity may dislodge these burgeoning beginnings, as does a tempest. At other times, it is said, if there has been enough serene quiet—as well as purposeful activity—leaves, flowers, and ripe fruit emerge.

XVIII

THE WAY
TO
ECSTASY
by
Dr. Bankey Behari

THE QUEST

I was awakened from my reverie by a gentle knock at the door of my humble cottage. As the breeze entered, it carried the melody of the stringed *rabab:*

> *The shades of evening mark the close of day*
> *The sunset fades, the world grows cold and grey*
> *Across the plains the lengthening shadows play—*
> *O tentsman, haste and strike the tents: I pray*
> *The Caravan is already on its way.*

A shiver passed through me, and my heart seemed to melt as, with tears in my eyes, I turned to greet the dervish, singing to his music. I looked at his effulgent face, his luxuriant white beard, and his lean form, shining like gold. I bowed, as he gave his parting message: "God and God alone. All besides is empty desire."

A great message and mighty words. I started on my soul's lone adventure, with an aching heart, yearning to receive His leaven that changes, His medicine that cures. I offered my soul to Him.

But it was a hazardous march, a dreadful flight from the Alone to the Lone; without the courage instilled by His beloved saint, I would never have been able even to start.

Something urged me to make haste, as into my mind came the words of the Arabian mystic:

> Our nights and days around each other spin
> And we, like planets, end where we begin
> Our feet are on the heads of those that passed
> And, as the cradle cries, the graves all grin.

Mutability is writ upon the earth's face, and I am a solitary sojourner on the Path that leads to the Eternal.

I entered a forest, far from other men, and lay on a bed of dry leaves, beginning with a song from the great Sufi, Sheikh Saadi: "Even living to the Day of Judgment, in the end/annihilation, in the end annihilation . . ."

The king does not survive in the world, nor the Moon in the sky; the sky, too, does not survive, it too knows death.

Where is Adam today, or Eve, or the grain of wheat that lured them?

One moment and then the next, thus time passes away.

Where is the vessel of Noah today, and where its boatswain? Gone is the storm that surrounded it, all is past and over.

Where is King Solomon today—and silver-tongued David?

Where is the flying throne of Solomon and the love story of Zuleikha?

Where is the Valley of Canaan today?

Where is Leila and her lover, Majnun, where the glances and blandishments of Shirin?

Where are Farhad and Khusru today—all have entered the Valley of Death.

Rich was Alexander, and he dwelt in sky-kissing mansions:

World-renowned was his majesty and might: but today all of it is come to nothingness.

Why dost thou lament, then, the loss of worldly wealth—or gloat over riches?

It comes and it passes away, nothing remains for ever.

It behooves thee to remember the Lord at every moment and to wash thy mind clear of all suffering and care; and to keep thy soul happy, knowing that all that the mortal witnesses is fleeting.

O my heart! Remember the Lord Truth constantly, and turn thy face away from all non-being.

Be not heedless, remain alert and wakeful, remembering that death hangs overhead to carry thee away at any moment.

Very sweet-tongued was Saadi, revealer of divine secrets was Hafiz, melodious were the songs of Khusru—all fell victims, just the same, to death.

This remembrance of the fact of death is the constant practice of the devotee Sufi, making him pledge every breath to the service of the Lord. What is the value of a single breath? Remember the tale of Alexander:

> When he was returning from his conquests in the East he fell ill. The doctors told him that he would not survive more than an hour. He said: "I offer half my kingdom if this can be extended to one day, so that I may arrive at my native land and see my beloved mother." Soon after the doctors said: "Sir! There are but five minutes left of your earthly existence." Alexander exclaimed: "Alas! What foolhardiness is mine! Today I realize how many years of my life were wasted in conquering kingdoms—and I cannot now buy even one breath in exchange for them!"

The Indian mystic Kabir sings: "Verily the truth I state, and over and over again, even to the beat of the drum: every breath that you draw must be passed in remembrance of the Lord—it is worth more than the value of this world and the next."

Al-Ghazzali illustrates the point in this way:

> A man gets a gem. How much will he be pained if he loses it? The anguish, and the hurt, will be much greater if, in addition,

he is murdered by a thief who steals it. The value of the breath is very great: because it can purchase eternity. [Al-Ghazzali continues:] The world continues because of the ignorance of people. Fools are running the world. If there were no fools, the bazaars of the world would close. If you are wise, consider yourself one of the company of the dead.

A few years ago, in Banaras, India, at an assembly of poets, a young man recited this: "None knows the hour of his death; and look at his shortsightedness; he collects provisions for a hundred years, although he is not sure whether he will survive until the morrow."

An aged poet, as soon as he had heard these words, stood up, patted the youngster, and suggested a correction to the final lines: "Not to speak of surviving until tomorrow—there is no knowing whether one will survive the next moment."

So the Sufi ecstatic urges one to start now, and not to rest until the goal is reached, since there is no certainty that a man will draw even his next breath.

THE ELECTION

Life is a precious gift, and this is the moment to make the election. Says a Sufi: "It is sure that you will have to part one day from life. Make your choice therefore; would you prefer voluntarily to sacrifice it at the altar of the Beloved Lord of Love, or to let it be snatched away by the cold hand of death?"

CASES OF CONVERSION

Habib Ajami was a banker, lending money at extortionate interest rates. His rapacity distressed even his wife. One day she was cooking some meat that he had brought in, and the pot became full of blood. He asked what it was. She said that it was because of the way in which Ajami dealt with his clients, and at this he felt sad.

As Ajami was walking along the street a little later, he overheard some children saying that they should get out of the way of Habib, the extortioner; for his shadow might fall on them, making them contaminated and henceforth sinners.

Ajami was so distressed by now that, full of repentance, he went to see Hazrat Junaid, the great Sufi. Junaid accepted and initiated him and taught him the divine Name. Habib was now a completely changed man; and as he was going home, he came upon the same group of children that he had passed earlier. One child said to his companions, "Pray remove yourselves from the way of Habib, lest our shadows fall on him, and *our* name be listed as sinners, for his repentance has been accepted by the Lord."

As soon as he got home, Habib gave away everything he had to the poor.

Hasan of Basra was a jeweler before he became an ascetic Sufi. Traveling to Asia Minor on business, he stayed with the Sultan's prime minister. The minister said: "We are going on a private mission with the Sultan, and you may accompany us if you wish."

They traveled until they came to a vast wilderness, in the midst of which a magnificent tent, guarded by soldiers, was set up. A strange ritual now took place. First the officers of the army entered the tent; then they came out, circumambulated the tent, and went away. They were followed by the most respected learned men of the country, who performed the same sequence of acts. Then a number of physicians followed the same routine. The doctors were succeeded by a troop of beautiful maidens, and again the same ceremonial was carried out. Lastly came the Sultan himself, with his ministers. Going into the tent, they spoke some words, came out, walked around the tent, and then withdrew.

Hasan now asked the minister the meaning of these actions. The minister said: "A most brave and handsome son of the Sultan died some years ago, and his body is buried within this tent. Every year all of us visit it, as you have seen, and follow the ceremonies that you have observed. First the officers of the army approach the tomb and say: 'If by the strength of our arms we could have saved thee from death, we would have done so, sacrificing our lives for you—but we are helpless against Death.' Then come the learned, who approach the tomb and say: 'If our wis-

dom could have averted thy death, we would surely have done
so, but before Death we are helpless.' Then the doctors say: 'If
our medicine could have saved thee, we would have saved thee
from the clutches of Death, but we are powerless.' And the beautiful maidens say: 'If by our beauty and blandishments we could
have saved thee from death, we would have sacrificed all, but we
are helpless in the face of Death.'

"Finally the Sultan and his ministers enter and the ruler says:
'My son! We tried our best, with our army, our physicians, our
scholars and all other means we had to help thee, but before the
divine ordinance we found that we were helpless. Now we bid
thee good-bye until we return in another year.' "

This incident made such an impression on Hasan that he decided to pass his life in prayer, and he spent the next seventy-five
years of his life in worship.

Hakim Sanai was the premier poet of Persia, whom Jalaluddin spoke of as his very eyes. He came of a noble family, and
was the court poet of King Bahram Shah. When the King was
making preparations for an invasion of India, Sanai composed a
poem in his praise, and was on his way to offer it to him. As he
passed a tavern he heard a dervish seated within say: "Saki! [Cup-
bearer] Fill the cup in remembrance of the blind Sultan Bahram,
and give it to me."

"Why do you call our Sultan blind?" asked the saki.

The dervish answered: "Is the Sultan not a fool, that he
wants to win further kingdoms, although he cannot control even
his own? He is a slave to his own desires, miscalls himself a ruler
and torments the creation of God."

Hearing this, Sanai listened further. The dervish, after draining the first cup, called out: "Saki! Give me another cup, in
memory of the blind philosopher-poet, Sanai!"

The saki asked: "Why do you call this distinguished scholar
blind?"

The dervish answered: "Can there be greater madness and
folly than to waste one's intelligence in praising kings, instead of
eulogizing the Omnipotent Lord?"

Now Sanai tore his garments, became a Fakir and refused to

wear even shoes. When the King asked him to return and marry his sister, he answered: "I have taken poverty as my bride, and I do not want a kingdom or a princess."

It was a hot summer day, while the Prophet was at prayer, and he heard the Divine voice say: "I have been ill for the past seven days, and you have not yet come to see Me!"

The Prophet answered: "My Lord! I cannot understand how you could fall ill."

The Divine voice said: "My beloved devotee Bilal is lying ill."

The Prophet Mohammed immediately started out in search of Bilal, but he could find no trace of him, and nobody seemed to know where he was. He went to the next village, where the richer citizens had assembled to meet the Prophet, but instead of greeting them, he said: "I have come to meet Bilal."

All were silent, and they stood there until at last the mayor of the town approached and said, "Sir, Bilal is the name of my servant."

"Take me to him immediately" said the Prophet. "I shall not enter his room" said the mayor, "as it stinks, it is in my stable, just opposite." So the Prophet went alone to the stable. From a small, dark room he could hear a voice repeating the name Allah.

Bilal was lying on a bed of hay, and the Prophet Mohammed spoke to him, apologizing for having left him alone so long, and added: "A voice from the Lord told me to visit you."

"Master," said Bilal, "repeat what the Lord told you."

The Prophet told him. Thereupon remarked Bilal: "Such a benevolent, merciful, almighty One is our Lord, who does not forget such infinitesimals as us, likening us to Himself. What can I offer Him save this soul?" Bilal fell at the feet of the Prophet and passed away.

Sari Saqati, the preceptor of Hazrat Junaid, was delivering a sermon one day when the Caliph arrived, in his full pomp. Saqati was at that moment saying, "Of all created beings the noblest is man and—although such a favorite of God—he yet commits in-numerable sins."

Returning to the palace, the Caliph spent a sleepless night, fearing divine retribution. Next morning he threw away his costly garments and dressed in a blanket; now garbed like a dervish he approached Saqati, and asked him for guidance. Saqati said that there were two possible paths of piety. The one enjoined in the scriptures, which required recitation of the holy Name, praying five times a day, making gifts to the deserving poor, and following all religious ordinances. The other, the shorter way, was to renounce the world and its obligations, to pass one's time in the worship of God, to seek nothing from anyone, and to accept nothing offered by anyone, taking only what was given by the Lord.

The Caliph heard this and, choosing, made his way into the wilderness. His mother later went to Saqati and complained that his words had turned her son into a dervish, whose very whereabouts were unknown. Saqati told her that he would return in due time. When the Dervish-Caliph did appear again, Saqati sent for his mother, and also his wife and child.

At the sight of the Caliph in the character of an anchorite, in such a wretched state of deprivation, they wept, and begged him to return to his family. When, however, the Caliph refused and started to go away, his wife said: "At least take your little son with you." The Caliph took off the child's clothes, and put a blanket over him. But the mother could not endure this sight. She took the child back, and returned to their palace.

Now the Dervish-Caliph was soon back in the jungle, and not long afterward someone arrived to tell Saqati that he was soon to die and wanted to see him. Saqati found his royal disciple lying at the point of death. As Saqati took his head on his lap, the dervish murmured "You are a little late," and died.

As Saqati was returning to his village to collect materials for the burial, he met crowds of people rushing into the jungle. They had just heard the Divine voice calling out that they must go to attend the last prayers for His most beloved devotee, who had just given up his life.

A certain saint records how, on his spiritual itinerary, he passed through a village that contained three tombs. On the first tombstone was written:

When a person knows that on his death the Lord shall question him about his sins and will punish him for them, and will recompense him for the good deeds which he has done, how can he lead a life of comfort and ease?

On the second tombstone was inscribed:

One who believes that Death can overtake him at any moment without warning, and will deprive him of the freshness and beauty of his body, and of all wealth, and will lead him to the darkness of the tomb, where he shall stay for an indefinitely long time; how can he take an interest in the joys of this world?

On the third tombstone was written:

Whoever shall have to proceed one day to the tomb, wherein, once lodged, his youth shall lose its luster, and the glow of his face shall disappear—how can he enjoy this world?

Coming upon an old man in the village street, the traveler enquired the meaning of these strange inscriptions.

The old man told him that these were the graves of three brothers. One was a merchant, the second a man of property, the third a pious man. When the pious man's time had come, his brothers went to him, and offered to give him money for the poor.

He said: "I need no money of yours. But promise me one thing. When I die, wrap me up and entomb me and write certain words on my tombstone." These were the words that the traveler had seen on the first tombstone.

After the burial, the second brother visited the grave. He heard a terrible hammering sound coming from it. That night he had a dream, in which his brother explained that he was being struck with a hammer because he had failed, in his life, to help an honest man, one who was being thrashed by an insolent assailant.

The second brother called the third, and said: "This inscription on the tomb is meant for me." He passed his days and nights thereafter in the wilderness, in prayer. Now, when the time of his own death approached, he knew it and called the last brother, saying, "Place such and such an inscription on my grave." This was the wording already seen by the traveler. He added, "Visit my grave daily, perhaps you may receive some beneficial instruction therefrom."

When the last brother did visit this tomb, he heard such a strange and penetrating sound issuing from it that he could not endure it, and he fell senseless. That night he dreamed that an angel came and explained, "Your brother has attained Paradise because he passed his time in worship. As for the instruction you seek, I tell you that a man gets what he sends in advance to the next world."

The last brother gave up all his wealth to be given to the poor, and called his son. He gave him orders to have the inscription that the traveler had seen put on his tombstone.

A son of the Caliph Harun al-Rashid of Baghdad was strikingly handsome. He was usually to be found in the company of the dervishes, wearing a woolen cap and coat of sparse wool. He was often seen meditating among the tombs.

One day as he passed through the resplendent court of his father, dressed as usual as a dervish, the proud nobles seated by the King said to one another, "This prince has brought shame upon his father. Would that the Caliph could take him to task for his waywardness, so that he might improve."

The Caliph called the prince and said: "My child! You are dragging my name in the mud." The prince was silent for a time, and then addressed a bird seated on the balcony of the palace before them, saying: "I order thee in the Name of my Creator, God, to come down and to settle on the palm of my hand."

The bird obeyed. Then the young man said: "O bird! In the Name of the Creator, God, come and sit on the palm of the hand of the Caliph." But the bird did not move.

Then the prince said: "It is you, Father, who are putting me to shame, by loving and attaching yourself to the world."

The Dervish-Prince left the palace, and went to Basra, taking only a copy of the Koran and a ring that his mother gave him as a keepsake. He took employment at the equivalent of four pennies a day, working only one day in the week, and spending half a penny each day on his upkeep.

The well-known preacher Abu-Amar one day went in search of a mason to repair his walls, and came upon the young prince at work. When he asked: "Will you work for me?" the answer was: "For what else are we born but to work?" The prince made the proviso that he should be allowed to stop working during the five times of daily prayer.

When Abu-Amar went to see what the youth was doing, he was surprised to find that he had done the work of ten laborers, and yet would not accept any more than the agreed day-wage. Abu-Amar went again, on a subsequent day, to find out how the prince worked so well. He was amazed to find that the young man simply sat on the wall, while the stones and bricks flew of their own accord to him, and the mortar applied itself. This is the way in which the works of the Perfect Ones are performed, and Abu-Amar wondered at it.

Soon afterward, Abu-Amar was told that the boy was lying ill in a dilapidated hut at the outskirts of the town. He was dying, and told Abu-Amar to beware of vanities and to be ready to answer for his acts before a righteous judge. "Wrap my body in an old cloth when you bury me," said the prince, "for the living have greater need of new cloth."

Then he gave these instructions: "Give my basket and headdress to the gravedigger, take the Holy Koran and the ring to the Caliph Harun al-Rashid. Give them into his own hands with yours, and tell him that they are the trust and properties that a young pilgrim gave you with a message. The message is: 'Do not die in the middle of the ignorant life that you are living, and do not be a victim of the vanities of the world.'"

The preacher went at once to Baghdad, where he could not get near to the imperial pomp of the Caliph. He climbed a tower when a royal procession was passing. Ten squadrons of the cavalry went by, each comprising a thousand men in full ceremonial uniform. Then came the Caliph, gorgeously robed and attended.

Amar shouted: "In the name of the Prophet! Here is a copy of the Holy Koran and a ring held in trust by me belonging to a youthful pilgrim, to be handed over, and a message to be given in private!"

The Caliph stopped, and ordered the preacher to be brought to his palace. He questioned Abu-Amar about the pilgrim and the manner of his death and burial. The Caliph then immediately went to Basra and visited the tomb of his son, drenching it with tears and reciting couplets in honor of the Pilgrim of the Path.

Amar slept that night in the tomb, and, in a dream, saw the Pilgrim, who said: "Amar! May God grant you His grace for the good offices that you have rendered to me in the last hours of my pilgrimage on earth."

Fariduddin Attar was a druggist before he turned dervish. One day he was busy in his shop when a Fakir who had come for alms, and who had been waiting for a long time, said: "Attend to me."

Attar replied, "I have no leisure."

The Fakir answered, "How shall you find leisure to attend to Death?"

Attar said: "I shall die, just as you, too, will die."

"Will you stand by what you say; if I die, will you?" Attar said that he would.

Hearing this, the Fakir lay down on the ground, put his begging bowl under his head, repeated the *Kalima* (*La Ilaha Illa Allah*)—No God but God—and died.

Attar immediately distributed all he had among the poor, put on a woolen sack, and became a Sufi recluse.

Jalaluddin Rumi was a professor of eminence, adept in rituals, and a master of the sacred writings. One day he was seated by a pool pondering over rare manuscripts. At the same time the great dervish Shamsi Tabriz was praying for someone to be made known to whom he could communicate.

A Divine voice asked: "If We confer upon you such a friend, what will you give Us?" Shams said: "My head"—and all know that he proved true to his promise in the end.

The voice showed him the way to the pool, and Shams stood behind Rumi as, unnoticed, he seized and threw the precious manuscripts into the water.

Jalal turned, saw the fiery eyes of the saint, and said: "O

Dervish! What a great loss to the world has been caused by your destroying those writings."

The saint of Tabriz smiled and, extending his hand, took the books from the water, dry and not in any way affected by their immersion.

Jalal fell at his feet and asked: "Where did you acquire this Knowledge?"

"I have come to teach you that" said Shams. They spent two months in study together after that, and Jalal emerged a perfected Sufi, reciting this poem in honor of his teacher:

> He is my Preceptor and my disciple. He is my pain
> and he is my medication;
>   I speak the truth when I say this, that he is my
> Sun (Shams) and my God.

Jalaluddin Rumi in his *Mathnawi* tells an allegorical story of "Moses and the Washerman." Moses, it runs, was sitting one day at his evening prayers, and he prayed the Lord to lead him to the person who was the meanest in the world, and the object of divine anger.

A Divine voice said: "Meet, in the early morning, the first man going to the river." Eager to see this detestable creature, Moses went early to the riverside, and there he found a short and swarthy washerman, with a load of clothes on the back of his donkey, striking it with his stick and shouting abuse, his eyes red with the drinking and sensualities of the previous night. Seeing him, Moses was satisfied, and returned home.

That evening, it occurred to Moses to ask the Lord to show him the object of his infinite mercy, his dearest devotee. The voice again spoke, saying, "Go and see the first man who approaches the river in the morning."

The following day, Moses was astounded to espy the very same washerman. This time, however, the man had no stick, and there was a much lighter load on his donkey, which he was patting affectionately, and was in tears, chanting the name Allah!

Moses decided to go to the man's home, to ask about him from his wife. Moses explained to her that he had noticed a tremendous change in the man in such a short space of time, and asked what spiritual practices had changed him in such a dramatic manner.

The woman explained that, until two days before, her husband had been, for the thirty years of their married life, a sinner and a most objectionable person. Then, two days ago, when he returned from the river, he had started to curse her as usual, as she gave him his food. Then, as he lay on his bed, she massaged his feet. While she was doing this, tears fell from her eyes, and he asked her the reason.

She said: "I want to ask you a question."

He said: "Ask."

She asked: "What is the greatest thing in the world?"

He said: "Earth."

She said: "And greater than earth?"

He said: "The seas."

She asked: "And what is greater than the seas?"

He said: "The sky."

She asked: "What is greater than the sky?"

And he shuddered, and said: "My sins."

Then the woman questioned him further: "What is greater than your sins?"

He said: "His forgiveness."

"Ever since then," said the woman, "he has been a model of repentance, ever in tears, and has asked everyone to forgive him."

The worship of the ecstatic Sufi, when he seeks to woo, as it were, his Beloved, transcends all rituals. When the Emperor Bahadur Shah of India was asked about this aspect of worship, he answered:

I am an infidel of Love, I do not need formal religion. I need no initiation into the faith of Islam. Every one of my fibers thrills to Love's note; I need no rosary to count the beads; I am a bondsman of my Lord, and I care not to roam free in the garden. The red wounds of separation glow in my heart as veritable rosebuds. What dread should there be for lovers on the Day of Judgment: their business and concern is in seeing the effulgent face of the Beloved, who shows his face to them. O my heart! Rejoice, for the Beloved has decided to sever thy head tomorrow with His sword, in the marketplace of Love, although He has made no promise to confer the priceless gift of His Vision! What matters it if there is no captain, if He is there to steer my boat clear of storms? If God plays the helmsman we shall plough the turbulent waters of the world and surely we shall reach home. The world complains that Khusru has turned infidel and an idol worshiper. He says, "I do not care what the world says—my only concern is my Beloved."

The goal of the devotee Sufi is the vision of God. If it demands, as in the case of Khusru, the offering of formal religion, it demands of Zuleikha her love and surrender to Joseph.

Amir Khusru, when very young, was taken by his father, the minister of the ruler of Turkestan, to India when he became Wazir to Emperor Allaudin Khilji. The father took Khusru to the great saint Nizamuddin Awliya to seek his blessing. Nizamuddin saw in the child a disciple and future saint, and asked the father to tell him something about him.

The Wazir said: "Sir! My wife died when Khusru was a year old, and since then I have taken care of him myself. When I take him to the bath, I notice that his shirt is burned every day where it covers the heart, such is the heat of the pangs of separation that the child feels."

Tears flowed from the eyes of Hazrat Nizamuddin. Raising his arms to the sky, he cried: "Lord! For the sake of the pangs of separation that burn in this child, forgive me on the Day of Reckoning, and accept me as Thine Own."

Mansur al-Hallaj had a sister who dwelt in the wilderness outside Baghdad, where she performed her orisons in solitude. When she had finished her vigils and prayers, it is related, an angel would bring her a cup of celestial nectar for refreshment.

One day Mansur passed the night by her side, and when the nectar arrived he begged a draught of it. She refused, observing, "You cannot endure the passion of Love." But Mansur, as soon as she had drunk, snatched the cup and drained the last few drops. The drink immediately had its effect, and he rushed about shouting *Anal Haq!* "I am the Truth!"

His sister gave a sigh and shed a tear, and then she said: "Alas! O one of little capacity, you have disgraced both me and yourself!"

After he had been condemned to death for his words of apostasy, his sister followed him to the gallows and said: "Did I not tell you that you would not be able to digest the fire of Love? You told the Secret, and now the gibbet has been your lot."

When people began to praise Mansur as a great hero of the Path of Love, the sister said: "O ignorant ones! If Mansur after quaffing a draught is styled by you a martyr, what would you call me, for I, for over twenty years, have been draining cups of this ambrosia and calling every time for more?"

Once Ibrahim Adham was making his way through a wilderness when he came upon seventy blanket-wrapped dervishes. Sixty-nine of them were dead, and very little breath remained in the last one. Ibrahim asked the seventieth dervish the meaning of this strange scene.

This one answered: "Very difficult is the path of spirituality. Tread it most cautiously. Provide yourself with a jug of water and a mere roof for shelter. Depart not too far from, nor approach too near to, Reality. Beware lest you be indiscreet or impertinent in following His Commandment.

"Know that we were a group of dedicated Sufis. We vowed to keep silence and not to hold discourses with anyone, to conform to certain rules and to take notice of none but God. When we reached Mecca, however, we met Khidr, and this made us very happy. We saluted him and said how happy we were that our efforts had been rewarded to such an extent that we had met this great Guide.

"Scarcely had these words left our lips than we heard the Divine voice reprimanding us: 'O ye defaulters! Breakers of vows! Was this your decision, that you forget the Creator at the company of the created? For this fault you are deprived of your lives!' All those whom you see have been consumed through their love for Him! Ibrahim, decide now whether you will pursue this Path farther, or whether you will return home."

Ibrahim asked the last dervish how it was that he had escaped the sudden death, and was left with some breath.

"I," said the dervish, "was still a raw youth and a novice, but *they* were stalwarts in the Path and fully ripened." When he had said this he, too, gave up his life.

This reminds us of the attitude of Rabia Basri. She, similarly, stressed that exclusive devotion tolerates no other affection. When the Prophet Mohammed appeared to her in a dream and asked her whether she remembered him as a friend, she answered: "Who does not recognize you as such? But how can I have friends when the love of the Lord has so filled my pores that no room is left for loving the creation or for hating evil."

Therefore the Sufis have the recital: "Look at the One, know the One, speak of the One, desire the One, feed from the One, and seek the One."

Ibrahim Adham took a lesson from the words of a slave whom he once bought. Asked his name, the slave answered: "It is that name by which you are pleased to call me."

Ibrahim asked what he would like to eat. The slave said: "Whatever you will give me."

"What work" inquired Ibrahim, "would you like to do?"

"Whatever work you require me to perform" said the slave.

"And what do you wish to have?"

"I am a slave, how is it that you and I can have separate wills?"

Ibrahim exclaimed: "Would that I could be a slave of the Lord and surrender to Him as this slave can surrender!"

How the most devout can be taken to task for departing from this rule in their lives is beautifully illustrated in an anecdote of Rabia of Basra. One day, after a fast of eight days, she felt hungry. Someone appeared with a sweet drink and placed it in a corner. She took it up, and as she was about to light a lamp a cat overturned the glass, so she thought she would be able to manage with a little water instead. As she was reaching for the pot containing water, the light went out and the pot fell and all the water spilled onto the floor.

Rabia gave a sigh and said: "Why dost thou treat me like this?"

The voice from the Invisible said: "Rabia! If thou seekest the gifts of the world we are willing to offer them to thee; but we would deprive thee of our sorrow. The gifts of the world and our sorrow cannot lodge both at once in the same heart. Rabia! You will one thing and we will another. Two separate wills cannot coexist in the same being."

After that she would pray: "Let thy will prevail, not mine!"

When her maidservant said: "Mistress, come out and enjoy the beauty of Creation in the Season of Spring!" Rabia said: "Come within, rather, and witness the beauty of the Creator. I see Him, and cast no glance upon the Creation."

Bayazid says: "For thirty years I sought God. But when I looked carefully, I saw that in reality God was the seeker and I was the sought."

Al-Ghazzali says that God remarks: "My devotees seek me as the shepherd seeks the flock; they seek the approach of night as the bird seeks its nest. When it is night the people make supplications to me. Therefore it is my promise to them that 'If you shall adopt me and make me the aim of your life, I shall adopt you who follow my commands. If you will truly seek me, I shall meet you. O Dwellers upon the Earth! At present you are living under a delusion created by that world, forsake it and attain my companionship and my nearness. You remember me constantly and I shall remember you at every moment.' "

Hearing these words, says Ghazzali, who would not say: "I seek Thee because of Thee, we seek nothing from Thee. . . ."

Prayer, to be effective, must come from a pure heart. Therefore it is necessary to consider the methods employed by the devotee Sufis to purge themselves, and thereafter to pass from the purgative to the illuminative and then ultimately to the Stage of Union.

Meekness, humility, and charity are essential. The loud or silent recitation of the Divine Name with full unswerving faith that it will enable the goal to be reached demands other factors for its success. These are solitude, fasting, night vigil, and silence. Poverty and detachment from the world and from possessions are other necessities.

In the case of poverty in its literal sense, a most thought-provoking case is that of Uwais al-Qarni, a contemporary of the Prophet. The two never met, yet the Prophet considered him a perfect dervish, and after his death Hazrat Ali and Omar, the then Caliph, went to find this man whom their master had so esteemed.

When, after ten years, the pair found him, Qarni exclaimed: "Alas! Why didst Thou, O Lord, disclose my identity?" He was regarded as mad, wore clothes retrieved from rubbish dumps, and prayed constantly, while children threw stones at him.

The newcomers described how they recognized him by the signs described by the Prophet, and asked Uwais if he would like some better clothes.

Qarni said: "As far as I am concerned, this ragged cloth is good enough for my purposes—unless you two can guarantee me that I shall live longer than it takes for the cloth to fall into pieces. If you can do that, I shall accept the new clothes."

"Would you not like some money?" he was asked.

"These two coins which I have earned as wages for my laboring are enough for me, as far as I can tell, and I do not need any more—unless you can tell me that I shall live long enough to need more" he said.

When Omar heard these words, he threw down his purse and the seal of the caliphate, crying out: "Would that I had never been born! Who will take up this money and this caliphate!"

Qarni asked: "Why should you care, when renouncing something of this world, who will get it after you? If you have given it away, it is not your concern anymore."

As to humility, when Hazrat Wasi was asked how he was, he replied: "How can you ask this of someone whose days are decreasing while his sins are increasing?"

Someone mocked at the tatters of Daqaq and asked him what he had paid for his clothes. He gave a cry and said: "I bought this suit at the price of the whole world, and I would not part with it in exchange for the bounty of every paradise."

Solitude is the foundation of all worship. Solitude enables a person to judge whether he is independent of associations that bind him to superficial things. To learn how to detach from the world is the highest form of philanthropy. In a characteristic illustrative interchange, Rabia asks her maidservant: "Is there anyone who can show me the way to Truth?" The woman answers: "Keep away from the world, for it has separated you from your beloved."

These further quotations from Sufi training materials underline this phase of dedication:

"Moses," said the Lord, "there is no greater sin than to meet the worldlies." Moses used to say: "He who shall recognize the world (for what it is) shall renounce it." The prophetic tradition has it, on this subject: "The world eats faith, like fire eating fuel."

Ahya ibn Ayaz termed the world "The Devil's workshop"; and al-Ghazzali said that spiritual experiences are never gained by those who are not able to renounce the world and its people.

Detachment from the created and concentration upon the Creator is represented thus, in a passage attributed to Jesus, the son of Mary:

> My food is fasting, my natural condition is fear, my dress a sack made from wool. My hearth is the Sun in Winter, my light in the night is the Moon, my conveyance is my feet, my food the berries of the forest. When I go to sleep, I have nothing with me; when I rise I am empty-handed. None is richer than me on the Earth. I advise you to concentrate your attention upon God, and give up meeting people. If you have a towering aspiration to meet God, concentrate upon Him. Remember: "If one employs all energy to attain an aim with high-mindedness, even a thorn may be turned into a rose garland."

Having worked to purify himself by the above activities, and by fasting and night vigils, the individual on the path of the ecstatic Sufi turns to the practice of the Divine Name.

Abul Hasan prayed, "I take to the remembrance of the Name and cherish no thought of the world besides this." He added: "I pray to the Lord to lead me to the person who knows how to pronounce the Name of the Lord as it should be spoken, that I might earn his blessings." Hazrat Junaid says that whoever repeats the Name of the Lord, the Name merges with him, and the Name merges into the Lord. Attar records that it was the habit of Shibli to fill the mouth of anyone who repeated the Name of the Lord with sugar. When his ecstatic state developed further, he would offer gold *mohurs* to whoever would repeat the name before him. And, when he developed still further, he carried a naked sword with him to smite anyone who took the Name of the Lord. When asked the reason for this strange behavior, he said: "Once I thought that people took the Name of the Lord genuinely with interest and desire for enlightenment, but then I discovered that they repeated it from habit, formally, or in ignorance."

Sheikh Abu-Bakr ibn Ismail Farkhani says:

I performed great austerities; so much, indeed, that my body became pale and emaciated, and I would often fall senseless through weakness. I prayed to the Lord to send someone who would initiate me in the Divine Name.

One day I was seated on a bridge at Damascus when I saw two persons enter a mosque. Something within me told me that they were angels. Then they came to me and said: "You want to be initiated in the Divine Name. We may impart the lesson to you." I answered in the affirmative. Then one said: "Say Ya-Allah (O God)." I thought that I had been initiated, so I rose to go, when he stopped me, saying "That is not the way, it must be repeated with truth and without self. You should repeat the Name as one drowning in the water, who has no support in that state and cries to the Lord for succour."

Then he recited a story. A devotee went to a saint for initiation in the Name, but the saint, looking at him, said, "You are not fit for the initiation." When he insisted that he was ready for initiation, the saint told him to go to the gate of the town and to report what he saw happening there connected with the first man to enter the town.

When he arrived at the gate he saw an aged woodcutter with a load of fuel trying to enter. A soldier went up to him, snatched the bundle of wood and beat him. The observer was made very sad by this, and went and reported the incident to the master. The saint said: "What would you have done, had you been in the place of the woodcutter?" The disciple said: "I would have killed the soldier." "But," said the saint, "The old woodcutter, who endured insult and beating, is my own preceptor, who himself taught me the Name."

As al-Ghazzali says, the Name may only be repeated after the dissolution of the subjective, commanding self, the *nafs-i-ammara*.

The ecstatic condition, engendered by the practices carried out in the right manner and with the right preparation, and not otherwise, is portrayed by Jalaluddin Rumi to the following effect:

> When the lamps are lit and the tables are spread, after the evening prayers, I am engrossed in thoughts of the Beloved, drawing sighs and lamentations. I perform my ablutions with tears, and the gates of the mosque shrivel with the heat of Love's fire kindled in me. Very curious are the prayers of the Love-intoxicated, which disregard all their appointed times and places. Very astonishing are the verses of the Koran that they repeat; their repetition is not by the tongue, but by the pining heart. When I am deprived of a working hand and heart, how can I knock at the door of the Beloved, since he has stolen my heart and hand? From Him I seek protection (against these vagaries) and such is my condition that I do not recognize the Mullah who is leading the prayers, nor the verses with which he is ending the prayer.

Jalal says: "If such is the beauty of Thine Eyes, and thus shine Thy Brows, and so piercing are Thy Glances—I say farewell to all my piety and rituals, and bid good-bye to my intellect and my religion."

The enlightened mystic poet of Majlis-i-Ushaq sings:

> *The itinerary is so strange*
> *That science is beggared*
> *And intellect becomes a Dervish.*

Therefore he advises one to close the subject, and we do so in these words:

For the fire of divine love shall not be borne by the pen, which shall break; the ink shall spill and the paper shall burn by the sighs that shall come. All love of the world and that due to the performance of rituals may be discussed, but not the experience of the greatest love.

So, pleasing to the Lord, girt with humility, fortified with meekness, let us live the supreme experience: FOR ME GOD IS ENOUGH.

The way in which the parables of such great mystics as Jalaluddin Rumi have been unveiled from their mystery and presented by Idries Shah has called forth this writing on the ecstatic Way as portrayed by the great Sufis, and the manner of its following.

Full recognition should be given to the services rendered by Shah, to the Seekers of both the East and the West, for his heart-enrapturing work, which places before the real Seekers the wine drawn from such great names—to mention but a few: Hafiz, Jami, Attar, and Khayyam—among the Sufis.

Idries Shah: you have provoked in me the desire to place before you a dish I have prepared; and by offering it to you I expect thereby to secure your blessings, to bring me close to the lotus feet of my Lord and bestow on me a place in the eternal Divine Abode.

XIX

FILLING A GAP
IN
KNOWLEDGE
by
Sir Razik Fareed

The works of Idries Shah have accomplished the difficult task of serving readers from both the Eastern and Western worlds. This scholar has shown unusual capacity in treating some of the most difficult subjects in a manner easily understood by the layman, providing that he is prepared to approach them with the minimum of preconceptions. The Saiyid has opened up realms of knowledge that ignorance and lack of effective communicators have mistaken for "black magic," since really advanced thinking tends to fill those who are too far behind it with something akin to horror. Thus the communications-gap, which allowed such misconceptions to flourish, has now to a very great extent been filled.

No informed reader should imagine from the foregoing that

there have been no writers in the West working on the exposition of Islamic mysticism, which is generally called Sufism. Reputable workers in this field have included Redhouse, Nicholson, and Arberry; but most of their material can only be termed secondary, and this for a variety of reasons. In the first place, not being Sufis themselves, they could not be expected to know how much, and what kinds, of Sufi materials are currently relevant. Again, a curious ambivalence hovers around their writings, as though they preferred some aspects of the subject to others. Many of these Western writers tend to concentrate upon one or more Sufi exponents to the exclusion of the rest. The result has always been that one would gather from them, unless informed to the contrary by Sufis themselves, that Sufis do not constitute a whole body of people, each accepted by the others.

Idries Shah, especially in such of his books as *The Sufis* (1969), *The Way of the Sufi* (1968), and *Tales of the Dervishes* (1970), points out the true characteristics and objects of Sufism, illustrating these by stories, parables, and other writings from the Sufi masters. His illustrative technique takes careful note, in the Sufi manner, of the value of portraying Sufis and their doings in the light of the requirements of his major audience. These requirements govern his selective treatment of the originators of the Sufi techniques.

Now, what really is Sufism? This is probably the first question asked by those who have been attracted to some kind of study of this path of Truth. Answers to this question, as to many others, are readily found in Idries Shah's works; and the different definitions are seen to correspond with what the questioner has in mind when he asks the question.

Some will say that it is an attitude to life, others say that it is a state of soul, yet others consider it a relationship with God. Sufism has three important features: it accepts poverty, it is generous without thought of gain, it is uninterfering and subject to the will of God. Sufism, in other words, can mean sacrifice, an empty hand, self-discipline, loss of the greed of self and of self-will, and finally attaining Divine Love, the love of God and love for one's fellow beings. For a Sufi, the love of God is placed first in the steps on the ladder of this mystic Way. According to Sufis, love alone can pass the flaming barriers and unsurmountable obstacles that obstruct man in his search for the Truth.

In the strife-ridden world of today, Sufi thought in such a form, put into practice by individuals and nations, could bring to man most urgently needed peace, friendship, and help; for one can clearly see that Sufi thought embraces generosity without any idea of personal gain. If each individual and nation were to help another in this way, their needs could be fulfilled without much difficulty. Again, if one individual or nation does not unnecessarily interfere in the affairs of another, many complications, wars even, could be avoided. Last, though not least, if the creed, the love of God and of his fellow beings were practiced by man, the world would be a happier place to live in.

Parables have often been said to be earthly stories with heavenly meanings, and fables teach us morals. The writings of the Sufis are allegorical and symbolical, in general; and some Sufis even explain the meanings, the spiritual significance, of their stories.

Idries Shah's *Reflections* (1969), while not conforming to one of these categories, yet prompts one to reflect. The story about "The Donkey and the Cactus" appeals to me as one that gives an insight into the suitability of what one relishes. What is delicious to one is abhorred by another. Why is this so? When one reflects upon this, varieties of modes come into one's ken. The next step is the selection of one of these. The analytical assessment, empowered by intuitive spiritual wisdom, helps one to discern the Truth, which alone leads to Reality. So many features of Sufism are so clearly illustrated by Idries Shah in his works that we should honor him as one of the great modern contributors to a better understanding of Sufism.

XX

POSSIBILITIES
OF
EASTERN MORAL INFLUENCE
ON MODERN
CIVILIZATION

by

Dr. Hilmi Makram Ebeid

If, because you wield power, you can commit acts of injustice against your fellow beings, do not forget that God's power supersedes your own. This maxim, deeply embedded in the thought of the peoples of the East, is of paramount importance. In his fifteenth book, the Saiyid Idries Shah has quoted a succinct version of this concept attributed to Ali, the great pioneer of Islam:

> *The rights that others have over you: remember them.*
> *The rights that you have over others: forget them.*[1]

Since World War II, the threat to earthly life resulting from disregard of these principles has invaded almost every area of

[1] Idries Shah, *Thinkers of the East* (London: Jonathan Cape, 1971), p. 3.

social concern. Whether it be international war, arbitrary destruction of human rights, pollution of the environment, or one-sided propaganda of a totalitarian nature, we are all under constant threat, and that threat is growing stronger daily.

It need hardly be observed that if the vital principle of consideration for others had been taken as the guiding light—not only as an ethic but also as an operational guide—the world would have been spared most of its present misery.

Idries Shah joins those who stand up for real values, and strengthens the front of humanity as distinct from self-deluding and deluded systems. This ardent message from the East to which I refer is, of course, the call for self-denial, and for the profound concepts of service that he has ever upheld, which are embedded in the Sufi tradition.

As an Arab of the Christian creed, and as a citizen of the world, I feel that the dynamic of Sufi thought and activity is such that merely to treat this phenomenon historically in the conventional manner is of limited interest when as an alternative we can investigate its beneficial potential for a world that sorely needs help.

Both past and present abound with indications that within the Sufi context men and women of all backgrounds can combine in a common front with the clear object of eradicating malicious and senseless rivalries among both nations and individuals. To this end, a concerted campaign should be organized to sustain Saiyid Idries in his effective propagation of Sufi ideas as living and nutritious concepts, which, quite apart from their religious content, can provide the moral and practical habit of mind essential to the preservation of man as a civilized being.

In spite of plausible arguments to the contrary, the desire for peace and justice pervades the very depth of the human soul, and this desire can be stimulated and assisted. It only took a Ping-Pong ball, apparently an insignificant object, to help restore the contact of China with the United States. No power on earth can destroy this sincere desire for progress and harmony. Sufi ideas in the past have united people from different cultures and creeds who were as bitterly opposed as any we find today. Few people in the West realize the far-reaching implications in their own contexts of Rumi's Christian disciples, of Ibn-el-Arabi's doctrine of the irrelevance of differing religious forms, of the acceptance of the Jew Sarmad as a Sufi, of the use by the Hasidim of Sufi methods of study and illustration, of the well-known influence of Sufi thought on Hindu Bhakti mysticism, upon the formation of the Sikh religion, and the common reverence paid by Christians to Saint Therapion and by Dervish Sufis to Turabi—one and the same individual.

The youth of the world today are not overinfluenced by old attitudes; they can more easily accept the ideas we call Sufi, without the prejudices that imprison many of their elders. An old friend of mine from our university days, Dr. Frank Marston, a most distinguished pedagogue, maintains an irrepressible optimism on this account, saying in a recent letter that if modern youth seem intent on "smashing everything," this may be a prelude to their desire to build the world anew. The Sufis' traditional opposition to hidebound formalism closely parallels this concept.

The main credit for Sufism as for Christian monasticism certainly goes to the East. If Sufism can be compared with certain aspects of Christian monasticism (and the Sufis accept Jesus on the highest footing, indeed, being called Christians by bigots for whom this is a pejorative), with certain differences of formulation that need not detain us here, it is a historical fact that the form of worship practiced by the Egyptian monks, bound to absolute contemplation and irrevocable surrender to God's will, started in the rugged austerity of the Egyptian deserts. This lends weight to the belief of our author that Sufi thought derives directly from experiential materials "although of course it may be linked with other esoteric traditions." This is why the Saiyid firmly holds that Sufism did not have direct Hindu or Christian sources.

From its desert surroundings, the Egyptian doctrine traveled far and wide to the West, where it gained extensive influence. And there is no doubt that Islam helped to mitigate excessively rigorous asceticism by leading more liberal-minded Christians to question the advisability of imposing overstringent vows upon monks.

No such doubts assailed European minds before their contacts with Islamic civilization, both in Syria and in Spain. But with the growth of these contacts, the doubts thus engendered about the monastic establishment moved from a dormant stage to active criticism of the institution itself. It was not until the sixteenth century that differences in Christian doctrine came out into the open when the Council of Trent [2] prohibited the marriage of the clergy irrespective of grade, thus inspiring Luther to an act of open defiance in marrying a Catholic nun and in formulating the tenets of the Protestant religion.

Contemplative desert dwellers, gaining experience of that science of the soul so widely known to early Christians and later to the Moslems, contributed an essential element to both creeds, enriching them in a manner that some subsequent commentators have sought, without justification, to reduce in importance.

In his book *Monks and Monasteries of the Egyptian Deserts*, Otto F. A. Meinardus, the German Protestant pastor and Associate Professor at the American university in Cairo, says:

> Those who live in Egypt have a different understanding of the desert from those who live in Europe and America. In some parts of the world, the desert has become a testing-ground for nuclear energy, and of the variety of means of destruction, annually tried out, to prove their effectiveness in killing men. But here in Egypt the desert is a blessing of God, for it is the desert that has provided from time immemorial a testing-ground for the souls of men. . . . Go to the desert for food and drink, and you will describe it as a barren waste. Go to the desert to listen to the Voice of God and you will receive insight, understanding and wisdom. To be a desert, it has to be silent, it has to be apart, it has to be different. Thus, the desert conveys a picture, waterless and featureless, yet overwhelming to the senses.

At one time the total number of monks in Egypt may well have exceeded half a million; and in the twelfth century five different national communities were represented in the Wadi Natrun Monasteries. The influence of these international elements who came together to undergo voluntarily the harshness of life in desolate conditions, for the worship of God, must have been important in contemporary society. They still remind those of us who cherish spiritual values that nothing should be left undone to

[2] December 13, 1545 to December 3, 1563.

overcome the evils of materialism that are unfortunately gaining ground day by day.

Our author gives deserved prominence to Saint Anthony as a prototype of Coptic ascetism and of Christian monasticism in general. His impact has been truly international and intercultural, and though he belongs to the Alexandria Patriarchate, the Church has been greatly enriched by the example of this one solitary monk, whose biography was written by Athanasius the well-known theologian and Bishop of Alexandria. It was translated into Latin twenty years later and his life was studied even in far-away Gaul.

Meinardus adds, "St. Antony's motives, his struggle, his strength have been a theme in the studies of depth-psychologists, anthropologists, painters, and writers."

Other Coptic monks, who suffered martyrdom during the Roman Diocletian persecutions, include St. Warina, St. Victor (Buqtor), St. Felix, and St. Regula, who are the object of special veneration to this day in Switzerland.

When I was admitted to Cambridge University, I was allowed to join St. Catharine's College; named after a saint from Alexandria who was subjected to persecution and martyrdom. A monastery still exists in the Sinai Desert to commemorate her life. Though my college was small compared to Trinity College, the largest of them all, undergraduates, from Trinity, in the distant days, were asked to doff their mortarboards when passing by St. Catharine's College.

I came to know this symbolic detail only a few weeks ago in a letter from another college friend of mine, Group Captain Leslie Bonnet, playwright and man of letters, when he learned that my son Sherif had been awarded a research studentship in Electronics by Trinity College, and Bonnet hoped, as an incurable fellow optimist with Frank Marston, that such traditions might not be allowed to decay.

There is no doubt that the East is a cradle not only of religion but also of moral philosophies. Through contact with Eastern civilization, after the conquest of Spain and other parts of southern Europe, the West slowly left the darkness of the Middle Ages, and learned from the Arabs the legacy of ancient Greece, which they had faithfully guarded and enriched, notably in

Spain. But it is wrong to suppose that the writings of the Islamic thinkers consisted only of studies translated from the Greek. A generation of Muslim writers, Persian in large part, not only analyzed the treasures of the Greek heritage, but criticized them in detail, thereby providing profound and constructive alternatives to the original data and to the conclusions derived therefrom. Scholars of Persian origin, who have left an indelible mark on Islamic history, include such figures as the physician Razi (Rhases), the philosopher and physician Ibn Sina (Avicenna), and Al-Biruni, a profound and original scholar described by Bernard Lewis in his book *The Arabs in History* (1966) as physician, astronomer, mathematician, physicist, chemist, geographer, historian and, indeed, one of the greatest intellectual figures in medieval Islam.

Europe also drew upon sources of Arab culture from the caravans that reached the West through Constantinople, from areas occupied in the Arab East by the Crusaders, and, of course, from Spain and Sicily, where the standard of cultural development grew to remarkable heights. Dante himself is held by Western scholars to have been influenced by Arab culture; he had resided in Sicily during the reign of Frederick II, who was enamored of the beauty of Arab culture.

There is now a movement, initiated by the late Egyptian poet, Ahmad Shawqi, which tries to remind Arabs, by verse and prose, of the great achievements of Arab and Berber Spain. These were so impressive that the Arabs, who were, and still are, singularly free from racial animosity and intolerance, could not help noting a difference of social and cultural level between the southern Europeans, already in contact with Arab culture, and northern Europeans who were in greater need of such help. The tenth-century geographer Mas'udi, quoted by Lewis in the book already mentioned, says:

> The people of the North are those for whom the sun is distant from the Zenith . . . cold and damp prevail in those regions, and snow and ice follow one another, in endless succession. The warm humour is lacking among them, their bodies are large, their natures gross, their manner harsh, their understanding dull, and

their tongues heavy . . . their religious beliefs lack solidity . . . those of them who are farther off are the most subject to stupidity, grossness and brutishness.

An eleventh-century Qadi of Toledo is also quoted as having remarked of the "Northern Barbarians": "Their bellies are big, their colour pale, their hair long and lank. They lack keenness of understanding and clarity of intelligence and are overcome by ignorance and foolishness, blindness, and stupidity."

These unflattering comments may be exaggerated, but with their customary liberalism and toleration, the Arabs managed not only to produce remarkable achievements in Spain, where they made their longest and most enduring conquest, but also to win the hearty cooperation of the country's original inhabitants. They had a say in the government of their country and succeeded in setting up a Hispano-Arab community. This was enriched, through its contacts with the Arabs, by proficiency in agriculture, art, architecture, music, and literature.

It is now generally admitted that ancient Egypt was instrumental in bringing to Greece knowledge in the domains of sculpture, administration, engineering, medicine, astronomy, and literature. It was through this medium that refinements of civilization, moral and intellectual, reached Rome through its contact with Athens, and were eventually transmitted to Western Europe, during the Middle Ages and the Renaissance, thus stimulating the march of progress, and striking off the shackles of relative ignorance.

Egypt in fact has had a positive and fruitful share in the eventual buildup of European civilization, by her own knowledge as well as by the ethical background evolved in Pharaonic Egypt, Coptic Egypt, and Arab Egypt.

This interpretative review, short and incomplete as it is, shows that the Arabs, in spite of the gigantic upheavals that struck at the very basis of their history, were not only receptive of moral tenets, which became the cornerstone of their civilization, but were eager to transfer the benefits of this civilization to other lands, including, of course, to the peoples of the West.

The part played by Central Asian civilization, in this respect and many others, is amazing for its magnitude; but since this has been given careful consideration by Saiyid Idries Shah, in my commentary I have stressed the Arab and Egyptian world to which I belong.

The far-reaching advances in war and peace, which were attained by the West from the beginning of the sixteenth century, and which have reached, at the present time, the zenith of their progress, coincided with the decline in the material and cultural possibilities of the Arab world and other Eastern countries. These patent discrepancies encouraged Western ambitions, in the first place, to gain a commercial footing in Arab areas, first by skillful diplomacy and then by acquiring judicial privileges (called the Capitulations) from the Ottoman powers, which exercised a dwindling sovereignty over these areas. Eventually these areas came under colonial rule, through the expansion of the Western Powers (more especially Great Britain, France, and Italy)—a state of affairs that came to an end after World War II.

Saiyid Idries Shah has shown—and I warmly agree—that with the passing of the colonial period, Eastern literature, in relation particularly to moral principles, has again become valued for the merit of its content and is no longer treated as an interesting product of a dead culture.

It is a happy augury for advocates of Eastern ethics that the work of Idries Shah should have been welcomed by many scholars and men of letters. Misgivings about Sufi and Eastern traditions have been corrected and the importance of these traditions has been recognized.

One essential condition for propagating spiritual ideas is that they should be seen to emanate from an environment in which they prevail. If we Arabs, and Orientals as a whole, wish to convince the world of the value of our ideas, we must ensure that an atmosphere of service lies at the basis of our mutual relations. In default of this, how can we call upon others to give us their moral support when we are incapable of helping ourselves? Logically speaking, a minimum official *entente* should have persuaded Arabs to found a Common Market, comparable with that of Western Europe, which aims at attaining complete political unity on the full realization of this great economic project.

A beginning has been made in the shape of the important

Federation of Arab Republics with Libya and Syria, comprising a population of forty-two millions, and when augmented by the almost certain adhesion of the Sudan, totaling more that half of the population of all the Arab States combined.

Consolidated as it would be by spiritual values, and aided by our heritage of inspiration, there is little doubt that it could provide a radical change in the outlook of the West on the East and of the latter on the former.

The salient principle that Egypt offers the world, as a nation composed of a Muslim majority and a considerable Christian minority, is that these two elements of the population live in perfect amity, and present an exemplar of mutual toleration that is a source of pride to followers of both religions.

This complete absence of religious intolerance has flowed from the innermost conscience of a people who are intent to defeat any attempt to foment strife on this account. Foreign observers do not hide their admiration at the sight of pious Muslims lighting candles at churches and frequenting these places of worship on many occasions.

On the death of my late brother, Makram Ebeid Pasha, on June 5, 1961, President Anwar el Saadat, known to be a devout Muslim, entered St. Mark's Coptic Church in Cairo, where the funerary service was held, and gave a long and eloquent eulogy of my brother's life as a combatant for national independence.

Current problems have not deterred the expert elite, which is exceedingly large, from undertaking its task of widespread reform and regeneration, in which Sufi thought could play a large, perhaps decisive, part. Our four universities, and the immense number of secondary institutions, produce annually a great many graduates in all spheres of learning, and they are so numerous that Egypt can afford to delegate thousands of them to the Arab world and Africa, as welcome experts in scientific and cultural fields.

The Egyptian has learned to emigrate. This is a most unexpected peculiarity in a country where people could not be moved from their birthplaces. . . . It is estimated that there are at least one hundred thousand Egyptians now living abroad either as emigrants or experts. Compared with the forty "effendis" chosen by Muhammad Ali to make the "adventurous" trip from Alexandria to Marseilles, this is indeed a pattern of the strides made by Egyptian initiative since then.

One other channel of communication to foreign eyes, ears, and minds is of course tourism. As the Egyptian Minister of Tourism has said, "We have sun, sand and water and a civilization seven thousand years old." This surely is enough to attract tourists from the whole world, who should logically come in even greater numbers.

We Orientals are hospitable to strangers, but are rather diffident about translating this hospitality into acquaintanceship with them, even if we know their languages. This is a barrier that we should endeavor to remove if we desire to abide by the Egyptian prime minister's advice that these tourists should be our ambassadors in foreign lands.

I wish to mention, in proof of this, an incident that conveyed to me, as a tourist, an excellent impression of Austrian character. When I was in Vienna, some years ago, I asked a passerby to guide me to well-known sites of the city. The conversation was in French, which my interlocutor happily knew. He indicated to me the locations of these places, but did not stop at that. He offered to give me explanations of their characteristics, which I thankfully accepted, thinking that he was a professional guide, a supposition that was reinforced by his very simple dress. When I offered him his fee on the completion of the visit, he politely refused it by telling me that he did this merely as a service to a foreigner and that he occupied the post of professor at the Faculty of Arts. I thought that this attitude was more effective than hundreds of advertisements portraying the attractions of the land to which this professor belonged. This gentleman became Austria's ambassador of hospitality and goodwill, not only to my acquaintances, but of course to myself!

The East had, indeed, instilled wisdom and moral and religious precepts into Western minds in their hour of need. It is high time now to employ every conceivable means, not only in the East but everywhere else, to implement the idea that just as the Dark Ages in Europe were ended by the Eastern contribution to civilization, so the need is even greater now for the West to cultivate the wisdom of the East, abandon materialism, and forswear force as an instrument of policy.

There is evidently no better means to dissuade the unjust from pursuing a policy of injustice than by setting the example of our passion for civilization and freedom, cemented as they are by our traditional attachment to service—as exemplified by Sufism and other divine commandments—and generously rendered to ourselves and to others. Then and then alone can there be any hope for this world of ours.

I believe that the Sufi doctrine's primary object, as exposed by the Saiyid, is to solve problems of conduct by recourse to suitable means of treatment. This ranges from the incomparable subtleties known only to Sufi students of psychology and sociology, from their many-sided researches in the spheres of science and literature, to folklore, art, and proverbs, and to such anecdotes as those of Mulla Nasreddin, which run deeper than their laugh-provoking surfaces. Wisdom, in all that this expression conveys to mankind, possesses profound significance and can produce far-reaching results.

These are some of the reasons that I believe, more and more strongly, that a movement with such stupendous possibilities as those contained in Sufi studies should not be confined but should break out into the farthest corners of the world, and should form the nucleus for universal action, and, under one name or another, should be adopted by men of all creeds and nationalities.

First among those who should come forward in support of this initiative would be reasonable-minded Christians of all denominations, who ought to welcome an alliance with all who appeal to human conscience for a better world. They will be inspired by many sources, including the desert monasticism of Egypt, which has ever been a faithful guide to spiritual values.

Monks may now be few in number, but the stringent tests for their selection, the conditions of their admission, qualify them for the confidence of all believers because of their continuous communion with God and their surrender to His will. Many of the theologians and leaders of religious thought, venerated by history, have been recruited from the ranks of monks. The Coptic Pope, Kyrillos VI, who died recently, was before his elevation to the papal throne a simple monk; and his successor has no other wealth but his faith and austere way of living.

It is now for the East to press for a more determined acceptance of its moral responsibility and to act upon the conviction that one day idealism will be an integral part of people's lives. Once the East helped in terminating the stagnation of life in the Dark Ages. It is now for the East and all men of goodwill to help in arresting the spiritual decline of materially advanced countries.

The roads trodden by Islam and Christianity, Sufism, and monasticism toward this goal may differ in form. One community may move with the world, while another may pray for it in seclusion. But there can be no doubt that, by their fundamental faith in God, which is their common heritage, they will converge into one common front of spiritual endeavor destined to render service to all.

XXI

ISLAM, SUFISM,
AND
TOLERANCE
by
Professor Ahmed Emin Yalman

Idries Shah is spreading the light of Sufism in a foolish world, where fanaticism, hypocrisy, hatred, and intolerance still prevail, in spite of the general advances in material civilization. For long I knew him only by name. Now that I have been able to read several of his books and to learn the trend of his varied activities, I am glad to discover in him a worker in a field that is too often neglected.

Religion in its ideal sense must mean a will to climb above material appetites and an urge toward lofty aims, through self-denial, love, charity, and virtue, to please God. The obvious thing for those engaged in this effort is to love each other, to cooperate for the sake of the common aim, and to show tolerance toward each other.

Unfortunately, religions so often become vehicles of fanaticism, lust for influence, power, and self-interest that their true purpose is forgotten. The great merit of Sufism is that it lays stress upon this purpose, and attacks such evils as hypocrisy and intolerance.

From this point of view, Idries Shah emerges as a defender of the true spirit of religion. To Muslims it is gratifying that he is a direct descendant of the Prophet and that he is facing his task in this capacity.

THE PATH OF THE PROPHET

The Prophet Mohammed must rank among the greatest revolutionaries in history. To him religion meant honesty, charity, cleanliness in every sense, wisdom, progress, conformity to changing conditions, and the supremacy of free reason. The conditions that he created in a primitive and retarded environment promoted rapid development and quick absorption of the treasures of science, law, and experience created by the Roman and Greek civilizations. The dynamism thus acquired reached over to the northern frontier of Spain to knock at the door of Europe, then slumbering in the dark decline of the Middle Ages.

Through shortcomings of human nature, this splendid advance did not continue; various abuses and conflicts broke out. It was Sufism that provided a refuge in the days when the "gate of free reasoning was pretended to be closed," when any sort of criticism of the obscurantism of the orthodox was silenced by violence.

TURKEY AS A BATTLEFIELD

Turkey provided a crucial field for the contest between orthodox fanaticism and the creative forces of Sufism. Hadji Bektash was one of the main organizers of the Turkish system of thought and administration during the rise of the Ottoman Empire. The system discouraged fanaticism and hypocrisy, set a high ethical standard, instituted a system of selection of the fittest, and insisted on a high conception of duty, order, and justice. The door was open to any man of merit; but a strict and successful professional training was essential.

When the downfall and dismemberment of the Ottoman Empire started in the seventeenth century, fanaticism triumphed. The Sufi orders were persecuted and obliged to go underground. Then started a continuous contest between the patriotic Young Turks who opposed fanaticism and the would-be heirs of the "Sick Man of Europe" as Turkey was then called.

SECULARISM THE HOPE

After the Revolution of the Young Turks in 1908, Turkish patriots came to the conclusion that the secularism practiced in their home countries by the imperialistic powers, but carefully denied to the nations under their domination, was the only conceivable course to follow. Ziya Gökalp, professor of sociology at Istanbul University and a member of the Central Board of the influential Union and Progress Party, took advantage of World War I to introduce a gradual secularism. He published a weekly religious paper to promote the following idea:

> Those who like to devote their entire life and interest to worship God and prepare for the afterlife are free to do so, but they should not stay in our way, when we try to progress and to grant rights to our women and to use our reason in connection with our rational beliefs.

After the War of Independence in Turkey, Kemal Atatürk finally introduced secularism, and the caliphate was suppressed to avoid duality of authority in the country. Religious seminaries, and all the varied religious orders including those of Mevlana and Hadji Bektaşh, were closed down. This system, although largely avoiding dogmatic interference in politics and education, made religion the monopoly of orthodox Sunni theologians. At the same time religious instruction went underground and lost quality, so that religion fell under the absolute influence of what Ziya Gökalp called the "Black Power."

Happily the Mevlevi and Bektaşhi organizations are now again treated with toleration.

"THE CANNIBALS OF THE SOUL"

I should like to relate an unusual experience I had while studying sociology and history at Columbia University in New York (1910–1914).

I attended, as a sideline, some courses at the new School of Journalism and found, to my agreeable surprise, that Dr. Talcott Williams, the first director, had been born in Mardin, Turkey, as a son of a missionary and had lived there the first sixteen years of his life. He told me that he had a debt to pay to his country of birth and that he would do it by putting me in close contact with personalities and institutions in America, an opportunity not usually available to a foreign student. In this connection, he took me, early in 1914, to the Student Volunteer Convention in Kansas City, Missouri, which had been organized to recruit educational and medical missionaries among young students.

I found a most fanatical spirit at the convention. The maps of the countries inhabited by Muslims were painted black, and in speeches delivered in a crusading tone students were urged to have a hunger for souls, especially Muslim ones, without paying any attention to the pain inflicted on the families of those converted. The spirit of hostility against Islam was unbelievably violent. When I was asked by Dr. Williams and by others what I thought about the gathering, I said: "I kept shuddering, I felt myself in the presence of barbarous cannibals of souls."

About thirty years after this experience the Secretary-General of the Congressional Board in Boston, which managed missionary schools and hospitals in Turkey, came to Istanbul with the determination to close them all because they failed to convert Muslim Turks. The manager of the Bible House suggested to him that he consult a few Turks, before acting. Since I was on his list, he came to see me and asked me what I thought about it. I gave him the following reply: "It is your problem. I have no opinion to offer you, but I should like to tell you a story. Do whatever you like after listening to it."

Then I told him the story of Ohannes Ferid, a young Armenian inhabitant of Aintep, southern Turkey, who was anxious to obtain enlightenment and asked Munif Effendi (later Munif Pasha, Secretary of Education) whether he could give him some guidance. Munif answered that he was sorry not to have any time himself, but recommended to him that he go and see Hasirci Hodja, a prominent teacher at the local religious seminary. Ohannes Ferid was thrilled by the wise guidance he received and told his teacher that, in comparison with the Armenian priests, he found him so superior that he had decided to become a Muslim.

Hasirci Hodja replied: "If you do that, I will never allow you to kiss my hand as your teacher. If you like to follow a straight path, you can do it in your own religion. You are not allowed to inflict pain on those who love you by becoming a convert."

The Secretary-General, one of the cannibals of souls whom I had seen in Kansas City, did not say a word, but the valuable schools and hospitals have continued to exist in Turkey for twenty-five years.

THE NEED OF A NEW DEPARTURE

We are facing materialistic tendencies in the youth of the world; they seem to ignore the true function of religions. In this situation, all religions should forget old rivalries and hatreds and cooperate to safeguard religious enthusiasm as a source of good against evil and as a prop of civilization.

In this connection, I remember the following words I heard in 1953 from Dr. Jean Nussbaum, Secretary-General of the European branch of the League for the Defense of Religious Liberty:

> Up to recently, we were accustomed to consider Islam as the enemy of religious liberty and tolerance. Now we must admit with shame that the contrary is true. Islam is the only religion exercising total tolerance and respect for other religions. The proof of it is plain. All sorts of non-Muslim religious communities have survived and prospered in Muslim countries, while no single Muslim was allowed in Spain and some other Christian countries to survive.

This makes it clear that any new era of religious peace and tolerance calls for Muslim leadership. I am of the opinion that Idries Shah has already undertaken this line of activity with considerable success.

XXII

SHAH:
KNOWLEDGE, TECHNIQUE,
AND
INFLUENCE
by
Professor M. Y. Shawarbi

Toward the end of 1971, a gathering of scientists assembled to see a series of films about science. Their motive was to "assess what is new for physics, chemistry and biology." [1] The program of films included Professor Bernal's *Water;* Sir William Bragg's *Faraday; Ion-Dipole Dynamics* by the NASA (American space authority) Film Unit; and the award-winning educational space-satire *The Dermis Probe.*

On the face of it, there is nothing remarkable about a number of modern Western scientists studying developments in science in London. What is, however, noteworthy is that *The Dermis Probe* (1970), an adaptation of a thirteenth-century work by the

---

[1] "Science Research by Cinema," presented by the Director, London University Audio-Visual Centre.

Sufi poet Rumi, was written by Idries Shah, who has specialized for years in transposing ancient Eastern thought into contemporary teaching frameworks.

Take another instance: a sociologist responsible for recruiting brains with unusual capacities for nonlinear thinking, in a filmed interview,[2] revealed that the sources he used in his work with the Rand Corporation "think-tank" (probably the most advanced center of space-age thought in the United States) were the works of Idries Shah, who had in several important books, superficially of mainly entertainment value, extrapolated materials from, among other sources, the Koran.

These instances could be multiplied; but my purpose in choosing them is to contrast them with an opinion, recorded a little over a decade ago, in a standard work on the Middle East, where it is held that such an occurrence as I have just described is a complete impossibility:

> The Islamic poets are no more than lyrical sensualists, and neither the Sufi texts nor the Quran, the chief literary work of Islam, provide any foundation for an intrinsically oriented evaluation of the problems of the modern world.[3]

Moreover as lately as 1961 there was published in Britain (and it was still to be bought in 1970) a book containing the statement: "The Arabs are the greatest liars and deceivers on earth. Their tongues know not the truth."[4]

This kind of thing, if it is to be taken as typical of the literary intake of people in England, might not be regarded as propitious for the prospects of an Eastern writer, especially one of aristocratic Arabian extraction.

In 1960, stressing the archaic nature of the thinking of the Middle East and its consequently supposed inability to respond to the challenges of a modern world, an Orientalist could claim that the East had lost the initiative over four centuries be-

---

[2] J. Kermisch, *The Dreamwalkers*, documentary transmitted on BBC-2, December 29, 1970. See also *The Guardian* (London), November 26, 1970.

[3] Georges Ketman, *The Middle East in Transition* (London, 1958), p. 483.

[4] S. A. Handford, trans., *Fables of Aesop* (London: Penguin, 1954, 1956, 1961), p. 156.

fore: "The most striking feature of the intellectual history of the century 1450–1550 is that during this period the West at last caught up with and overtook Islam." [5]

Less than a decade later, in 1969, Imam el-Arifin was able to show, quoting from such sources as the journal *New Society*, something of the revolution that Shah's work had caused in those few years.

> The result of Idries Shah's writings can only be described in superlatives. Every single one of his books published in English (and not all of them on Sufism), as if by some magic spell, rapidly became accepted as a significant work in the field with which he dealt. Poets, scientists, professors of physics and of literature, anthropologists, each in his own area, claimed that here was something of undoubted value.

> Orientalists and other scholars, who had until then regarded the study of Sufism as their peculiar preserve, were amazed to find that Idries Shah's books, unlike those of the "specialists," were being reviewed with enthusiasm in the mass-circulation press. But this was not all. Solemnly serious sociological journals averred that this material, formerly supposed to belong to a vanishing cult, was of prime importance in solving current human problems in advanced societies. In book after book, Idries Shah revealed Sufic facets and theories which were seized upon by the most unlikely variety of readers, both specialist and otherwise, as being of significance to social, scientific, and other fields today. [6]

By the spring of 1970, *The American Scholar*,[7] while noting that initial reactions to Shah's work had been confused, had registered the spread of the new knowledge: "At first it was poets and writers who tended to recognize its importance, but now its influence is spreading where long overdue—among scientists, psychiatrists, biologists and so on." Less than a year later, the British Broadcasting Corporation had contracted to use instructional tales by Idries Shah in its educational programs; American

---

[5] J. J. Saunders, ed., *The Muslim World on the Eve of Europe's Expansion* (Englewood Cliffs, N.J.: Prentice-Hall, 1966), p. 129.

[6] Imam el-Arifin Sheikh Imdad Hussein el-Qadiri, introductory essay to Johnson Pasha, trans., Mahmud Shabistari's *The Secret Garden* (London, 1969), pp. 15–16.

[7] *The American Scholar*, Vol. 39, No. 2, p. 330.

companies had snapped up the paperback rights in all his works, he was listed in *Two Thousand Men of Achievement*—and Orientalists were vieing with one another to write tributes to his work in a celebratory volume.

The spread of Shah's ideas and their application to almost every area of study and literature are accelerating rather than slowing down. His first fifteen years of work are worthy of examination, both in their internal pattern and also in the context of the revolution in thought that seems likely to increase the influence of ancient Eastern knowledge upon East and West.

There are several strands that seem worth viewing individually if we are to understand the phenomenon of Shah's emergence as a "maker of the modern mind." In the first place, as Professor T. P. O'Neill notes, a mind of this caliber does not exist in a vacuum, being rather the product of an environment and at the same time able to exercise leadership over it:

> Makers of the modern mind, then, are men who ride the intellectual tide of their time. They accept the age's fundamental assumptions, protest against what it condemns, promise what it most desires. They articulate the age's thoughts and desires. They are nevertheless important figures in history. For the world is never the same after them that it was before. They act as foci for many ideas which without them would not be combined as strong forces for change in history. They can be likened to a glass which focuses the otherwise harmless, scattered rays of the sun to produce a single burning beam . . . the world is changed because of them.[8]

The reception that Shah's work has received in the East well illustrates the character of a "role in search of an actor," which has recently become a much-quoted phrase. Arab literary men have likened him to al-Ghazzali and to Jamaluddin al-Afghani: praise indeed whose importance the Western reader may judge if he realizes that these names are as important to the East as Rousseau and St. Augustine are to the West. Shah's penetrating philosophy of action, conveyed in the relevant passages in his *Reflections* and *Caravan of Dreams*, recalls the personality and

[8] T. P. O'Neill, Ph.D., *Makers of the Modern Mind* (Milwaukee, 1949), p. 369.

the "role of destiny" passages in Miles Copeland's book, when he talks about Gamal Abdul-Nasser:

> His exceptional self-confidence, which is strongly communicated to anyone who meets him, arises from his belief that, like these prototypes, he is merely one who happens to fill the "role in search of an actor" as he explains it in his *Philosophy of the Revolution*.[9]

I reserve, for this stage in my chapter, the information that I have known Idries Shah and his family for nearly a quarter of a century; and I do feel that such personal knowledge helps in studying both the synthesizing mind that he brings to his work and the background that led to the achievements now being discussed.

Almost since his childhood, Shah has made it his task to study certain factors of human life and thought that are normally seen only piecemeal. While most scholars specialize either in the Arab or the non-Arab sides of Islam, he has always been fascinated by the interaction of the two; while Western scholars are normally less than at ease in the East, he is very much at home in the West. His analyses of the Orientalists' view of the East, instead of being influenced by it, as are so many Eastern thinkers, have been objective, descriptive, and highly perceptive.[10]

He embarked on a twelve-year program of study of the thinking patterns of Asia and Africa, which resulted in two books: *Oriental Magic* and *Destination Mecca*, both worthy of close attention.

Originally entitled *Considerations in Eastern and African Minority Beliefs*, the comprehensive survey of thought and practice, *Oriental Magic*, was published in London and Paris in 1956 and 1957, and has been in continuous demand ever since. It combines scholarly research at the British Museum and elsewhere with periods of fieldwork carried out in Asia and Africa. Having originally encouraged Shah in the production of this extensive work, Professor Louis Marin, head of the School of Anthropology

---

[9] Miles Copeland, *The Game of Nations* (London, 1970 ed.), p. 110.

[10] See Shah, *Special Problems in the Study of Sufi Ideas* (account of his Sussex University Seminar) (1st ed.; London, 1966), *passim*.

at the University of Paris, contributed an enthusiastic foreword, calling the book "a real contribution to knowledge." In this judgment he foreshadowed the wide public and scientific welcome that was to follow all of Shah's later writings. It is interesting to note that the sober scientific journal *Nature*, favorable notice in which is one of the coveted accolades in the learned world, welcomed the book. Shah's theme was that there is evidence of a possibility that human faculties higher than those ordinarily admitted are capable of development.[11] "A point of view" said *Nature*, significantly, "of which too little has been heard in the past." Today throughout the world, scientific research, both private and supported by governments, is in full swing in that direction.[12]

Oriental Magic, in spite of its popular title and sponsorship by a general publishing house, claimed serious scholarly attention, as did its successor dealing with Western esoteric thought—*The Secret Lore* (1957), a bibliographical companion volume.[13] But the converse was also true—in spite of its serious content and intent, this book claimed the applause of such literary journals as *Time and Tide* ("heaped with jewels"), the *Times Literary Supplement* ("wealth of illustrative matter"), and the interreligious periodical *Hibbert Journal*, which called it "fascinating and illuminating." This acceptance in the specialist and general press was to be the invariable hallmark of Shah's subsequent work. He had, it seemed, caught the mood and devised the method of providing important materials in a manner that was acceptable to both "worlds." *Oriental Magic* is difficult to analyze. It has an extraordinary range and content, and is a conspectus of belief with an encyclopedic quality, its conciseness and accuracy are

[11] Fourteen years later (in 1971) the famous author Colin Wilson unaccountably came in for a great deal of literary derision for postulating a similar capacity—called by him "Faculty X." Perhaps the acceptance of an unfamiliar idea still owes more to its mode of presentation than our conceit will admit.

[12] E.g., Professor Claudio Naranjo, *The Unfolding of Man*, Stanford Research Institute, March, 1969, for the United States Office of Education—a survey of over one hundred and fifty educational methods, including Sufic thought. The Esalen Institute has released tape recordings made by Dr. Naranjo on Sufi materials for psychological study.

[13] Its original title, *Some Materials on European Minority-Belief Literature*, lies buried by the exigencies of commercial publishing practice.

married to great readability. It covers a period ranging from thousands of years before Christ to the present day.

Destination Mecca [14] was also first published in 1957. It was presented as a book of travel and adventure in the Middle East, and was the product of years of study and residence in the Persian, Turkic, and Arabic cultures of the area. Its public appeal was immediately recognized in its adoption by the Travel Book Club; and on his return to Britain, Shah was interviewed on television by Richard Attenborough. He spoke on and showed film of the holy cities of Arabia, and gave his views on an area which was at that time of the greatest international interest.

This book, which features experiences with princes and peasants, with sorcerers and guerrillas, in jungles and palaces, is compulsive reading. Like the other Shah works, it quickly established itself as an authoritative source of academic material. It figures, indeed, in the Saudi Arabian documentation in the Human Relations Area Files associated with Yale University, and is sponsored, since 1959, by no fewer than sixteen other universities, alongside such authoritative sources as *The Encyclopaedia of Islam*, the *Encyclopaedia Britannica*, and the *Yearbook* of the United Nations.[15] Twelve years after its first publication this book continued to earn plaudits, such as this one, from the *Times Literary Supplement:*

> Like his father, Sardar Ikbal Ali Shah, Sayed Idries Shah has done much to explain the world of Islam to Westerners, and, in particular, to promote the study of Sufi philosophy among English-speaking people. Both are great travellers, with the knack of penetrating into places, and meeting personalities, often entirely inaccessible to other writers. . . . His lively observation and his powers of description make this "personally conducted tour" of the Middle East as exciting as a good novel, especially as the author's Afghan origins and distinguished lineage secured him access to quarters which no European traveller could hope to reach. Much of what he writes illuminates factors of permanent importance in the Middle East: and no one can read this book

[14] Many reprints and editions; the latest (illustrated) edition: London, 1971.

[15] G. A. Lipsky, *et al., Saudi Arabia: Its People, Its Society, Its Culture,* "Survey of World Cultures" series (New Haven, 1959).

without carrying away a lasting impression of the vigour and vitality of Islamic culture . . .[16]

Shah's books on the East, and on little-known beliefs, started to appear at a time when sociological and psychological interest was turning toward a reexamination of traditional forms of thinking, and when the obvious limitations in the pedestrian work of a few uninspired scholars were becoming more clearly visible to the public. His Oriental works incurred their share of criticism in some circles; but oddly enough this criticism was far milder than the strictures that many conventional scholars reserve for one another. One has only to read the viciously patronizing onslaughts on professionals by professionals in this field to realize that Shah has escaped lightly indeed.

His work on Western esoteric thought and its relevance to that of the East was welcomed by students of the behavioral sciences for its freedom from propaganda and bias, maintaining as it does an objectivity that much literature on supernatural beliefs and practices still tends to lack.

Concurrently, Shah did what he calls "Western fieldwork." One part of this was to study filmmaking, from the production floor upward, to determine whether it was a suitable vehicle for the communication of traditional ideas. The fruit of this study was the development, in conjunction with the eminent film producer Richard Williams, of the award-winning *The Dermis Probe*, and to set in motion the production of a multimillion-dollar version of *Mulla Nasreddin*, in full-color animation, which involved five years of training for the production staff alone before a single foot was shot.

Shah's Western activities, developed while dividing his time between East and West, show a balanced interest in the cultures and institutions of both worlds. His position in the Eastern world has already been noticed; in the West he also has a distinct place of his own.* He is prominent in humanitarian causes; he is an active member of many learned societies and institutions. He pioneers research in electronics; some very advanced discoveries in the field of negative ionization are associated with his name.

[16] *Times Literary Supplement* (London), June 19, 1969.
* See Note A at the end of this chapter.

These activities in the realm of what are sometimes called "practical affairs" surprise some Western observers who think that a man who expounds Sufi philosophy and practice with such distinction should never leave his ivory tower. Such an assumption betrays ignorance of the tradition of participation in contemporary affairs side by side with cultural activities that is inherent in Shah's background. In Islamic society, the Prophetic tradition is paramount: Mohammed himself was a prosperous merchant. Many of the ancient Sufis, Shah's ideological forebears, encouraged mundane achievements as an index of the development of human capacity on higher levels.[17] This long-established practice of achieving objectively measurable excellence, characteristic of the family of Idries Shah, has been discussed by William Foster [18] and is supported by other evidence.

For example, in the late 1960s, Shah's father, my old and most respected friend the Sirdar Ikbal Ali Shah, died.[19] At that time, though partially retired, he was still exercising official responsibility for Indian cultural connections with the enormous territory of West Asia and North Africa, as Council Professor appointed by the Indian Council for Cultural Relations. In accordance with custom, he designated Idries as heir to the wide-ranging connections, official, learned, and social, which he had acquired over half a century as an outstanding personality of the East. With this heritage behind him, Idries Shah began to prepare more philosophical and social materials for publication.

He had effectively started his Sufi exposition with *The Sufis*, which Robert Graves had encouraged him to write. Fittingly enough, the first reference to the book that can be traced is its enthusiastic recognition in the official publication *Afghanistan News*.[20] In other places it was a revelation.* Tracing historical, literary, organizational, and psychological connections between East and West over many centuries, it covered an extensive field.

---

[17] E.g., Sahl commenting on a recluse: "He has established himself upon a mountain/So he has no work to do./A man should be in the market-place/While still working with true Reality." (Cited in *The Way of the Sufi*, Jonathan Cape, 1968, p. 226).

[18] "The Family of Hashim," *Contemporary Review* (May, 1960).

[19] *The Times* (London), No. 57,712, November 8, 1969.

[20] Vol. 7, No. 81 (May, 1964).

* See Note B at the end of this chapter.

The Listener (October 29, 1964) echoed many commentators: "The Sufis must be the biggest society of sensible men there has ever been on earth."

Within a year of its first publication, the book figured in an honours examination at Oxford. It encountered some criticism on the pretext that it was drawing Sufi thought from its traditional place among academic Oriental studies. The difficulty that some rigidly orthodox scholars found in adjusting themselves to the realization that Sufism has a practical, and not merely an academic, content was explained by Shah in an address to graduates at Sussex University the following year:

> What I had done was to collect the results of whole lifetimes of other people's academic research, often buried in monographs and seldom-read books, always by respected Orientalists and specialists. . . . It was too rich a mixture for some readers. And yet many of them should have been more familiar than I was with work already done in their own fields.[21]

There is no doubt that this remarkable book set in train a rapid appreciation of the importance and value of Sufi traditions and learning systems to the West and to all developed countries as well as to the East. This appreciation was encouraged by a number of factors. Literary critics welcomed the two collections of Mulla Nasreddin tales [22] centering on the "Oriental Everyman" figure who illustrates human thinking in all its phases. This helped to establish both Nasreddin (known as Goha in Arab countries) and Idries Shah in the literary world.

The Nasreddin joke-books, dealing with a character long thought to be nothing but a buffoon, were now revealed as an ancient psychological and scientific instructional instrument.[23]

---

[21] Idries Shah, *Special Problems in the Study of Sufi Ideas* (2d ed.; London, 1968), p. 9.

[22] Published in Great Britain by Jonathan Cape; in the United States by Simon & Schuster, by Dutton Paperbacks (1971, 1972), and by Penguin (1972).

[23] Coral Gables Conference on High-Energy Physics, University of Miami (San Francisco and London: W. H. Freeman, 1965); R. Simac, "In a Naqshbandi Circle," *Hibbert Journal*, Vol. 65, No. 258 (Spring 1967).

They marked a further stage in the recovery of formerly unknown or forgotten materials.[24]

The choice (on the BBC "The Critics" program) of two
of Shah's books (*Reflections* and *The Way of the Sufi*) as "Outstanding Books of the Year" created a popular demand for them
that has continued to accelerate.

In comparative religion and metaphysics, the release of over
five hundred "teaching stories," in *Tales of the Dervishes* (1967),
Wisdom of the Idiots (1971), and several other books was recognized in religious and philosophical journals as elucidating a
hitherto very imperfectly known system of teaching. Further,
the popular mass-circulation *Evening News* of London told its
four million readers that here was a "Multi-IQ" system. Thus one
and the same book may be read by a housewife, may figure on
the list of a university course in sociology, and may be cited in
an encyclopedia as a reference work.

Several important men of letters have undoubtedly played a
significant part in contributing to a wide recognition of the value
of Shah's work. Robert Graves (*The Poor Boy Who Followed
His Star*, 1968), Doris Lessing (*The Four-Gated City*, 1969),
and Alan Sillitoe (*The Death of William Posters*, 1965, 1969)
have all made use of stories or extracts from his books. The title
story of *The Poor Boy* was, in fact, an adaptation of a single tale
that appeared as one of the eighty pieces in Shah's *Tales of the
Dervishes*.

Such recognition in the literary world was not confined to
the West. The eminent Syrian man of letters, Dr. Zeki el-Mahassini hailed Shah on behalf of the Arab world in an article published in the influential cultural journal *Asda'* of Beirut. As one
of the foremost Arabic poets, his dedication of an ode (*Qasidah*)
to Idries Shah marked a milestone in inter-Oriental letters.

Shah's *The Book of the Book* (1969, 2d ed., 1970) was some-

---

[24] The Naqshbandi *Silsilah* (chain-of-transmission school) is tradition-
ally associated with Shah's family. His great-grandfather, Nawab Moham-
med-Ali Shah, is buried in the Delhi shrine of Khwaja (Master) Baqi-Billah.
In Sufism, the Naqshbandi is "probably the earliest of all mystic *silsilahs*"
(Emeritus Professor M. Habib, of Aligarh, in his Foreword to Saiyid A. A.
Rizvi, *Muslim Revivalist Movements* (Agra, 1965), p. ix.

thing wholly novel in form. Its nature can best be summarized in these review extracts:

> Contains a two and a bit line preface, nine partially printed pages and approximately two hundred and sixty-three pages which are totally blank. . . . By his very concept Idries Shah makes a reviewer's job impertinent and superfluous. . . . Perhaps we have laboured too long under the misapprehension that there is a pre-existent truth and that the art of communication lies in finding the technique to trap it.[25]

The tale contained in the first few pages of *The Book of the Book* explains how people judge things only by appearances, and become indignant when the appearance proves to be fallacious. *The Sunday Telegraph* (March 15, 1970), realizing this, says: "Actually it is—among other things—an extraordinary psychological test, in that it predicts the complete range of possible responses to itself."

Such explanations did not stop one or two reviewers from reacting violently. A thick book, they felt, refusing to read it, *must* contain printing on every page. In fact humor of this kind, allied to astonishing expertise in projection, promotion, and timing, is worthy of the Sufi tradition.

Examination of Shah's work shows that he is trying to supply materials of value to the audience that is receiving them. He is not trying to reproduce textually chapter and verse of Sufi materials in a written form originally designed for the very different public of ancient times.

In this connection a significant point was his direction of attention to the fact that Sufi literature contains what a modern technologist would call a "fail-safe" type of mechanism. Sufi ideas are conveyed in accordance with the needs of the community to which they are directed, independently of the personal equation of the person conveying them. This is what the Sufi thinkers call the dictum of *Zaman, Makan, and Ikhwan*—the right time, right place, and right audience or participants.

Study of the great Sufi authors proves that they belie the

[25] *The Inquirer*, February 21, 1970.

patronizing theory of outside observers, symptomatic only of "judging others by oneself," that a Sufi is merely reacting against society, or preaching a personal, inner compulsion. A Sufi teaches only because there is need for his teaching.[26]

A study of Shah's works reveals that they consist of literature and applied philosophy, designed to produce a specific effect. They are not mere scholasticism; they are sources of inspiration, although an outward observer may fail to discover it.

Because of this characteristic, the present chapter cannot replace a study of the books themselves, though it may serve to highlight some of their content. But to illustrate some of the riches they offer, it is only necessary to look at, say, the first hundred pages of Shah's sixteenth book, *The Magic Monastery* (1972). This is a collection of over a hundred and fifty tales and dialogues.

These pages bring home to the reader what he no doubt already knows, but at the same time tends to ignore: that people seeking mere knowledge often assume that there is some secret that can be confided to them, something that they can acquire, as one takes possession of a material object. Yet experience shows that it is the development of understanding that converts ignorance into knowledge, and that *that* is the inner truth of the matter. The passage "Service" (p. 94) underlines this in a manner difficult to forget.

One of the most beguiling characteristics of the collection is the steady presentation of those aspects of human thought and behavior that most societies ignore, or recognize under misleading names, but never put in true perspective. Worth reading again and again, is the tale called "Six Lives in One," which ends with this implacable truth: "Now that you know that it is not the experiences that you *want*, but the ones which you *need* which are significant—you can perhaps start to learn" (pp. 90 f).

The essential neuroticism of many self-chosen seekers and the futility of their posturings in an ineffectual "search after truth" is brilliantly portrayed in the recital attributed to Ramida (p. 74).

[26] Perhaps one of the first recognitions of this fact by a modern scholar is to be found in Robert Cecil's recent book *Cultural Imperialism* (London, 1971).

In "Kindness" (p. 63) the profound teaching that is found in the story of Moses and Khidr in the Koran, and in "The Horseman and the Snake" in Rumi [27] finds very powerful expression. This is summed up in the memorable dictum: The well-intentioned man may give away sweetmeats; the physician bestows curative medicine, whether people think the medicine is bitter or sweet.

The unthinking student, like the less mature human being everywhere, will be attracted to what is pleasant or easy, or looks "good" or "reasonable"—including what he imagines to be "valuable suffering." The Sufis, in contradistinction, have for centuries pointed out (al-Ghazzali did so frequently) what is only now becoming generally recognized in modern culture: namely, that experience is necessary, and that it may come in any form. Stylized efforts, conventional "sacrifice," and so on do not lead to real experience and certainly are not themselves experience.

The true function of what are often called "spiritual exercises" (*Dhikr* or *Wazifa* in Arabic and in the terminology of most Sufis) is explained in the instruction of the great teacher Bahauddin Naqshband (who died in the fourteenth Christian century) in the passage on "Exercises" (p. 34). There are no magic keys; here is something written from knowledge, not from the mechanical repetition of dogma:

> There are three phases of all exercises.
>
> In the first, exercises are forbidden—the aspirant is not ready; exercises would harm him. This is the time when he generally desires exercises most.
>
> In the second, when time, place and brethren are suitable for the exercises to have effect—they are indicated.
>
> In the third, when exercises have had their effect—they are no longer needed.
>
> And no Master ever performs exercises for his own progress on the way, for all Masters have passed the third stage.

The same precept, from a slightly different angle, is found in "Eating and Wonderment," in which a teacher fasts to make his

---

[27] Koran, Chapter 18; "The Cave" in *Tales of the Dervishes* as "The Man Who Looked Only at the Obvious" (pp. 198–200); "The Horseman and the Snake," *ibid.*, pp. 140–141.

pupils admire him, so that he can show up the hollowness of mere admiration of externals (p. 32). This lesson, rare at any time, though not so uncommon among the Sufi classical writers as elsewhere, is of the greatest possible value to those wishing to penetrate beyond outward forms.

"Catharsis" illustrates the sophistication—advanced even by twentieth-century standards—of the traditional Sufi master, who is able to set aside his own apparent self, as well as his concern for his own "image." Jan-Fishan Khan (Idries Shah's great-great-grandfather) acted thus in the episode (p. 60) of the man whom he wanted to shame by imitating him. The man's reformation was made complete when he saw the utter ugliness of his own behavior acted out by another person. Incidentally, this tendency of Sufis to mimic the actions, and even the views, of others for illustrative purposes—like a living cartoon—explains many of the catastrophically inaccurate assessments of them made by humorless critics, who have imagined that this behavior, which has only been assumed for teaching purposes, reflects the Sufi's real ideas.

The dramatic difference between the farsightedness and lucidity of the Sufi teachers and the obscurantist attitude of those who simply operate esoteric cults is hammered home in "Absurdities" (p. 36) by relating the devastating advice of the mystic who sent his pupils first of all to study the behavior of some "pure" scholars:

> A certain Sufi sent all would-be disciples to hear and write down the harangues of his detractors, who for the most part were narrow-minded scholars.
> Someone said: "Why do you do this?"
> He said: "One of the first exercises of the Sufi is to see whether he can perceive the absurdities, partiality and distortions of those who imagine themselves to be men of wisdom. If they can really see through them in this way, descrying their selfish and bitter natures, then the disciples can begin to learn about Reality."

The superficiality of conventional students of inner thinking is trenchantly displayed in the allegory entitled "Appearances" (p. 30), which, in the form of a conversational fragment, efficiently dissects the situation, ending with these memorable words:

Until they trouble themselves to exercise another capacity (than superficial self-assessment) they will be at the mercy of appearance. Total disregard for this fact means that people are placed out of communication with us in reality and have to depend upon what they can obtain from our outwardness.

The folly of hoping that information can be useful if the person studying it lacks the basic training or earlier knowledge necessary to interpret it or benefit from it is well illustrated in the passage called "Vine Thought" (p. 29), which at the same time can be used to criticize—constructively—the source of the information and the observer alike.

Much of the paradoxical behavior of Sufis, which has traditionally worried other people, and still disturbs their equanimity, is explained by the sentence (p. 80): "If you want your food to be safe from the greedy, tell them that it is poisonous." The subtlety of this technique of "applied aversion therapy" is more mature, as one sees it in these pages, than in similar references in the literature of today. To make one man avoid another by allowing the former to conclude that the latter is unpleasant is a far cry from the relatively juvenile desire to please or prevail at all costs and at all times, which is taken elsewhere as a precondition of human behavior.[28]

Innumerable stories, in this collection as in the other Shah books, show how little people have changed through the centuries. As so many sociologists have remarked, we are still in need of the identical strictures that were applied to Eastern orthodox bigots of the Middle Ages. This may be particularly true of the West, because of the current assumption, which is, alas, erroneous, that there is no obscurantism in educational circles.

One of the hardest-hitting passages is the short, terse illustration of self-deception, so often exemplified in book reviews and political or religious discussions, where it is implied that something deprecated is really not of importance because "present company is always excepted":

A would-be disciple said to a sage: "I have been listening to you for days now, condemning attitudes and ideas, and even conduct,

[28] Cf. *Tales of the Dervishes*, p. 27.

which is not mine and never has been. What is the purpose of this?"

The sage said: "The purpose of it is that you should, at some point, stop imagining that you have not been like any of the things I condemn; and to realize that you have a delusion that you are not like them now" (p. 20).

How does the dervish training system work? "Greed, Obligement and Impossibility" (p. 19) deals with self-deception and how, in a social parallel, a person can be brought to the realization of his own rationalizations.

One constant contemporary problem is neatly dealt with in "The Self-Congratulating Fruit" (pp. 17-18). The value of reading and the foolishness of spurning things that can be read in books through the vanity of looking for things that are "not in books" is clearly illustrated.

"The Sun and the Lamps" is important in showing that Sufi study can really only be carried on by Sufis and with Sufis, because monastic and similar institutions provide only partial, if at times suitable, opportunities for it. "The visible places of Sufi study are like lamps in the dark. The inner places are like the Sun in the sky. The lamp illuminates an area for a time. The Sun abolishes the dark" (p. 81).

The title tale of the collection *The Magic Monastery* (pp. 13-16) shows how the philosopher can produce all kinds of reactions in people, to indicate their changing moods, and also to portray their shallowness of thought if they abide by conventional methods of approach and interpretation. It also shows how they may be unable—or unwilling—to profit from such lessons.

Sufi studies, then, are taking on a new lease of life. In the past they have suffered many ups and downs. Quite a number of Western scholars have automatically adopted the attitudes of those Eastern bigots who saw, from time to time, a threat to established thinking patterns in the work of the Sufis—a threat that al-Ghazzali showed, a thousand years ago, was nonsense. Echoes of this attitude still persist here and there. As an example you could have read, as lately as 1964, the following opinion by the renowned Orientalist of Budapest, the late Ignace Goldziher:

Ibn 'Arabi, one of the most prominent Sufis in the Spain of the sixth/twelfth century, was not so much a mystic as a spiritist and a swindler, profiting by Spanish Arab credulity and superstition for egoistic purposes.[29]

The real truth is that Ibn 'Arabi, called Sheikh al-Akbar (the Great Teacher), is recognized as one of the outstanding mystics of all time, by both Eastern and Christian commentators.* His work has been the subject of much attention and analysis. Unfortunately cultural xenophobia of the kind shown by Goldziher is displayed on page after page of work even by some of the most prominent Orientalists, especially those of the past.

"It is an amusement to me to take what liberties I like with these Persians," said, incredibly, Edward FitzGerald. He continues, astonishingly, to write in this way of some of the world's greatest men of letters, most of them Sufis: "who (as I think) are not poets enough to frighten one from such excursions, and who really do want a little Art to shape them" (*Letters*, 1960, pp. 249 ff).

Since this kind of malady does not deeply afflict the present generation of Orientalists, it is not surprising that they continue, in increasing numbers, to align themselves with the Shah projection of Sufi ideas. If, in a minority of instances, this has had the effect of isolating the ultrapedants, there are compensations.

It is pleasant to record the gradual acceptance of Shah's work, which shows that many educators are reasonable men. Shah made it clear in his Sussex address † that Sufis, who traditionally oppose pedants, only take to task those who are too narrow to allow the development of human ideas. The record of the succeeding five years amply proves that these are only a minority. It should be noted that over one hundred acknowledged authorities and scholars of repute have cooperated in the present *Festschrift*.

Note A: Shah's reputation as a specialist in human thought, methods of learning, and transcultural communication caused him

---

[29] J. de Somogyi, trans., in *The Muslim World* (January, 1964), p. 38.
* See Note C at the end of this chapter.
† See Note D at the end of this chapter.

to be appointed Director of Studies of a society—the Institute for Cultural Research—set up in 1965 to pursue the study and teaching of human knowledge and to further its accessibility to the public. The ICR was registered as an educational charity with the Department of Education and Science in 1966. In common with major institutions of educational repute throughout the world, the ICR is listed in the authoritative publication *The World of Learning*.

The educational interest aroused by Idries Shah's books and courses among scholars has enabled the Institute for Cultural Research to develop contacts and to cooperate with bodies working in public education in many countries. Many professors and other men of distinction have associated themselves with its work, and expressed admiration for it. It now commands widespread respect and influence.

Note B: The Sufis examines contacts between people of different cultures, and the persistence of certain forms of intellectual and experiential approaches to human problems, including the education of the individual and the mass, both in religious and literary areas. It deals with the methods of thought, personalities, organizational structures, and sophistication of thought of major Eastern thinkers such as Rumi, al-Ghazzali, Ibn al-Arabi, and Saadi; and their influence upon the thought and output, as discerned by scholars, of such individuals as Dante, Ramon Lully, Roger Bacon, and the Schoolmen, of initiatory societies and methodology in philosophy. It also links with the Celtic and other Western forms of thought, comparing and contrasting them with the major Eastern forms of thought represented by Indian, Persian, and Arabian, as well as Hebrew, philosophers.

Note C: Ibn al-Arabi (Sheikh al-Akbar, Doctor Maximus). "Nor did all those who borrowed his ideas call themselves Muslims. He inspired, among other medieval Christian writers, 'the Illuminated Doctor' Raymond Lull, and probably Dante." Professor Reynold A. Nicholson, *A Literary History of the Arabs* (Cambridge, 1966), p. 404, quoting M. Asin Palacios, *Islam and* the "*Divine Comedy*" (London, 1926). See also M. Asin Palacios, *La Escatología Musulmana en la "Divina Comedia"* (Seguida de la Historia y Critica de una Polemica) (3d ed.; Madrid: Instituto Hispano Arabe de Cultura, 1961); and Sirdar Ikbal Ali Shah, *The Spirit of the East* (London, 1939), pp. 148 ff.

Note D: In 1965, Idries Shah was invited to conduct a seminar in the School of European Studies at Sussex University. His course was concentrated upon the strengths and weaknesses in study, attitude, and education to be found in the field of Middle Eastern and medieval European thought both in its interchange and also in its approach, typical of the quasi-religious attitude, to the problems of the identity of man and his place in life. He also dealt with the intercultural diffusion between the West of the Middle Ages and the southern Mediterranean world of the Saracens. This invitation proved to be the first of many from universities, schools, and broadcasting authorities for his contributions to general and specialized educational fields. In 1972 Shah was named a Guest Professor in ecumenical studies at the University of Geneva.

APPENDIX I

NOTE ON TRANSLITERATION

Quotes from some authorities on the transliteration and spelling of Eastern words:

There is no universally accepted system of transliteration for Arabic names.

WALTER S. LAQUEUR, *The Middle East in Transition* (London, 1958), p. xix.

As regards the transliteration of Arabic words I deliberately reject the artful and complicated systems, ugly and clumsy withal, affected by scientific modern Orientalists . . . the devices perplex the simple and teach nothing to the learned.

SIR RICHARD BURTON, *The Book of the Thousand Nights and a Night* (London, 1897), pp. xxix f.

. . . to differentiate these letters by dots or commas . . . however useful for purposes of translation into Arabic, Persian, Turkish, or Urdu, is only bewildering to a reader unacquainted with the Arabic alphabet and pronunciation.

SYED AMEER ALI, *A Short History of the Saracens* (London, 1949), p. xi.

T. E. Lawrence "of Arabia" made a classic comment on the problem of transliteration . . . "There are some 'scientific systems' of transliteration, helpful to people who know enough Arabic not to need helping, but a wash-out for the world. I spell my names anyhow, to show what rot the systems are."

I do not myself believe that all of the systems are rot, but I readily admit that they are a wash-out for those who don't know the Arabic alphabet.

PROFESSOR JAMES KRITZECK, *Anthology of Islamic Literature* (London, 1964), p. 29.

Every scholar thinks that to show himself worthy of his salt he must devise a system better than any system already in use. Agreement to use a standard system thus becomes extremely difficult to reach, even on a national plane, and how much more so on an international one?

J. D. PEARSON, A.M. (Librarian, School of Oriental and African Studies, University of London), *Oriental and Asian Bibliography* (London, 1966), p. 230.

APPENDIX II

BIOGRAPHICAL NOTES ON THE CONTRIBUTORS

A. REZA ARASTEH, PH.D., M.R.S.M.

Formerly Professor of Analytical Psychology at the University of Tehran, Dr. Arasteh has been a member of the faculty of the Department of Psychology, George Washington University Medical School and also Director of Interdisciplinary Research at the Psychiatric Institute of Washington. His contribution to this symposium, as "Sufism: The Way to Individuation" was first presented at the C. G. Jung Foundation in New York in 1971. Professor Arasteh is author of the psychological Sufi study *Rumi the Persian: Rebirth in Creativity*, with a preface by Erich Fromm. He has also written *Final Integration in the Adult Personality* and *Creativity in the Life Cycle*, published at Leiden. He is currently a senior advisor to the United Nations Institute for Training and Research. He is listed in *American Men of Science* and in the *International Encyclopaedia of World Scholars*, and is a member of the American Psychological Association and the Royal Society of Medicine (London).

MIR S. BASRI

Educated at the Alliance School at Baghdad, Mir Basri has carried out studies in Sufism and Hebrew mysticism. He is a poet and the author of many books and articles in the cultural field. As a scholar he has represented his country at numerous world gatherings, including two Orientalist congresses. He has been a Chief of Section and Head of Protocol at the Iraqi Ministry of Foreign Affairs. His major works include poetry sharing the versification of the *Taiyyah* of Ibn al-Faridh (A.D. 1181–1235), the major Arabian mystical poet. His *Precursors of the Iraqi Cultural Renaissance*, studies of thirty eminent personages, has been published recently by the government of Iraq. He has been a member of the Royal Asiatic Society for over twenty years. Mir Basri is also a celebrated economist. He has been Director of the Baghdad Chamber of Commerce, and is the author of books and papers on economics.

THE VENERABLE BANKEY BEHARI, D.THEOL.

Originally trained as a lawyer, Dr. Behari is the author of two standard legal texts. Between 1930 and 1966, he wrote over twenty books on religion and comparative mysticism in the East. In 1940 he became a Hindu monk. Dr. Behari is the translator into English of several Persian Sufi classics. These include a translation from Attar's *Memoirs of the Saints* (3d ed., 1971), an abridged translation of al-Ghazzali's *Revival of Religious Sciences* (3d ed., 1972), and a translation of Rumi's *Fihi ma Fihi*—in which work he was encouraged by the late Professor Reynold Nicholson. His *Sufis, Mystics and Yogis of India* (2d ed., 1971) was encouraged by Pandit Nehru. Other works are *Bhakta Mira Songs from Bhartihari, Mysticism in the Upanishads, Minutes with the Mystics of Iran,* and *Sufi Poets of Iran* (1939), as well as the two volumes of *Minstrels of God* (1954). He has recently completed *Immortal Sufi Triumvirate: Sanai, Attar, Rumi, Tuhfa,* and *The Table-Talk of Sufis,* which are in press. He is now a hermit at Vrindaban, India.

SIR EDWIN CHAPMAN-ANDREWS, K.C.M.G., O.B.E., K.ST.J., K.C.S.G.

A British diplomatist, Sir Edwin was educated at University College, London, the Sorbonne, and St. John's College, Cambridge, where he studied Oriental languages. He is a fellow of University College, London. Apart from service in the Foreign Office, Sir Edwin's career has been entirely in the Middle East where he served his apprenticeship, as he calls it, in the Levant Consular Service. He has been Minister in Cairo and Ambassador in Beirut and Khartoum and he has lived and traveled throughout the entire region. He has an extensive knowledge of the way of life and traditions in those countries that were within, or contiguous to, the former Ottoman Empire. He was a vice-president of the Royal Central Asian Society and is a member of the Council of the Anglo-Arab Association. After his retirement from the diplomatic service, Sir Edwin was Chairman of the Committee for Middle East Trade and a member of the British National Export Council. He is now a business consultant.

JOHN H. M. CHEN, M.A., M.S., M.S.L.S., PH.D., ED.D.

Professor Chen has carried out graduate and advanced studies at Columbia University, New York University, Virginia Polytechnic Institute and Virginia State University, University of Wisconsin, University of Denver, and the Pennsylvania State University, as well as in the Far East. He has held the posts of Professor of Education and of International and Asian Studies in various universities in the United States, and is a noted Orientalist. He is at present Professor of Library Science and chairman of his department at the University of Southern Mississippi. Dr. Chen is the author of over twenty-five books and numerous monographs, and has won many literary and academic awards. He is an authority on the storage, retrieval, and automation of literary materials and library services, and is deeply read in the literature of East and West, including the thought of the Middle East. Among his better-known works are the prize-winning *Originals of Oriental Peoples, A Study of Population in Asia* and *From Near East to Far East.* He is a member of a number of learned societies, such as the American Library Association, American Society of Information Science, and Chairman of the Executive Council of the International Institute for World Studies and Intercultural Research in New York.

HILMI MAKRAM EBEID, B.A., LL.B., LL.D.

Dr. Ebeid comes from a renowned Coptic-Christian family whose members have been active at the heart of Middle Eastern events for many years. After Victoria College (Alexandria), he was graduated from Cambridge, later obtaining his doctorate from the University of Dijon. He has been Vice-President of the Cairo Mixed Court and then judge of the National Court of Appeal. For most of his life he has been closely connected with social, spiritual, and philosophical affairs. His career has been marked by a struggle against xenophobia; and in his legal work he has always opposed the application of the letter of the law as against equitable solutions. Guided by such ideas, he has always warmly supported the call for universal service and brotherhood. This, he says, is why Sufi thought is particularly appealing to him.

SIR RAZIK FAREED, KT., O.B.E., J.P., U.M.

A Ceylonese educator and sponsor of cultural activities, Sir Razik is known as a man of letters and a parliamentarian. He has served as a member of the Senate and also of the State Council in Sri Lanka.

NASROLLAH S. FATEMI, M.A., PH.D.

Born in Persia, a descendant of the Prophet Mohammed, Professor Fatemi holds the title of Distinguished Professor of International Affairs and Director of the Graduate Institute of International Studies at Fairleigh Dickinson University in New Jersey. He has taught Diplomatic History and Iranian Civilization at several centers, including the Asia Institute and Princeton University. Dr. Fatemi has been Mayor of Shiraz (Iran), Governor-General of the Province of Fars, and has served as Vice-President of the Legislative Council of Isfahan Province, and member of the Persian Parliament. He has represented Iran at UNESCO, and has been a member of, and adviser to, the Permanent Delegation of Iran at the United Nations. He has also taught and traveled as a university representative in Europe, Africa, the Far East, the Middle East, and Central Asia. He has contributed extensively to scholarly journals. Among his best-known books are *Diplomatic History of Persia*, *The Contemporary Middle East*, and *The Biography of Hafiz* (the classical Persian Sufi poet), *The Dollar Crisis*, *The Oil Diplomacy*, and *The Humanities in the Age of Science*.

A. K. JULIUS GERMANUS, D.PH., D.LITT.

A specialist in Persian, Turkish, and Arabic, Professor Germanus has taught at Aligarh and Delhi Universities as well as at the University of Budapest. He has been a visiting professor at nine universities in eastern Europe. A member of the Orientalist Committee of the Hungarian Academy of Sciences, he is also a member of the Academies of Cairo, Baghdad, and Damascus. He was educated at the universities of Vienna and Istanbul, and studied at Budapest under the illustrious Orientalist Arminius

Vambery, and did his basic Arabic work under Professor Ignace Goldziher. He has contributed to two volumes in honor of eminent Eastern thinkers. He has served as a non-Party member of the Hungarian Parliament and as a member of its Foreign Affairs Committee, in addition to his membership in the Hungarian Committee for UNESCO. Dr. Germanus is the author of over sixty works in the Orientalist field, among them *Le Nationalisme arabe* (1918), *La Langue et la Civilisation Turque* (1925), *Bektashi Dervishes* (1928), *Modern Movements in Islam* (1930), *India* (1933), *Modern Arabic Literature* (1950), *Legacy of Ancient Arabia* (1963), and *Ibn Khaldun, Precursor of the Philosophy of History* (1967). His work has appeared in many languages, including Arabic and Urdu.

SIR JOHN GLUBB, K.C.B., C.M.G., D.S.O., O.B.E., M.C.

Glubb Pasha lived for thirty-six years in the East and is one of the best-known authorities specializing in Middle Eastern history. He has written thirteen considerable works, among them *Britain and the Arabs* (1959), *The Empire of the Arabs* (1963), *Syria, Lebanon and Jordan* (1967), and *Life and Times of Muhammad* (1970). He has lectured extensively and has been a visiting professor at several universities. Firsthand material on the thinking of the people of the Near East is found in his monograph *My Years with the Arabs* (1971).

Sir John Glubb has also written: *The Story of the Arab Legion* (1948), *A Soldier with the Arabs* (1957), *The Course of Empire* (1957), *War in the Desert* (1960), *The Great Arab Conquests* (1963), *The Lost Centuries* (1967), *The Middle East Crisis* (1967), *A Short History of the Arab Peoples* (1969), and *Peace in the Holy Land* (1971).

SALEH HAMARNEH, PH.D.

Dr. Hamarneh is Senior Lecturer in Arabic at the Jagiellonian University at Cracow, which was founded in 1364. He is a member of the Orientalist Committee of the Polish Academy of Sciences in Cracow, and a Fellow of the Institute for Cultural Research in London.

He spoke on the work of Idries Shah at the Assembly of the Twenty-First Congress of Polish Orientalists in June, 1971.

MOHAMED YAHIA HASCHMI, PH.D.

Educated at the universities of Berlin and Bonn, and at the Technical University of Stuttgart, Professor Haschmi is both a noted scientist and the author of works dealing with the Sufi tradition. His publications include a consideration of atomic theory in Sufi thought, alchemical literature, ion-exchange in Arabian writings, and a symposium on Jalaluddin Rumi. He is President of the Society for Scientific Research at Aleppo, and has taught and published extensively in the fields of the relationship between traditional and contemporary literature and science. He has also written on Islamic arts. He has participated in many international conferences, presenting treatises on scientific history and world understanding. He has taught at both the Syrian University and the Technical University of Stuttgart, and has published extensively in Arabic, German, English, and French.

THE HONOURABLE MR. JUSTICE HIDAYATULLAH, O.B.E., M.A. (CANTAB.), LL.D.

Pro-Chancellor of Delhi University and Chancellor of the Muslim National University of New Delhi, Dr. Hidayatullah has been both Chief Justice of India and Acting President of the Republic. He has been a member of the faculties of several universities, Dean of the Faculty of Law at Nagpur, and has won many academic awards. A delegate to many international conferences, he has written books on law, biography, and constitutionalism. His knowledge of Eastern thought and Sufi philosophy is based upon wide contacts, study, and an upbringing in the atmosphere of Indian, Persian, and Arabian culture in an illustrious Eastern family. Justice Hidayatullah is a member of the Executive Committee of the World Assembly of Judges, a member of the International Institute of Space Law, and the Vice-President (Asia) of the World Peace Congress. He is an Honorary Bencher of Lincoln's Inn and holds the Order of the Yugoslav Flag, with Sash.

JAMES KRITZECK, M.A., PH.D., LITT.D.

Director of the Institute for Advanced Religious Studies and professor of Oriental Languages and History at the University of Notre Dame, he was formerly at the Institute for Advanced Study at Princeton, and was a professor of Oriental Languages at Princeton University. His *Anthology of Islamic Literature* (1964) has been widely admired. It contains extracts from al-Hallaj, al-Ghazzali, Kalabadhi, Attar, Rumi, Saadi, Hafiz, and Jami, among the Sufic writers. In 1965 Pope Paul VI named Professor Kritzeck to the Papal Secretariat for Non-Christians, and he attended the Fourth Session of the Second Vatican Council. He was also a delegate to the Munich (1957) and Moscow (1960) Congresses of Orientalists. A member of many scholarly societies, Dr. Kritzeck has contributed frequently to both Eastern and Western journals. He has traveled extensively in the East, including Soviet Central Asia. He is coeditor of *The World of Islam* (1959). Among his major works are *Sons of Abraham* (1967), *Modern Islamic Literature* (1968), and *Islam in Africa* (1969). He has been a visiting professor in Morocco, Egypt, and Japan.

ROM LANDAU, D.HUM.LITT.

Rom Landau has been an acknowledged authority on religion, metaphysics, and the Arab world for over thirty years. His *The Philosophy of Ibn Arabi* (Ethical and Religious Classics of East and West, No. 22) (London, 1959), on Sufi thought, is one of his more important works. He collaborated with the late Professor A. J. Arberry, the Arabic specialist, in editing *Islam Today* (1943), and is himself author of fifty-one books. He has lectured at many universities, including Princeton, Yale, Harvard, and Stanford, and was professor of Islamic and North African Studies at the American Academy of Asian Studies and the University of the Pacific. Professor Landau's international best seller is *God Is My Adventure* (rev. ed., 1964) and among his important scholarly works are *The Arabesque* (1955), *Arab Contribution to Civilization* (1958), *Islam and the Arabs* (1958), *The Arab Heritage of Western Civilization* (1963), and *History of Morocco in the Twentieth Century* (in Arabic, 1963). He has contributed to *The Times* (London), *The New York Times*, and numerous literary journals. In recognition of his scholarship, he was made a Commander of the Order Wasm Alawite by King Mohammed V in 1956. He resides in North Africa.

ZEKI EL-MAHASSINI, D.LITT., LL.D.

One of the foremost of poets, authors, and literary critics in the Arab world, Dr. Mahassini has been Syrian Cultural Attaché in Cairo, and has served in senior posts in the Ministry of Education at Damascus. He is a professor in the Faculties of Letters and of Education at the Lebanese University and Professor of Literature at Damascus. He is internationally celebrated for his contributions to learned journals, for his work at the Ministry of Culture in Cairo, and for his part in the Arab Literature Conference at Mecca. A doctor of both laws and literature, his thesis on Abu al-Ala, the mystic poet, was published in Cairo (1945) and Beirut (1964). In addition to producing fourteen full-length research works on classical literature and on major figures in the world of letters, he is the author of numerous monographs and lectures, and is also a noted broadcaster. His latest work, which has received much acclaim, is *Arab Epic Poetry* (new ed., Cairo, 1971). In 1970 he published *Inspired Legends*, about classical figures; and another important book is *Abu Nuas, Poet of Genius*. Among Dr. Mahassini's shorter works is an essay on Ibn Taimiah and several Sufi poems. He is a Corresponding Member of the Spanish Royal Academy of Literature, and of the Academy of the Arabic Language, Cairo.

ADNAN MARDAM BEY

Adnan Mardam Bey is a poet and dramatist who has taken many of his themes from Sufi historical sources. He is the author of two poetic dramas dealing with the saint Rabia and the martyr al-Hallaj; and the former piece has been described as the most brilliant in Arab theatrical history. The family from his mother's side (Hamzawi) is descended from the Prophet Mohammed and also from Prince Mohammed Ali al-Kourmoushi. Literary critics in the Middle East hold that Adnan Mardam Bey's work is probably the best in contemporary arts in the area. Selections of his poetry and prose are becoming known in the West, though so far only through scholarly translations. Some of his pieces have been translated in Spain and Brazil, and an English version is in preparation at Indiana University.

ISHTIAQ HUSAIN QURESHI, M.A., PH.D. (CANTAB.)

Vice-Chancellor, University of Karachi, President of the Institute of Central and West Asian Studies, Professor Qureshi has studied and taught in Asia, Europe, and the United States. He has been Chairman of the International World University Service at Geneva, a professor at Columbia University, and Dean of the Faculty of Arts at Delhi University. As a major Orientalist and historian, with degrees in Persian and history, he has been Director of the Central Institute of Islamic Research. He is a member of the Council of the Pakistan Institute of International Affairs, University Professor of History, President of the Historical Society, and a member of the Advisory Council on Islamic Ideology. He has held three ministerial appointments and three professorships. During the past forty years he has been responsible for a dozen standard works on Eastern thought and history. In 1964, he was decorated, in recognition of these and other services, with the Star of Pakistan (S.Pk.). He has made a deep study of Sufi thought with special reference to its historical, philosophical, and practical aspects.

AHMAD SAIDI (IMPERIAL IRANIAN ORDER OF HUMAYUN)

Ahmad Saidi was born in Khoy, Iran, and educated at Tabriz, in the United States of America, and in Britain, where he was engaged in research and reading toward the Doctorate of Philosophy. He is the compiler of a Persian-English dictionary, and has had great interest in Sufi studies for many years. He has been active for over forty years in educational, cultural, and community relations linking East and West; a process that has been helped by his extensive expertise in English, Persian, and Turkish, and a knowledge of Arabic and French. His Imperial Majesty the Shahinshah of Iran conferred the Order of Humayun on him in 1962, and he is included in *Two Thousand Men of Achievement* and numerous other reference works. In addition to the intensive study of Middle Eastern literature, he holds degrees in international relations and economics. Mr. Saidi served as Chairman of the Export Promotion Centre of Iran at Tehran and was a member of the High Economic Coordinating Council. He has also held other official appointments with the United States government.

His work has been used in graduate seminars at George Washington University, where he did postgraduate studies. He has extensive professional and economic interests, and is the author of numerous articles in Persian and English. He is editor of the *Iran-American Review*.

M. Y. SHAWARBI, PH.D.

Professor Shawarbi is a member of the Supreme Council on Islamic Affairs in the Federation of Arab Republics. Closely associated with major figures at the heart of affairs in Europe, Asia, and Africa for many years, he is an authority on the outstanding personalities of the East. He has been active for three decades in intercultural relations, both within the Eastern world and in its relations with the West. Educated in Egypt and Britain, Professor Shawarbi has been director of the Islamic Center in New York and a member of its Board of Trustees. He has held three visiting professorships in the United States and was chosen to deliver the Islamic Resolution in celebration of the tenth anniversary of the United Nations. Among his present appointments is that of Secretary-General of the International Society for the Dissemination of Islamic Culture. A distinguished scientist and author as well as a man of letters, he holds a chair at the University of Cairo, where he is head of his department. The professor, as his surname denotes, is a member of one of the most distinguished families in the Near East.

THE REVEREND SIDNEY SPENCER

A graduate of London University, The Reverend Sidney Spencer took an honors course in Comparative Religion at Oxford under Dr. J. Estlin Carpenter, and has studied and published on this subject for many years. He is a Unitarian and a specialist in mysticism. He has edited and published William Law's books, *The Spirit of Prayer* and *The Spirit of Love*, and contributed to the article on Christian mysticism in the *Encyclopaedia Britannica*. He is the author of *Mysticism in World Religion* (1963), in which he traces, *inter alia*, the growth and trends in Sufi teaching. This comprehensive work contains the result of studies of the work of Professors A. J. Arberry, E. G. Browne, and R. A. Nicholson, and others in Sufism, and is based upon his course of

Upton Lectures (entitled "God and Man in Mystical Religion") delivered at Oxford in 1950. He has been a minister at several churches in Britain, and is noted for his *Deep Things of God: Essays in Liberal Religion* (1955). He was Principal of Manchester College, Oxford, and tutor in Comparative Religion and Philosophy of Religion 1951–1956. He is at present engaged in the preparation of a volume expounding his spiritual outlook.

EMIR AREF TAMER, D.LITT.

Educated in Syria and Lebanon, Dr. Tamer is an authority on Islamic culture, as well as a poet, novelist, and historian. He has published twenty full-length works, among which are included scholarly historical and literary studies. A member of several learned societies in the East and West, including the Royal Asiatic Society of London, he is the son of the Emir Tamer El-Ali, head of the Ismailia Community in Syria.

L. F. RUSHBROOK WILLIAMS, C.B.E., M.A., B.LITT., F.R.S.A., J.P.

Professor Williams is a Quondam Fellow of All Souls' College, Oxford. While University Professor of Modern Indian History at Allahabad, he built up a school of Mughal studies. A major historian and authority on South Asia, he has been a minister in an Indian State, was Eastern Services Director of the B.B.C., and served for many years on the editorial staff of *The Times* (London). He has also been a government adviser on Middle East affairs, and has received many scholarly honors and awards. In addition to writing standard works on history and the East, he contributes to such learned periodicals as the *Royal Central Asian Society Journal*, and writes for the *Encyclopaedia Britannica*. He has been interested in the background and writings of the Sufis for over half a century.

He resides in Britain and travels frequently to the East, where he is widely known and respected. He has for many years been adviser to certain Eastern royal houses.

AHMED EMIN YALMAN, PH.D.

Professor Yalman was educated at Columbia University and became, on his return to Turkey in 1914, first associate professor of sociology, and then professor of statistics in Istanbul University. He also engaged in journalistic activities. In 1919 he was exiled to Kutahia, by the order of the sultan and in 1920 to Malta by the British Occupation forces. On his release, the national government in Ankara offered him the post of Director-General of Press and Information with the promise of being sent to Washington as the first ambassador after the peace. He asked to be excused because he wanted to stick to his journalistic work. He took an active role in the development of his country from a feudal sultanate to a modern democracy. Dr. Yalman has known many of the controlling minds of the East and the West for half a century.

He was one of the founders of the Liberal International in 1947 and the International Press Institute in 1950. The awards he received include the Golden Pen of Freedom of the International Federation of Newspaper Publishers. The Gold Medal of the British Institute of Journalists and those of several American universities. He has published three books in English, one in German, and more than ten in Turkish, including his autobiography in four volumes.